LEE SHORE BLUES

SEX, DRUGS AND BLUEWATER SAILING

Snapshots from a life at sea, from sailing pilot cutters to cruise ship captain, from commercial fisherman to single-handed ocean racing

Written and published by
Peter M. Heiberg, Canada

Lee Shore Blues: Sex, Drugs and Bluewater Sailing

© 2014 Peter M. Heiberg

Library and Archives Canada
ISBN 978-0-9936922-3-9

Also available with colour photographs:
ISBN 978-0-9936922-0-8

Also available in electronic formats:
ISBN 978-0-9936922-1-5 Kindle edition
ISBN 978-0-9936922-2-2 ePub edition

Written and published by Peter M. Heiberg, Canada

To order or to contact the author, please email: leeshoreblues@yahoo.com
Snail mail address: Lee Shore Blues, Box 62, Gibsons, BC CANADA V0N 1V0

Designed/edited by Jane Keyes (www.page-perfect.com)

Front cover: *Waves*, 24x20", oil on canvas © Winnie Shepardson
(www.winnieshepardson.com)

All photo images by the author unless otherwise credited.

This book is dedicated to Christy, without whose love and patience it never would have happened. Also to my two wonderful kids, Sarah and Gunnar. Through it all...still my two wonderful kids. Finally, to the memory of my mother, who taught me that security is an illusion, and whose life was more exciting than mine.

INTRODUCTION

I have a confession to make.

Although this whole book is something of a confession, the confession I want to make at this moment is that the following pages were never intended to be a book. The strands that came together were from widely diverse concepts, and it was only late into the various projects that I thought I could perhaps stuff both feet into one gumboot and make a book.

If there has been a tragedy in my life, it has been that I didn't have the opportunity to raise both my children. I have good relations with both of them and I wanted them to have some idea of how their dad wasted his life. My mother, with my encouragement, wrote a small book before dying. Not only is it a cherished possession, it's also an historical document of life, love and war in the generation before mine. It's also pretty damn exciting, involving her travels on North Atlantic convoys, being attacked by German U-boats, living through the London blitz, and breastfeeding my brother in the London tube as the bombs walked around at street level. My father flew Spitfires during the Battle of Britain and was shot down at least once. I thought that the least I could do for my kids was leave a similar (if less exciting) record of my life at sea. That's one strand.

Another important strand was the fact that I bought, rebuilt, and owned for thirty-five years a type of sailboat that became fairly famous among the cognoscenti. This was a Bristol Channel pilot cutter, arguably the finest ocean-going small vessel ever built during the age of sail. After rebuilding the boat, I sailed it from Cornwall in the U.K. to Vancouver, Canada, without benefit of an engine or virtually any modern navigation gear. The current owners of this boat compiled an incredible history of the vessel (built in 1899), included here as Appendix 1. I was determined to add my two cents to the history of *Carlotta*, as I owned the boat longer than any other owner and sailed her the farthest. That's the second strand.

As my commercial career at sea developed, I had the psychological equivalent of the feeling you experience when you have one foot on the dock and one on the boat…and they're drifting apart. My life had been sailing, but the money was in fishing, towing, large yachts, and cruise ships. For years I had two résumés. When being hired for a yacht delivery, I would never let the owner see that I ran towboats or fished commercially. When being hired to run a towboat, I would never admit to spending years under sail.

So this was the third strand (with a decided left-hand lay). The problem was, I knew I could write a book that would interest the many people interested in pilot cutters. I knew I could write an interesting addition to *Carlotta*'s history. I have had a few interesting experiences as a fisherman, and I knew commercial fishermen would probably get a laugh out of my endless blundering. But could I put it all together so the fishermen would appreciate my struggles rebuilding and sailing a really old wooden sailboat? Could I interest the pilot cutter aficionados in the struggles of someone learning to fish commercially?

Obviously, both situations had the sea in common, and that should interest most of the seamen. For the rest, I just threw in a bunch of sex and drugs. If you're not interested in boats, the sea, sex or drugs, we'd probably have nothing to talk about anyway.

— Peter M. Heiberg

Then I looked at all the works that my hands had worked, and at the labor that I had labored to do; and, behold, all was vanity and a chasing after wind, and there was no profit under the sun. — Ecclesiastes 2:11, *World English Bible*

…one must still have chaos in oneself to be able to give birth to a dancing star.
— Nietzsche

I'd like to be a hero,
But I ain't got the nerve.
— Roy Orbison, "Chicken Hearted"

CONTENTS

CHAPTER 1

....

FEAR

Never be afraid of being terrified. — Paul Johnson

We are all scared balls of puke. — Anonymous

Talking to people who have never spent any time on the ocean, the question invariably arises: "Are you ever afraid?" It is not really the right question to ask, however, as it requires too simple an answer. There is fear, but there are also years of tedium, months of anxiety and, yes, even a few instances of joy. I'm now at the stage of life when I can look back at virtually all of my many voyages and not recall having been afraid very often. There has certainly been danger, but danger frequently occurs when there is an accident, and an accident occurs without anticipation. Fear, as many know, generally resides in the anticipation of danger.

As an example, only a few years ago I was taking my boat, *Scaramouche V*, from Vancouver, Canada to San Francisco to take part in the Pacific Cup race to Hawaii. As is often the case, the wind was blowing great guns off Cape Mendocino, and continued to blow hard all the rest of the way to San Francisco. Fortunately, it was behind us, so the ride, while "enthusiastic," was not unpleasant. We were on the starboard gybe, but as we approached Drakes Bay outside of San Francisco it was necessary to gybe over to port. This is a pretty routine manoeuvre, but does require some care in a big breeze. There was absolutely no anticipation of danger as I went forward and cast off the preventer. If there were to be any danger, it would be when I returned to the cockpit and passed through the "death zone" (as I like to call the area swept by the boom during a gybe).

There was not much to worry about: both my crew were well experienced, and I had sailed many miles with them with no mishaps at all. Before entering the death zone, I made eye contact with the helmsman, and said, "Make me safe." Translation: bring the boat slightly upwind so there is no possibility of a gybe. To this day I am not sure what happened, but just as I ducked under the boom as I was moving aft, the boat *did* gybe "all standing," as the expression goes. The mainsheet tackle caught my neck. It picked me up, hurled me all the way from where I had been on the port side, across the bridge deck and completely across the cockpit, where I landed on my neck and head between the primary and secondary winches on the starboard side.

It was all over in half a second, but — despite the extreme danger — I felt no fear at all. The helmsman, on the other hand, may have felt a wee bit as I graphically described what I would like to do to him and his future progeny. Around the actual event, however, there was no anticipation of danger, so there was no fear.

I should probably add that I was totally unhurt by this event: not even the smallest bruise. A few months before, this same thing had happened to someone on a voyage between Mexico and the Marquesas. In that case, the upper mainsheet block had ripped out a large portion of his throat, and his life was saved only by a major rescue and extraction effort.

My one story of real terror afloat involves neither a long passage nor an ocean crossing. Instead, it occurred on a short coastal cruise in a GP 14 — a small, open, fibreglass sailboat built in the U.K. (How I came to own this boat also involves some real terror, but that is not a story for these pages.)

After my university education was complete (more than complete, I felt at the time), I was splitting my time between the U.K. and Vancouver. When in Vancouver, I often departed the city to enjoy Lasqueti Island, one of the Gulf Islands located in the Strait of Georgia, about sixty miles north. My pal Jim and I would hang out with our friend Blood Sugar Sam, and, since Lasqueti Island was one of the main production centres for marijuana, home brew, and magic mushrooms (*amanita muscaria*, if memory serves. I remember, after eating my first amanita mushroom, someone handing me a mushroom book that informed me that, while they were poisonous, they "were seldom fatal"; this cheered me considerably), we had a hell of a time. Summer in the Gulf Islands was — and still is — the best.

On this particular occasion, instead of driving north on Vancouver Island to French Creek and taking the ferry (a ferry I would skipper at a much later date for a very short time), Jim decided he wanted to bicycle to Lasqueti, something we had done previously. I suggested I should sail there in our GP 14 dinghy and then we would switch: he could sail home and I would bike.

The plan began well. It was great weather as I sailed west out of English Bay. When night fell, I would tie the dinghy somewhere secure and find a likely looking place to camp. I should point out that, in Canada, any area below the high-tide line is Crown property and open to anyone's use; at that time, there was so much foreshore that nobody could possibly have found a way to stop this kind of camping. My only issue was the tidal range, and making sure the dinghy would be afloat in the morning. I'd developed a method of hauling the boat out toward a small anchor so that it would float all night and I could easily retrieve it in the morning (one of my many great inventions that had been invented all over the world about five hundred years earlier).

The trip took four or five really pleasant days, with almost no rowing and the light breezes typical of the area. Rain didn't seem to exist, heralding the start of a love affair I have to this day with the coast. Once on Lasqueti, I found my way to what we used to call Earl's Cove (only 'cause Earl lived there; not the real Earl's Cove), secured the boat, and walked up to meet Jim and Sam. At this time, Allen Farrell — a West Coast legend who designed and constructed boats out of driftwood and then made South Pacific voyages in them — was building boats on the island. It was fascinating to get a chance to sit at his feet. Thus far, all had gone well on our little island getaway.

Some days later, we decided it was time to be heading home. I walked down to Earl's Cove to help Jim rig and launch the boat. Although the weather had seemed settled at Sam's house, by the time we got down to the water it was clear that there was a very strong westerly blowing. Now, at this time, Jim had a lot less sailing experience than I did, so I suggested it might be safer if I sailed the boat back to Vancouver and he biked. He was fine with the idea, pushed me off, and headed back to the ferry on his bike.

There is a point reached in every downwind voyage when it is easier to continue on than to turn back. I can't remember when I realized I was well out of my comfort zone, but I do know that by the time I did, turning back was no longer an option. It was howling; short, steep, breaking seas pursued me angrily, with spume being blown off the tops of the waves.

I managed to get the mainsail down. Although I was going dead downwind, I sheeted the jib in hard to reduce the area. The geography here is such that, upon first leaving the east side of Lasqueti, you have some shelter from the island itself (as well as Jedediah and Texada islands). Of course, as you continue, this lee eventually narrows and disappears. I knew I was in trouble. What I didn't know was what I was going to do about it.

I decided I would try to make it to Thormanby, an island southeast of the tip of Texada. This meant I would be at a slight angle to the wind, but still generally downwind. I was truly afraid now, as it was Easter and the water was still very cold. I couldn't seem to make the Elvstrom self bailer work, but had a small bucket that I soon attached to a short line and threw overboard in an attempt to slow myself down, as I was overtaking the waves ahead.

Just when things seemed really desperate, a large Coast Guard vessel approached upwind; she would pass within a hundred yards and could hardly help but see me. I had never asked for help before, so I argued with myself about whether to wave my jacket to attract attention or just wait to see what developed. I finally decided that if she offered help I would take it, but otherwise I would try for Thormanby.

She steamed by at fifteen knots or so, completely oblivious to my existence. So much for keeping a good watch. There was no choice now: I had to make it to the beach at Thormanby.

Easing my weight from side to side as the waves and angle of heel dictated, I did manage to make the beach — and the beach, fortunately, was parallel to the wind direction, so I didn't have to contend with a major beach break.

Several times in my life I've had close encounters with death. Once, as a young teenager, while surfing in waves much bigger than I was competent to handle at Rincon in California, I wiped out on the biggest wave I had ever ridden. When I finally washed up on the beach, I was subjected to the commonly reported post-calamity high that makes the world appear brilliant in all its glory: colours were vivid beyond belief, the warmth of the sun on my cold skin was almost erotic, and just being alive made me euphoric.

Arriving at the beach on Thormanby felt similar. Although somewhat less vivid, it was somehow more…*intellectual.* The Rincon experience involved fighting madly for the surface and air only to find several feet of foam, choking on the white water, then being driven under again by the next wave, fighting with all my strength to get back to the surface only to find more foam and another wave towering over me, and trying desperately not to inhale water. In contrast, *this* near-death experience was centred around the awareness of what would happen if I capsized in a strong gust. Although uncomfortably real, at least it didn't involve the absence of oxygen at the moment.

But I did need to make a decision. Organize the boat, get the bailer working, and carry on? Camp on the beach until conditions improved? Hike overland to the summer cabins that were clustered at the north end of the island?

I gave myself half an hour to calm down and then decided I could probably carry on safely with just the jib, while towing a bucket, with a functioning bailer.

After a good rest, I relaunched the boat and headed south again. There is no point in trying to describe the next six hours. I don't think I swallowed once in all that time. The voyage, which had taken the better part of a week going north, took those mere, harrowing six hours going south. I hugged the shore where there was one to hug, and hoped for the best the rest of the time. Planing down the south side of Bowen Island, I realized there was no way I could alter course enough to cross English Bay to our dry berth in False Creek. There were some docks at the West Vancouver Yacht Club where I could at least gain dry land, but I hesitated because it was a rather snooty place that might not be quick to welcome a long-haired hippy who hadn't bathed in a couple of weeks.

I came up with a plan. If it turned out they wouldn't let me leave the boat there, I would simply abandon it at their dock and walk away. There was no way in the world I could make it across English Bay and live to tell about it.

I approached the yacht club and was spotted immediately by the dockmaster, who looked at me as if I were something repulsive he had just discovered on the bottom of his shoe. I blurted out that I had sailed from Lasqueti and couldn't go any further under these wind conditions. He was clearly shocked: "You sailed from Lasqueti in that?! Two thirty-foot boats have been dismasted just between here and Bowen. Of course you can leave your boat here. Do you need a ride to Vancouver?" A real gentleman, and a good lesson for me about stereotypes.

I phoned Jim, who was already at our house in Kits; that's because he'd had the same following wind on the bike and hadn't had to use any low gears, even on the uphill sections. He drove over to pick me up, and I told him about my six-hour brush with death. Forty-five years and a thousand voyages later, that remains my scariest adventure at sea — and all it took was a fourteen-foot plastic boat, a breeze, and some very cold water.

CHAPTER 2

·················

DEEP SEA

*There is not so helpless and pitiable an object in the world as a landsman
beginning a sailor's life.* — Richard Henry Dana

Self-knowledge is always bad news. — John Barth

Although this book is about some of my adventures in small boats, my first deep-sea experience was actually on a 16,000-ton bulk carrier. In 1968, I took a semester off from university due to some terribly important personal crisis that has not been retained in memory. I was living with a young woman — we'll call her Linda — who was a truly wonderful person. I still think fondly of her.

I had no work, but this was the sixties and work was easy to find. Living in a house full of other hippies, life was cheap and I had no worries. Sitting around one evening smoking far too much pot, someone I didn't know mentioned that he was working on a freighter in the harbour, and had just returned from Japan. This totally fascinated me. After listening to some of his adventures in foreign ports, I asked him how he had come by such a great job. He replied that there was nothing to it; in fact, they needed a new galley hand on his ship. And that is how I came to be employed on the MV *Kanangoora*.

Of course, my girlfriend just about shit, to be perfectly blunt. Here we were in a committed relationship and suddenly, without consulting her, I was headed to Japan by myself. I was so excited at the prospect of an adventure after several years of tedium at university that I couldn't see her viewpoint. We had been assured that the ship just sailed back and forth from Vancouver to Japan, so I would be gone only six weeks and then everything would return to normal. I didn't see the problem.

That is, I didn't see the problem until the ship, with me on board, exited the Strait of Juan de Fuca heading north, and two things happened: first, I was overwhelmed by lovesickness — absolutely stricken by the absence of Linda; and second, I vomited all over my shoes.

And I continued to vomit all over my shoes for the next two weeks. Every time a whiff of galley grease wafted my way, I vomited. Every time I tried to eat, I vomited. Every time I tried to work, I vomited. I vomited until nothing but a thin drool of spit would come up; still, dry heaves wracked me, and again I tried to vomit.

I have made a few ocean crossings in small vessels in my life, and on each voyage (at least when I was younger), I've experienced a bit of discomfort at the start. Occasionally, this involved vomiting. But, if you want pure, totally incapacitating, gut-wrenching, saliva-soaked seasickness, it's the *Kanangoora* every time. As the old joke goes, the first day you're afraid you're going to die, and the second day you're afraid you're not going to die.

I haven't mentioned it, but all of this took place in February, and the great circle route to Japan takes you north until you are actually in sight of the Aleutian Islands — that is, you'd be able to see them if you didn't have fog and low cloud racing toward you continuously. Were it not for the spindrift constantly driven over the whole ship as she crashed through one wave, and the next wave smashed over the fo'c'sle head and ran down the length of the ship, you could probably have seen all sorts of wonderful things.

Leaving Georgia Strait, green seas smashed, time after time, against the steel stormboards that were bolted over the lower superstructure ports, trying to find our weakness. Go on deck? Nobody had to tell you not to go on deck: it was impossible to force a door open against the strength of the wind. The green water rolled six feet deep down the decks, hit the superstructure, and burst upward completely over the bridge and radar antennae. Our normal speed of twelve knots was reduced to six, and then four, as we tried to force our way against a liquid bedlam. The water found some hidden weakness in the two-inch-diameter steel life rails, bending them like overcooked spaghetti. At the time, I made myself a solemn oath that I would never cross an ocean in a small boat.

Nobody was worried. The *Kanangoora* was built to carry iron ore, so a load of grain for Japan did not test her at all. *I* was tested, but the ship was fine. Inside, life went on as usual. The three-hundred-pound homosexual steward would get drunk and chase us around the galley trying to steal a feel. I became good friends with Henry, the chef, and he helped me plot my escape from the ship to get home to my girlfriend. If I sound like a total pussy, it's because I was.

It took two weeks to get to Yokosuka, Japan. By the time we arrived, the weather had settled down, along with my stomach, and I realized the world wasn't going to end if I didn't see my girlfriend for a few weeks. Now things improved rapidly. For one thing, while the ship (using modern facilities) had taken three days to load 16,000 tons of grain in Vancouver, the same 16,000 tons of grain were unloaded in individual hundred-pound sacks. Each sack was carried by a single man and placed on the back of an open truck; another man then stacked the sacks until the truck was full. What this meant was that we had two full weeks to explore Japan, view the sacred temples of Kyoto, get drunk, or do whatever our idea of pleasure dictated.

While all of this was happening, to the south the Vietnam debacle was taking shape. Yokosuka is an R&R stop for the U.S. Navy, so the bars were full of lost, young American kids wondering what the hell had happened to them. These guys were so anxious to talk to someone not in the military that it was impossible to buy your own beer. Although they were supposed to be relaxing, they were bored with the war and with each other; in fact, it's the only time I've seen fist fights in which both participants appeared bored.

I remember an anti-war demonstration taking place in the streets one day. Since I had been heavily into the peace movement back home, a pal and I tried to join in. We were firmly and not gently excluded. This was my first (but not last) taste of Japanese racism that is often masked by that culture's outstanding good manners.

On the other hand, a characteristic of the Japanese people that I admired greatly was their honesty. It is my understanding that up until the end of the Second World War — when the Americans instructed them differently — locks had not been required in Japan. Houses were not locked, boats were not locked, cars were not locked. At the time I was there, many things were still unchained, unbolted, unpadlocked, and I still cringe with shame when I remember stealing the bicycle of the ship's watchman as a prize for my girlfriend in Canada. He was just a poor working guy who didn't need a thief like me in his life.

You will start out standing
Proud to steal her anything she sees,
But you'll wind up peeking through her keyhole
Down upon your knees.
— Bob Dylan, "She Belongs to Me"

Of course, the culture that grew up around the American soldiers on leave was the same culture of camp followers that has existed throughout history. Bars and whores, cheap goods and cheap thrills were abundant. A trick the bar girls loved to try (in Japan and around the world) was to snuggle up to you when you entered a bar and get you to buy them a drink. The drink they got, of course, would be tea — which in a glass looks the same as whisky — and you would be charged some outrageous amount that they would then split with the house.

One night, while out drinking with Eddy, the third engineer with whom I'd become friends, we were in an unfamiliar bar in an unfamiliar part of town when the girls tried this trick. We wouldn't even let them sit down, so it was a bit of a surprise at the end of the evening to have the bill come and find that it included many dollars (or yen) for drinks bought for girls who hadn't even sat at our table. When we objected, suddenly nobody spoke any English. Then, when we tried to leave, the manager physically locked us in. However, Eddy was an Egyptian, and had grown up in a part of the world that was very poor. Not only was he familiar with every hustle known to man, he was big, and had spent years as a prizefighter in addition to his years at sea.

Eddy communicated to the manager that I would remain in the bar while he went to get more money to pay the tab. This was acceptable and he was allowed to leave; I didn't know what to expect, but I trusted Eddy wouldn't abandon me. My faith was justified when, after only thirty minutes, Eddy returned with a very stout Japanese gentleman who commenced to rant at the staff until spittle flew, his eyes bulged, and his face grew as red as a Second World War caricature of our Asian brethren. Then we were allowed to leave.

I asked Eddy what in the world he had done to orchestrate such a great solution to our problem. He explained that he knew a bar where all of the bar owners gathered to gamble each evening. He'd found the owner of the bar in which we were having the trouble and told our story. The owner said his employees would never do such a thing and refused to hear anything more about it. Eddy slapped a Ben Franklin down on the table, saying that if he were wrong the bar owner could keep it. That got the man's attention, as a hundred dollars was quite a bit of money in those days.

The owner, of course, was furious when Eddy turned out to be correct. However, as the third engineer said later, he was probably pissed mainly because his employees were doing it and not piecing the action off to him. For my part, I was totally impressed that a guy from Egypt would know where the bar owners drink in Yokosuka, and know how to take our aggravating situation to a satisfactory conclusion. It didn't work so well a few nights later, though, when someone in a camera store tried to rip Eddy off, failed, and rolled down some steel shutters to prevent him from leaving. Eddy tore the shutters out of the wall, knocked the clerk unconscious when he tried to restrain him, and spent the night in the grey-bar hotel for his trouble.

On the last night in Yokosuka, I spent a few hours in a meditative walk around the seaport. It had been a great adventure to see at least a small part of Japan. My best friend in high school was a Japanese American who was really proud of his Japanese heritage, and I got a kick out of getting to Japan before he did.

When I finally returned to the ship, it seemed as if the world had gone crazy. Almost the entire crew was falling-down drunk, music was blaring, people were passed out in the crew-quarter alleyways, and the smell of ripe vomit was overwhelming. It was a pre-departure blowout.

Back in the sixties, the crew's quarters were located below deck level, while officers' quarters were located in the superstructure. As a result, this kind of bacchanalian hell could go on in the crew cabins and the officers would be totally unaware. The officers on the *Kanangoora* were, for the most part, very uptight Swedes with that typical Scandinavian arrogance that believes Sweden is the centre of the known universe and all other peoples are lesser mortals. They would not have been amused at the debauchery taking place below decks.

When I arrived on the scene, there was one rather attractive but totally unconscious Japanese whore being passed from cabin to cabin. (I'm not entirely sure why anyone would want to have sex with an unconscious person. It certainly gave me an entirely new meaning for the term "stirring the porridge.")

Anyway, after everyone had their fun, the poor girl was tossed in a spare cabin and left to regain consciousness in her own sweet time.

What amused the hell out of me was that, unbeknownst to the crew, a new Swedish third officer had arrived some hours earlier. After the other officers had welcomed him on board in the officers' mess, they'd attempted to install him in his cabin in the superstructure only to find that the cabin hadn't been cleaned since the previous officer had departed. And it had been left in something of a… well, mess.

This was not a problem as long as the officer didn't mind spending one night in an empty cabin in the crew's quarters. He graciously said that would be fine. I happened to be standing at the bottom of the companionway ladder getting ready to leave the insanity of the crew's last night when I saw him appear at the top. He was still dressed in his spotless white uniform, blond hair in perfect array.

He recoiled visibly at the blast of rock and roll music that greeted him, but managed to persevere and descend the ladder. A drunken Filipino crewman flung his arm around the man's shoulders and breathed a vomit-laden welcome. Still the officer persisted, demanding to know where his temporary cabin was located. Finally, he was directed to the spare cabin, and thrust open the door to be faced directly with the hairy, naked genitals of the used-up hooker. Someone had tried to put a blouse on her, but one breast peaked coyly out from between the buttons. A small bubble of green snot pulsed rhythmically from one nostril.

The look on the face of the clean, upstanding young officer cannot be adequately described — horror, disgust, perhaps a touch of outrage at this sperm-bespattered vision of Japanese womanhood. "Not at all like we do it in Sweden," you could almost hear him thinking.

I made my way, chortling, to my cabin. Just another night in the ancient spiritual land of Japan.

....

It was time to depart Asia. I had learned how to deal with my seasickness, but because we had a partial load of Japanese automobiles bound for Canada, we took a much more southerly route in order to avoid damaging them in the weather of the high latitudes. While the good weather was great for me working in the galley, in those days when the weather was good the crew was out chipping rust on deck. Back then, we had thirty-two crew on a 400-foot ship, whereas today you might have twenty-one on a 900-foot ship.

The gay steward, who had never had any luck with me, set me to painting the pantry as a punishment. Every time I moved a box or carton, a dozen or so cockroaches would scatter in all directions. Instead of killing them, which made a mess and got boring quickly, I began to paint them green. I painted hundreds of them in the hope that they would be entertaining for the next kid who didn't fancy a 300-pound boyfriend.

CHAPTER 3

....

ON THE PATH TO
CARLOTTA

I've learned the last thing that I'll ever learn by rote,
That's the last time I'm going to throw away my vote,
I'm turnin' in my jacket for a coat,
Goin' to get myself a big old wooden boat.
— Rex Weyler, "Wooden Boat Song"

I had been sailing with my family from a very young age. In fact, my natural father had an Olympic sailing medal he had earned as the foredeck hand on the King of Norway's six-metre in the '36 Olympics. However, the vicissitudes of parental relationships took me away from my sailing roots, and for all of my teenage years I had basically "swallowed the anchor." My interest never waned, though, and I sailed and bought sailing magazines whenever the opportunity arose.

After finishing university, I found work in the U.K. When I wasn't working, I was looking for an old wooden boat.

Why did I want to own an old wooden boat?

The roots of this addiction are not entirely clear. Partly it was the nautical equivalent of the back-to-the-land movement of the sixties. One event that certainly contributed occurred while I was visiting my parents in Puerto Rico. I had bumped into some young guys who were delivering a wooden schooner (the *Buccaneer Prince*) to Nova Scotia. They asked me, and my pal Jim, if we would like to help take the boat as far as Bermuda. We responded by asking, "Does the pope wear a funny hat? Does Rose Kennedy have a black dress?" Thus, I met my pal and the skipper, Freddie Roberts, who will also appear in later chapters.

The trip across the dreaded Bermuda Triangle (I'm being facetious here) to Bermuda was generally uneventful. Good sailing, large patches of Sargasso weed, and good company made for an unremarkable but enjoyable first small-boat voyage. It was during this trip that I first heard of St. Barths, an island that plays a big role in this book and my life.

After we arrived in Bermuda, Jim and I hitched another ride on a Finnish aluminum sloop to the Azores. The skipper was a complete nutcase. I'll give you a few examples of his lunacy.

In Bermuda, he had some electronics repaired but refused to pay the tradesman, so the tradesman returned to the boat and "unfixed" everything. In addition to that, the skipper refused to admit that he'd forgotten how to do celestial navigation (if anyone ever asks you if it's possible to cross the Atlantic using only radio beacons, the answer is *yes*). He also had a gun on board, and anytime there was evidence of life in the sea, he would haul out his gun and blast away at anything that moved in, on or above the water. We would cower behind the deckhouse as bits of turtle were blown skyward for his own puerile amusement. Obviously, we were pretty anxious to get off that boat, but the experience didn't dim our enthusiasm for either sailing or wooden boats.

....

While this chapter concerns the events leading to my discovery of *Carlotta*, I will take a minute for a laugh (I hope).

When we got off the Finnish boat in the Azores, we took a ferry to Lisbon. On the way, it stopped at Madeira. The stop was only for a few hours, but long enough for us to have a drink (or two) at the famous Sports Bar. Then, being healthy young men, we thought we might have a look around for some local talent. Although Madeira is Portuguese, I thought my very elementary Spanish might do the trick, so I started approaching cab drivers, asking, "Donde esta el casa de puta?"

Due to a very heavy police presence during these years, most of the drivers wanted nothing to do with us. Finally, one grizzled old guy in a clattering deathtrap of a car, with a short, dead cigar hanging from the corner of a mouth that held only a few brown remnants of teeth, agreed to show us to the local whorehouse. We had a couple of hours before the ferry continued on to Lisbon, so we arranged to have the driver return for us, giving us just enough time to make it to the ferry.

The whorehouse was actually a large, open-air patio with, we presumed, the rooms in the back behind the bar. There were certainly plenty of attractive young women. We made our needs very clear to the proprietor, who agreed that everything was fine and indicated we should have a drink and look over the selection of women.

Keep in mind, now, that we were young men in our twenties. We had been at sea for some time, interrupted only by a few weeks in Bermuda — where most people seem to walk around with something uncomfortable jammed up their fundament — and now we were surrounded by attractive and apparently compliant women, along with as much booze as we could drink.

We bought the girls drinks, and we drank, passing the time in that delightful way in which sailors have passed the time since the first sailor rolled down a gangplank with a pocketful of change.

But…we were very aware of the passage of time. We had our favourite girls on our laps and were also buying loads of drinks for the also-rans. The sun was hot and life was good, but time was passing.

Finally I turned to Jim, "This is great, but if we're going to get laid we'd better get on with it. I'm going to talk to the boss."

I approached the proprietor and made it clear that it was nooky time. He made it equally clear that he spoke no English and had no idea what I was talking about.

We had now spent several hours and many dollars entertaining the ladies. We had played our role in the ancient ritual. I returned to the table and explained the situation to Jim.

Jim said, "Let me deal with it."

Jim is not a small man, but neither is he inclined to violence. On the other hand, we were both exceedingly horny and had a strong suspicion that we were getting ripped off. The women were also watching attentively as Jim approached the proprietor. They were well aware of the hustle and were not happy. They'd had lots of drinks and liked us in the way that young whores can still prefer certain customers to others.

Jim walked directly up to the boss and started explaining in very clear and loud language that we knew we had been hustled and were extremely unhappy. The boss backed away and Jim stepped closer, still in his face. What the boss couldn't have seen was that Jim had unzipped his fly and, while they argued, had begun pissing on the man's shoes.

By the time the guy realized what was happening, Jim was pissing up and down his pant leg. He began to slap ineffectually at Jim's dick. The women, watching the action, dissolved in laughter; it was apparent that they were entirely in sympathy with us.

This was my cue: grabbing tables, I threw them over. Jim tucked himself in and joined in the destruction. Glasses shattering, women screaming, we reduced the place to rubble while the women cheered us on.

At that very minute, as though it were a Hollywood production, the old codger in his broken-down cab showed up and we were gone. Arriving at the ship, we were the last passengers aboard. We laughed all the way to Lisbon.

....

From Lisbon I flew back to England to earn a few bucks and continue my search for a boat. It was at this juncture — when I found myself wandering around Hampshire, living in my Volkswagen van — that I stumbled across the Crableck Yard on the Hamble River. It was an early spring day with heavy dew, the mist still laying along the river: altogether a pastoral scene worthy of a Turner painting, with a few boats laying in mud berths alongside the banks of the gently flowing river and another row of yachts moored to a line of pilings down the centre of the river. The morning sun sparkled in the cobwebs that hung in their rigging, and blackberry vines dripping with morning dew crowded the footpath.

There were three 120-foot-long J boats in a row, two boats made of wood, and another, named *Velsheda*, that was constructed of steel. A little further along was a gentleman busily working away on another old wooden boat. I struck up a conversation. This was Les Windley and the boat was the *Marguerite T,* perhaps the most famous of all Bristol Channel pilot cutters. He put down his tools, invited me aboard, and we had a good gam about some of the pilot cutters I had read about but never seen.

Les and I became great friends, and I sailed often on the *Marguerite T,* eventually coming to the decision that a pilot cutter was far too much boat for me. I lived on board for a while and each evening we would row down to the Jolly

Sailor Pub, where Les was well known both for his love of women and for his talent on the banjo.

Of all the adventures we had, I will relate just one. One night, when we were both asleep, some unusual noise caused Les to awaken. He climbed out of his bunk and found himself up to his knees in water.

"Peter, Peter, get up! Get into the cockpit and start pumping like hell!"

Of course, we had both been "well away" before we went to bed after three or four hours at the Jolly Sailor. Manfully, I rose to the occasion and groped my way on deck. Les soon discovered that the problem was a missing fastening he had removed the day before and neglected to replace; as the tide rose, the empty bolthole was eventually under water, causing a bit of a problem. A wooden plug and plenty of pumping soon sorted things out and we went back to our bunks.

The next night, after another session at the Jolly Sailor, I got up in the night to relieve myself. As it happened, the head was right next to Les's cabin. The sound of me pissing into the head, which in effect was right beside *his* head, woke him up. He hit the deck running, hollering, "Peter, Peter, get pumping!" His reaction to discovering what had actually disturbed his sleep gave us both quite a laugh.

....

THE SHORTEST SEA VOYAGE EVER

The search for a boat led me down many strange paths. At one point, when I was living on the Hamble aboard *Marguerite T*, I saw an ad for a great-looking steel boat — if I remember correctly, it was an Alan Buchanan design. The picture in the magazine showed a sweet sheer and moderate overhangs, and the idea of a steel boat really appealed to me; plus, at forty feet, it seemed like one I could handle. These, you'll remember, were the days when I had decided a pilot cutter was just too much boat.

There was one small problem: the boat was located in Greece. In the seventies, of course, there was no Internet, and even phoning Greece from the U.K. was a big deal. I wrote the agent and was assured that the boat was "captain maintained" and in first class condition. He also sent me more pictures, from which I could see that she was, indeed, a beautiful boat.

Thus, one fine spring morning found me departing the Hamble, with Les howling with laughter behind me: I had found a discarded baby carriage among the blackberry brambles and converted it to a luggage/tool carrier. I tottered off down the path looking like someone from Steptoe and Son. I really believed this boat in Greece was going to work out, and consequently carried with me all the tools I thought a new boat owner should have on hand.

My good pal, Chillum John, with whom I had been living and working in London, was by coincidence also Greece-bound. We made plans to meet. We'd had a small "scopaz" factory in north London and, working in conjunction with an artist, had made a pretty decent living making reproduction art and selling it on our "pitch" in Green Park. Unfortunately, our artist had taken a vacation to the United States and been murdered. We tried to keep the company going, but in order to keep our pitch we had to be on station doing business every weekend, all winter long. Of course, there were very few tourists, so we would freeze weekend after weekend defending our proprietary rights to the pitch.

I should say here what we were doing was in no way illegal. The British Museum also sells scopaz reproductions, and I don't think anyone walks out of the museum thinking they have a piece of the Elgin Marbles under their arm. On the other hand, if a purchaser assumed he was buying original art, we wouldn't go out of our way to disabuse him of the idea.

In any case, John and I were both ready for a Greek vacation. He was bound for a friend's waterfront farmhouse on Ikaria, at that time a tourist-free Greek Island. I was headed for Athens, and from there I would find my way across Greece by train, with my baby carriage, to the small harbour where the boat was located. The owner would meet me there and I would live happily ever after with my new steel boat.

Naturally, this didn't happen.

The boat was on a mooring, but even from shore I could see that it was a badly maintained piece of rubbish. Rust streaks covered the hull. The rigging was slack and the halyards crashed around in the wake of passing vessels. Inside the hull, the ceiling (hull liner) was pegboard, the mattresses were mildewed, and the whole boat stunk of neglect.

To say I was upset would be an understatement. I swore at the owner and called him a lying piece of garbage. I unloaded my baby carriage from his dinghy and stomped off back to the train station to return to Athens. Once there, and having cooled down considerably, I contacted John and arranged to meet him at the ferry dock in Ikaria.

The journey from Piraeus to Ikaria was memorable if only because I have never seen so many people vomiting in a single location. It was only moderately rough, but, with an ocean of puke sliding from one side of the lounge to the other, it was all I could do to keep my dinner down. I was very happy to leave the ferry the next day upon reaching port.

The house we had been loaned was indeed waterfront but, as you will see in the photo of it, rather basic. Icarus had flown too close to the sun, the heat had caused his wings to melt, and he had crashed to earth only a few hundred yards from our abode…or at least that's how the myth went.

We had a great time, swimming, sunning, cooking and generally being lazy. This was at a time when the Colonels had taken over Greece and installed a Fascist government of the worst sort; read *A Man* by Oriana Fallaci to get a proper feel for this period. Paradoxically, rather than experiencing any of this police state, we three hippies (we had been joined by Gary, another friend from London) were left totally alone. The locals, who had probably never seen hippies before, were completely sanguine about our presence, and quite friendly. We tried to be discreet, but there was really no issue. On occasion we would even help the neighbours press their grapes. In borrowed gumboots, we would stomp around in a small stone pool and the juice would run out a drain into a plastic tub.

Once in a while we would go to Athens for supplies. I had never gone to the Acropolis before and it was a treat to go with John, who had spent substantial time in the country. The story he loved to tell was that, many years before, he had been studying in London to be a chartered accountant. He had taken two weeks off to have a vacation in Greece and, while there, someone had handed him a joint. He never looked back: "You've heard of the hippy trail to India? Well, I blazed it." He returned to London from his two-week vacation six years later. This was not John bragging; it was just the truth.

So, there we were at the Acropolis, and perhaps not in an entirely normal state of mind, with John instructing us about the Turkish invasion and how they had used the Acropolis as an ammunition warehouse. It had exploded, resulting in a tremendous amount of damage. The Greeks, over many years, had made several half-hearted attempts to repair the damage. I remember passing a collapsed Corinthian column that had a piece of modern rebar sticking out of it; John's comment: "That's a bit like scraping down the Mona Lisa and finding numbers."

The summer rolled on in this delightful fashion. At one point, Gary and I got the idea to go to Turkey. The ferry went from Samos, the next island over, to Izmir, Turkey. We got to Samos and were stuck there for a day or two waiting for the next ferry to Izmir.

As everyone knows, an idle mind is the devil's workshop.

We had heard that in Greece you could buy Quaaludes (Mandrax to my English brothers) over the counter. I had never taken the drug before, but many of my friends had. I thought this would be a good opportunity to "have a go," and, sure enough, the druggist sold us a bottleful. Early one evening, while sitting in a tavern near the commercial quay, we decided to swallow a couple and see what would happen. (I learned subsequently that alcohol is counter-indicated when taking Quaaludes, but who knew?)

We took our medicine and ordered a couple more ouzos. I recall we were playing chess in the warm evening air, and the tavern was full of happy Greeks drinking and shouting and slamming down dominoes. Nothing much seemed to be happening, and we were still playing chess when I noticed that Gary had taken on a pronounced list to starboard. I'm tempted to say that he crumpled off his chair, but that wasn't the case at all. He rotated with a perfectly straight back and it was actually his shoulder or head that made contact with the ground first.

The Greeks thought this was tremendously funny, but I was not so sure. I gathered Gary up and set him upright, tossed a bunch of money on the table, and got us out of there. We made our way over to the commercial dock area, which had no fence and was in fact part of the promenade. Both of us were now experiencing some pretty heavy weather. However, by grappling each other when necessary, we managed to maintain the vertical. Luckily, we didn't seem to be attracting too much attention in the poorly lit area.

There was a pretty little coastal freighter tied to the quay, and her crew was shifting cargo ashore. Gary said, "You know, Peter, I've never been on a ship before." I, of course, after my Japanese experience, was something of an old hand.

I replied that the Greeks were generally pretty relaxed and probably wouldn't mind showing us around. That indeed proved to be the case. The gangway watch welcomed us aboard and, although we had no words of Greek and they no English, they happily showed us the whole ship, from bridge to engine room. Meanwhile, of course, the bloody drugs we had taken were having a more and more deleterious effect on our navigation systems. We passed through one of the entryway doors from the engine room after our tour and arrived back on deck. We were trying to communicate with our guide when I began to sense that all was not as it should be.

There was a certain urgency in the sound of the conversation coming from the Greeks. They appeared to be trying to placate us, and the entire tone of their interaction with us seemed to be changing by the second. Just then I looked to where the gangway had been; not only was it gone, the ship was moving away from the dock. I hadn't spent years of my youth reading about press gangs and "shanghaiing" for nothing.

"Gary!" I yelled, "They've got us!"

The Greeks were now forcibly trying to restrain us, but I broke away, rushed to the open side of the ship and launched myself into space. I landed ass over teakettle on the dock, with Gary just behind. The Greeks were yelling, and I was cursing them in return. Gary was rolling around clutching his ankle, but at least we were free. And the ship? Well, it moved about eighty feet down the dock, where the crew secured it again. As it turned out, the conversation had only been to reassure us that they were just moving a short distance.

I got Gary to his feet. With the drug and his badly sprained ankle, we did an awkward dance pulling at one another, falling this way and that. I realized we couldn't go on. That is, Gary couldn't. First he sat down on the rough pavement, then he lay down. Not sure what else to do, I rolled him against the side of a building, covered him with an old piece of cardboard and went home to our B&B.

And that was the shortest sea voyage ever.

. . . .

It was back in the U.K., not long after this episode, that I resumed my search for a boat. At the same time, I was now also searching for a boat for my mother and stepfather and, while I failed to find a boat for myself, I did find one for them: a sixty-foot converted torpedo recovery vessel. I returned to Canada and my parents flew to England to close the deal. With three Gardner diesel main engines, it was easily capable of taking them back to the Caribbean. Bob, my stepfather, worked hard to complete the needed changes in Thomas's Yacht Yard in Falmouth, and it was arranged that I would join them for the trip to Puerto Rico.

The search for a boat of my own was proving more difficult than I could have imagined, and three months later I was back in Vancouver wondering what to do next, wallowing a bit in a windless groundswell. But, as is often the case when I'm not charging ahead and tilting at all available windmills, life stepped in and lent a hand.

I received a letter from my mother telling me that Bob had suffered a heart attack and I was needed. Of course, I dropped everything, flew to the U.K. and took the train to Falmouth, where Bob had been deeply immersed in the preparations for an Atlantic crossing.

I wasn't there long before the doctor discovered that, in fact, Bob hadn't suffered a heart attack, but instead had testicular cancer. Things went downhill very quickly, and this wonderful man, who had become my *de facto* father, died. A bright light was extinguished for all of us that day.

My mother was devastated, and it was left to me to arrange to bury Bob, sell the boat, and get my mother safely off to friends in Canada. While all of this was going on, I passed the time looking at — what else? — wooden boats. Lots of wooden boats. One day I saw an ad for a pilot cutter that was lying at Fowey. When I discovered that Fowey was only twenty-five miles up the coast, I thought I would take a look. I was not very hopeful, as by this time I had looked at hundreds of boats and been disappointed time and time again.

It was a beautiful Cornish morning with a slight mist hanging over the river and fields. John, the boat's owner, launched a punt and was rowing. I, of course, was in the stern, facing forward. And there, moored in the middle of the river, was this black beauty — no mast, no rigging, and even at a distance I could tell the hull was rough. But, God, was she beautiful. I can clearly remember thinking, I hope that's the boat we're headed for. I hope that's *Carlotta*.

I was lost from the first moment. Smitten. And I'll tell you something else: for the next thirty-five years and a million tribulations only touched on by these scribblings, I never, ever rowed away from *Carlotta* without thinking, God, what a beauty. I'm pretty sure that's why it's the custom to face backward when rowing: so you can have a last look at your beautiful boat.[1]

The sale went ahead very quickly. The owners — overjoyed that they had found a live one — and I — overjoyed that I had found my dream boat — inked a deal. The 2,500 pounds sterling seemed like a joke (about $5,000 in those days;

---

[1] The well-known writer and pilot cutter authority Tom Cunliffe once described *Carlotta* in his *Yachting Monthly* column as "the loveliest cutter of them all," so I like to think I was being objective.

at the time of this writing, the boat is for sale for US$310,000). My life was totally and irrevocably changed from that day forward.

Because I was still in possession of my parent's boat, I used it to tow *Carlotta* from Fowey down to Thomas's yard, where I was promised a berth alongside some dolphins. Her gear, which included spars and rigging, was left in a yard near Fowey for the time being.

When I eventually did recover the gear, I was charged a hefty storage fee, as well as being charged for her "legs."

Seems reasonable, I hear you thinking. Perhaps, but the whole story is that this yard had been responsible for fashioning the legs for *Carlotta* that very nearly put an end to her. In the U.K., it is common practice for boats to have vertical posts (or legs) that bolt securely at the boat's greatest beam. These are carefully formed and very strong, serving to balance the boat on the bottom when the tide goes out — sort of like a portable tidal grid that goes everywhere with you. When you want to sail you wait for high tide, unbolt the legs, and you're away.

Dick Twist, the famous owner of *Carlotta* prior to John, had warned him that they must never, ever put legs on the boat. Well, other people thought differently, and the yard in question had built the legs. The boat was left unattended to dry out for the first time. When the tide was fully out, one leg collapsed and the boat smashed down from upright.

To give you some idea of the force, the distance from the extreme end of the counter to the ground when the boat is resting naturally on her keel is thirteen feet. She displaces about thirty tons. Thirty-three individual futtocks (parts of the frame) were broken. The bilge stringer was broken. Untold months were added to the rebuilding project. Pay for the legs and storage? I'm not so sure.

However, I was young and, if not stupid, at least naïve. I got the boat safely to Thomas's with the help of George, a Cornish friend of my parents and something of a gofer. Although terribly helpful in my early days in Falmouth, it turned out he was madly trying to get into the pants of my newly widowed mother, while also remaining busy helping himself to parts off the boat I was trying to sell for her. The Cornish are a complex and interesting people.

All was set for the start of the rebuild — except that my dog was still in Canada, as was my girlfriend, Sandy. England was stupid about rabies in those days, so importing the dog legally was out of the question. I did have access to my mother's boat, though, and my girlfriend could just as easily come to Brittany in France as she could to Cornwall. Thus the great dog-smuggling caper began.

We arranged the rendezvous for L'Aber Wrach. We slipped out of Falmouth and crossed the channel. On board was George, along with a fisherman friend of his who may have made the trip before (we didn't inquire too closely), and Chuck, a hippy friend from Canada. All went as planned. After dodging the insane traffic in the English Channel, we tied up to a large public buoy alongside a French police boat. Sandy was waiting for us after a somewhat eventful train trip from Amsterdam with the dog. In actuality, there were two dogs. Since we were making the trip anyway, we had agreed to bring the dog of a young English gentleman who was engaged to an American girl. Apparently, she had made it very clear that the engagement would not proceed unless he figured out how to get her dog into England from the U.S. For us, five hundred quid was five hundred quid, so we agreed to bring the dog.

A quick trip ashore to enter and clear Customs and get some fresh baguettes and we were off, back to England. At that time I had a mooring in the Helford River near Falmouth that belonged to my mother's boat. The fisherman and George slipped ashore with the other dog, while the rest of us had a few beers and went to sleep. There would be plenty of time in the morning to report our arrival.

So, after a leisurely sleep-in and breakfast, I rowed ashore to report to Customs. But when I stepped out of the dinghy, cops and Customs officials came bursting from behind every tree and vehicle in the area. I was surrounded. Their own boat surged up to the dock with lights flashing. I was grasped very firmly by the upper arm in that irritating way the police have of demonstrating power and control, and we returned to our boat. Questions were flying. I remember the head cop saying, "What is it, Pakis or hash?" This referred to the smuggling of Pakistani refugees and hashish that was prevalent at the time.

Meantime, my dog snoozed, unbothered, beneath the cabin table. Something didn't compute. If they had caught the desperate band of dog smugglers, why were they asking us about hashish? (To be sure, Chuck had spent a very intense five minutes in the head flushing all our drugs away when he saw me being busted on shore.) Finally, I turned to my friends and said, "We answer no questions until they tell us what's going on." After another few minutes of frustrated yelling, they settled down and told us that the Coast Guard (in England at the time, this was the name for a network of informers who kept an eye on boat movements to prevent smuggling) had reported us up the River Fal when we declared ourselves in France.

I smugly informed them that when we were in France, we'd been tied alongside the French National Police boat, and that should be very simple to check. This took the wind out of their sails pretty quickly. Of course, they couldn't just say they were sorry and leave, but we definitely felt a shift; they became, if not polite, at least less aggressive.

It became apparent in time that we had nothing to hide and they started to leave. The overbearing jackass who had taken me by the bicep and exhibited the most aggression during the questioning turned at the door. Pointing under the table, he said, "That dog better not have gone ashore in France."

"Of course not," I replied, "We are well aware of the laws."

A few days later, I went to the Falmouth Customs office to (incorrectly) try to register *Carlotta*. Sitting at the desk was the same officious prick. Putting my palms up in a gesture of defence, I said, "No, no, I haven't come to confess." He was not amused.

CHAPTER 4

....

THE REBUILD

Where do you begin such a vast rebuilding project? I felt I was pretty well prepared, having taken eighth-grade wood shop. I had owned a boat before *Carlotta*, but it was nine feet long and made of fibreglass. I decided that polishing the running lights was probably a good place to start.

For years afterward, I laughed at myself for starting out this way, but I'm not so sure it was all that silly. The fact is, if you don't know where to start a big project, it's sometimes best to at least do something that does no serious harm while you figure out your first move. I like to take Robert Pirsig's quote from *Zen and the Art of Motorcycle Maintenance* and make it applicable to the sailing world: "The real [boat] you're working on is a [boat] called yourself."

What to say about the four years rebuilding *Carlotta*...

I moved her from Fowey to Cyril Thomas's, and this was her home for the next four years. She leaned against a few dolphins in a yard that was mostly a hard beach with several large sheds and railways. Cyril seemed ancient to us (but then, we were relatively young) and, like all Cornishmen, watched his money very carefully. And yet, I felt we did become friends over the years. Sometimes he would open the office safe and share dirty pictures with us. This was before computer porn. I remember once he trotted out some strange sex pictures. After a moment I burst out, "But they're fags!" He chortled and said, "Feels the same, just smells different." Funny old guy, Cyril.

When rebuilding a boat, it is a fact that no matter how much work one does on it or how much money is spent, it becomes less and less valuable until the very last coat of paint is applied. A great many people are defeated, and their lives destroyed, because they don't come out the other end. I did come out, mainly because I had some financial reserves, but also because this was the first big project I had ever undertaken and failure was simply not an option. The other side of the coin is that, once a young man completes a project like this, he will never again be intimidated ("The same fire that melts the butter bakes the bread").

I could put it off no longer; I had to pick up the tools. The boat had a very dark interior made of Japanese oak. I don't know what Japanese oak is, but I suspect it is what we call brown oak; it is more dimensionally stable than white oak, although much more prone to rot. The interior had been neglected for years, and had become darker and darker with age. Also, it had no dead lights in the deckhead, adding to the gloom. So here was the dilemma: I knew there must be serious damage behind all of this raised-panel joinery, because I knew she had fallen over. The issue was how to take it apart so that I could later reassemble the work of those master craftsmen of the 1920s.

I began with a series of small pry bars to lift the detailing, and then I could tap the stiles and rails apart. I labelled each piece with masking tape and a code indicating its position.

This method lasted about fifteen minutes. After this, I picked up a large wrecking bar that had some serious weight to it and had the interior out in an afternoon.

To this day, you can probably go into a pub in Falmouth or Penryn and there will be some old fart mumbling into his pint of bitter, "Oh yes, I remember Peter, he was the one who ruined the beautiful interior of *Carlotta*." Nobody talks about the assholes who let the boat fall over in the first place.

I'm not going to get into the whole rebuild. I was a lousy carpenter and did a lousy job, but I saved the boat. I think I replaced thirty-three futtocks and 300 or so feet of planking. Horn timbers, knightheads, deck beams, bilge stringers, counter, and on and on…and on again. I clearly remember thinking one day: the boat is only fifty feet long, there must be a finite number of problems.

But the real motherfucker was that I had never done a big job in my life. I didn't know if I could do it. Everywhere I looked, there were more problems. I remember waking up one morning after a serious acid trip with some local friends, all alone in the filth, looking around and thinking: I can't do this. There is just too much wrong. I've fucked up. I'm fucked.

There were no shower facilities in the yard, so I was constantly filthy. My living conditions were disgusting, and I had no refrigeration and only a very basic cooker. I had left one of the original bunks in place so that I had somewhere to sleep, and every night I rolled into bed exhausted and unshowered. An old copper exhaust pipe ran alongside my bunk, and most nights I would be awakened by rats running along the pipe to get to my makeshift galley; they had a particular fondness for cereal. Worse, I have an enduring vision of peeling off some strips of bacon for breakfast and finding a conical pile of squirming maggots between layers.

At about this time, when I was approximately one-quarter of the way through my rebuild of *Carlotta*, I became completely despondent — totally defeated by the endless work with so little apparent progress. I decided to take a couple of days off to visit Les, who now had the *Marguerite T* anchored in the Medina River in Cowes, on the Isle of Wight. This involved a train journey to Southampton, a ferry across to the island and, finally, a walk until I was opposite *Marguerite*. Once there, I sat down on the grass in a large pasture dotted with oak trees and stared down at a picture of loveliness floating in centre stream. Such a beautiful boat.

I sat for twenty minutes, realized I now had all the inspiration I needed, and walked back to the ferry. I got back on the train, returned to *Carlotta*, and picked up my hammer. I never did speak to Les, but I wrote him later and told I had come to visit, saying, "Thanks for the help." He laughed and understood.

....

As an historical note — for those interested in the *Marguerite T* — it was here, on her moorings on the Medina, that Les had the fire that destroyed the beautiful stained-glass windows that depicted marguerite flowers at the foot of the companionway (they were leaded glass and melted in the heat). Les had switched from burning coal in his solid fuel stove to teak scraps, without realizing they burned substantially hotter. He was ashore when friends saw smoke pouring out of the companionway and rowed out to save the boat.

....

Back to pounding nails on *Carlotta*.

Because of the difficulty (or impossibility) of finding grown frames for a whole boat, the futtock system was developed. In a perfect world, parts of the oak tree would be found whose grain perfectly followed the curve of the boat's hull. In the double futtock system, it was necessary only to find a length of oak that followed a single part of the curve; then, by staggering it with a sister frame lying alongside that followed a subsequent part of the curve, and then joining them together with a number of iron pins, you could approximate the strength of a single frame that followed a double curve from keel to deck.

For perspective, think of a wine glass. Now imagine it's eight or ten feet high and you are trying to find a length of oak that follows the curve formed by the sides of the glass. Still don't understand? Go buy a wooden boat and bang your knuckles for four years like I did.

In England, it was, and still is, illegal to cut down oak trees. When it was time to replace the futtocks, I made up templates that followed the curve formed by the broken futtock, and then travelled around the countryside trying to find boatyards that had a stock of filches of oak whose grain followed my template. I had some success, but was nowhere close to getting the thirty-three pieces necessary.

I had some friends at this time living in Mylor Creek. Once, while visiting them, I had noticed a whole row of beautiful, mature oak trees on the other side of the creek that had collapsed due to erosion of the creek bank. Since you were allowed to cut up trees that had already fallen, the plan was hatched. I found the farmer who owned the trees and explained my problem. He was more than helpful, saying I could take any of the limbs I wanted but would have to pay for the trunks. Given the fairly radical nature of the curves required, I had no use for the trunks.

There are two types of Cornishmen: those who are incredibly fucked up about money, and those who are generous and spiritually large. These oak trees were located across the creek from Terry Heard's boatyard, and he was one of the best: generous with his boat-building knowledge, generous with his tools, and, in this case, generous by allowing me access both to the creek and to his dinghy. I was saddened some years ago to learn of his premature death.

Thus I found myself early one clear, calm, soft summer morning, mist lying on the creek, with the only sound the occasional milk truck meandering down the lanes, launching Terry's dinghy with an armload of patterns and a Swede saw. Beaching the dinghy on the farmer's side of the creek, I took my time, but had no trouble finding the necessary curves. I would buck off the outboard end of the limb, buck off the inboard end, drag it to the water, and row it across to the yard. In less than three days' work, I had all my futtocks. Well, that's not quite true. I had tree limbs that were perhaps five or eight times greater in mass than the final futtock, but I had my wood. With the help of some friends in the yard, we strong-armed the wood into my old Bedford van and I drove it up to a mill whose owner understood about frames and had agreed to cut them. It all felt so organic: from tree to boat, with only my sweat in between and Cornwall at its best.

Before I began the rebuilding job, I had read all the books I could yet still had no real appreciation for the size of the project. In truth, I probably never would have begun it if I had. For a long time, it was a source of irritation to me that people would come along as I ripped off another plank or lifted another covering board, and say, "That's a big job you've got there." They said this when I first began the job in Falmouth in the seventies, when — no argument — I had an immense job in front of me, but they were still saying it as I spent a couple of hours splashing on a coat of anti-fouling paint in the nineties.

It took me a long time to figure out why this irritated me so much. First of all, I had a much better appreciation (before long) of the size of the job than they did. Second, I didn't understand whether they were giving me a warning, or communicating their superior knowledge of wooden boats. Finally, I hit upon the solution to shutting up these morons, and it's one I still use today. Whenever anyone would come along and say, "That's a big job you've got there," I would reply without looking up, "Yeah, you're right, I should probably be watching more television." I just knew the twits who were vomiting this nonsense were spending all of their evenings and weekends watching their lives drain into the unfillable television sinkhole.

At about this time, two things happened. One of them was personal and sad, and the other was significant to the success of the project.

The first was that Sandy, the Canadian woman who had brought my dog over, was mutually deemed unsuitable for the life of boats I had chosen. This was a person who had been my friend for years, and I'm sure I'm not the first to note that we lose a lot of friends to love. She was the kind of woman who would cause drunks to approach me in pubs and lecture me about how lucky I was, telling me I should take care of her, etc.; you've all heard it. She was fairly liberated and this irritated her even more than it did me. Still, she couldn't stand the feel of sandpaper on her fingers and, for better or worse, there was going to be a lot of sandpaper in my future.

The morning of her departure arrived. We were living on *Carlotta* at the time — as I did, stupidly, all throughout the rebuild — so were pretty dirty. It was dark and it was early. Neither of us felt good about what was happening, but we both knew it was necessary. My old Bedford van was not at her best, but we only had to get to the airport, a reasonably short distance away, and I was confident we'd be fine. Naturally, we were late, and hurrying, and both feeling rather shitty about what was happening. Adding to that, we were a little hung over, but we were both determined to get it over with.

So we did. We arrived at the airport, she left, and life went on.

....

WHEN THE STUDENT IS READY, THE TEACHER WILL APPEAR

The other thing that happened was that I hired Peter Divers as an assistant, and this turned out to be one of the smartest things I did during the rebuild. He was a wonderful guy who took great pride in being a shipwright and had no ego problems about instructing a protégé. You can read more about him in a book titled *Schooner Man*.

We worked together for almost a year. How about this: a qualified sailor/ shipwright working with you for ninety pence an hour? It was stupidly cheap even then. By the time he left *Carlotta*, we were replacing underwater planks… between tides. What this means to the uninitiated is that, as the tide fell, we would remove a plank that was eight inches wide, two inches thick and twenty feet long. Then we would take another plank, shape it to fit the hole perfectly, and have it installed, fastened and caulked before the tide rose again. The consequences of not finishing the job once begun do not bear thinking about. One time, after finishing a plank, I realized we had done the whole job without exchanging a word — the good side of male bonding.

I remember the first time we drove up to look at the rigging that had been removed from *Carlotta* when the mast came out. It was piled in a heap perhaps four feet high by eight feet across. To me it just looked like a rat's nest of rusting wire rope.

Peter picked up a piece: "Gaff span." Next piece: "Upper shroud." Next piece: "Inner forestay." Next piece: "Bowsprit shroud." And so on through the pile. I was dumbfounded. And, for the next eighteen months, he never let me down. If something was debatable or there were different ways to do it, he would speak up and give me both sides of the argument. Of course, I had to pay him: yep, ninety pence ($1.80) per hour. When he was surprised by something or something went wrong, he would roll back on his heels and say, "Well, fuck my old boots." Forty years later, when I'm surprised by something or something goes wrong, I roll back on my heels and say, "Well, fuck my old boots."

Probably a year had passed between buying the boat and finding Peter. As I mentioned earlier, and as anyone who has rebuilt a boat will attest, you start work and then the boat and conditions degenerate until you apply the final coat of paint. I'm not exaggerating. In other words, you buy a boat — it may be in terrible condition, but you saw something of value in it, so now you own it — and then you rip out the interior, tear off planks, rip up the decks, etc. All the time you're doing this, the boat is becoming worth less and less…and even less. In the meantime, you are spending more and more…and even more. Until you apply that last coat of paint, you may just as well be investing in a serious cocaine habit for all the good it seems to be doing.

But here's what's important: as you rip your dream boat apart, you'd better be fucking sure you can see the project through. If you don't, you're about to eat your lunch in a serious financial and spiritual way. The boatyard I live near now has a whole section of the yard referred to as "the field of broken dreams."

In this year before getting Peter on board, I had ripped out the interior, removed several covering boards, and made serious inroads into replacing the broken futtocks…but still.

Then Peter arrived on the job, not at all overwhelmed by the scope of it. For him, it was just another job. What was at least as good was that my pal Jim arrived from Canada to buy himself a wooden boat and sail back to Canada. (At the entrance to Falmouth Harbour is a rock with a light on it called Black Rock. Jim and I used to joke that sailing to Canada wasn't difficult; it was getting to Black Rock that was difficult.) With Peter's help, we found Jim and his (former) wife Marilyn a good boat. And there we were, three friends from Canada putting our boats together in Thomas's Yacht Yard under the able tutelage of Peter Divers.

For the year I had spent in Cornwall, a peculiar aspect of the Cornish had really begun to wear on me. In Canada, if you had a project going and got a nice bit of equipment, everyone would admire your acquisition. In Cornwall, everyone would want to know how much it cost and then would let you know how badly you had gotten ripped off. Once or twice I could laugh — I was not poor, so I could afford what I was doing — but for a whole year every single purchase was chewed over with the goal of making me feel like a fool, and this by knowledgeable people. Since I had no great confidence at all about the enterprise, it truly ground me down.

Jim was a like a breath of fresh air. He was raised in the Yukon, and was used to making lots of money (as a hard rock miner) and spending lots of money. "Fuck these Cornish dildos that have been poor for centuries," he said, "Let's get on with the job."

And we did. We persevered with our projects and had a thousand adventures and misadventures, some good and some really not so good. But we were young and doing what we wanted to do during the day, then having lots of fun in the evenings. It's hard to get better than that.

We would work on our boats every day, then go up to the pub every night. Work went forward at a satisfactory pace. Of course, I had my dog, Gravy, with me by this time and he was a truly great companion. Every night Gravy would come with us to the pub and, since I was now single, *I* chose the pub; naturally, I selected the pub frequented by the women who attended the Falmouth School of Art. It wasn't too long each evening before the pub was very crowded and very smoky. Gravy would get trampled on every few minutes, so after a while he'd decide it was not much fun and head out into the night to pursue male-dog activities. (I never asked, but I'm sure they were not much different from male-human activities.)

The pub closed at eleven. The dog gone, I would stagger, depending on my luck, either to my boat or someone else's home. At some time during the night — *every* night — Gravy would return to the pub to see how I was making out. Finding the door closed, he would scratch and scratch until the publicans who lived above the establishment would get out of bed, go downstairs, and open the door so that he could make his rounds of the interior looking for me. Finding me gone, he'd make his way back to the boatyard and bed. They would give me hell the next evening, but they never stopped letting him in to confirm that I wasn't there. In fact, the owners got up every single night after going to bed — wait for this — *for a year,* and let the dog in to look for me. Only in England.

One time Jim asked me if I had any wood so he could fashion some engine bearers for his boat. I had a stack of keruing I thought would be perfect for the job, so I told him where the stack was and thought no more about. Later that night, we were bullshitting at the pub and Jim commented that the keruing was a lot like teak to work with. I laughed and said, "Yeah, but teak is about twenty times the price." Oh Jesus, it couldn't be true. But it was. Somewhere in Western Canada, there is a very pretty little sailboat, formerly called the *John Cabot*, with quite beautiful Burmese teak engine bearers. Jim had misunderstood my directions.

Around this time, I began to come to serious terms with the difficulties of putting an engine in *Carlotta*. She had been built without one, which meant the shaft and propeller were offset to port. This in turn meant that the engine had to be situated in the middle of the bloody boat, just where you didn't want it. Then, of course, I had to deal with the shaft log, gland, A-bracket, shaft, propeller, clutch, tanks, primary filter, engine mounts and bearers, and so on, *ad infinitum*. And all this while I was reeling under a tremendous load of work as I continued to find more rot and other problems with the boat. It was enough to make a person go get stoned.

And that's how I found myself back in Mylor Creek on board Chas and Sue's boat, *Nell*, which had been built in 1886 and was, I believe, the oldest boat on which I've had the pleasure of sailing*. Old as it was, it was in beautiful condition. As we sat around one evening smoking some of Afghanistan's finest, I described in great detail the many hassles I was experiencing putting an engine in the boat.

In a great billow of smoke, Chas said, "Why not do without an engine? I'm throwing mine overboard."

My troubles fell away like a suit of clothes.

It was not long after this that Chas and Sue sold *Nell* and bought a farm. I ended up sailing for the next thirty-five years with no engine. There's a lesson in there somewhere.

---

* Chas, Sue and I, along with some other friends, had a wonderful sail to Ireland on *Nell* — the story of which will have to wait for another book. However, it was on that trip that I first experienced the joy of flopping around in thick fog with heavy shipping all around (not that a motor would have made that any better). At one point, Chas dragged out an old bellows-operated foghorn that, like *Nell*, was probably built in 1886. It wheezed reluctantly twice, and was quietly put away without further comment. It might have been helpful in the days of sail, but, in the days of fast, steel, diesel-powered ships, it was just an embarrassment.

CHAPTER 5

....

SELFLESS SELF-ABUSE

Oh, God, why did You give me such a talent for the ridiculous?
— George MacDonald Fraser

At one point I began living with Jane, a model from the art school. She'd had two or three thousand boyfriends before me, and had never become pregnant. This seemed like a bonus to me, as the last thing I needed was the decrepit wreck of a pilot cutter and a baby. She agreed that a baby was not in the cards, but she wanted to know if there was something wrong with her given that she had spent the last ten years awash in sperm with no pregnancy. (Those may not have been her exact words, but it was something like that.)

I thought that was reasonable and volunteered to assist her in any way I could, thinking along the lines of driving her to the hospital. At the Truro medical clinic, however, they informed her that before checking her plumbing they would have to run a sperm test on her boyfriend, for the simple reason that it was much easier.

A wiser man might have asked, "Easier on whom?"

As I said, though, I didn't mind helping, and I had often bragged that after my years at private school I knew seventy-two ways to beat off. After a week's abstinence, I was sure I could do it on a ski lift.

At the time all this happened, we were, of course, living on my filthy boat. The morning arrived when we had to be in Truro at seven o'clock in the morning for me to provide sperm. I still had my terrible old Bedford van (used exclusively to haul boat supplies but generally reliable enough to get me where I was going). We set the alarm for six. It was winter: dark and cold. I got up first to light the Tilly lamp.

For those of you who don't know anything about Tilly lamps, they are fuelled with kerosene (paraffin in the U.K.). The first thing you have to do is pressurize the tank with a small, built-in pump, hold a container of "meths" (methyl alcohol) under the mantle, and light the alcohol. Once the kerosene gains enough warmth to vapourize, the mantle will ignite and you can remove the meths.

All of this can be done very easily…unless it's six in the morning, dark and cold, you are hung over, and you spill the bottle of lighted meths, causing the flaming alcohol to run down under the lamp into the open drawer that contains your clothes, where the two proceed to combine enthusiastically with oxygen. In due time we got the fire out, got dressed (both of us feeling a bit pissy), and headed out into the drizzling Cornish rain to the truck.

The truck was a good truck, the way old trucks can be, but was not without its issues. One of the issues was that it tended to lose coolant. No doubt I could have fixed it, but I couldn't rebuild a boat and also fuck around with an old truck (or at least that was my thinking).

There is a long hill as you leave Falmouth for Truro. I was aware that time was now an issue following our firefighting activities, as I hadn't left a lot of leeway for fires in the cabin when I'd budgeted our time. Therefore, it was a little upsetting to see the temperature gauge slowly climbing into the red area. Fortunately, I knew that if we could just get to the top of the hill, there was a petrol station where they would surely have water.

We made it. The station was closed, but there was a water standpipe near one wall. I was sure we were safe. We pulled up beside the tap and I stood looking at it stupidly: here was the water and here was the radiator, but there was no hose. As I searched the immediate area for a vessel suitable for transporting water, I was becoming very mindful of the time remaining to reach my appointment to masturbate. I searched the truck. It was hard to believe there was no pot, no bucket, not a thing that would carry water.

Luckily I'm not totally without creativity (whatever you may think). I was wearing gumboots, and, since time was now pressing, I took off one boot and filled it with water from the tap, started the engine, and poured the water into the radiator. It worked fine, but didn't fill the radiator. I hobbled over the wet ground in my one sock, refilled the boot, and turned around just as the police were pulling into the petrol station.

Would you believe me if I said the first words out of the cop's mouth were, "Hallo, hallo, what's all this, then?" God's truth.

There is some rule of life that the surest way to make a cop slow down is to try to make him hurry up. I really didn't want to explain about my rapidly approaching appointment for self-abuse, but I did say we were desperate to get to a doctor's appointment in Truro. Meanwhile, he was idly picking bits of broken glass out of one of my headlights. That's another story, and just the sort of thing to interest a copper.

We were finally able to get on our way, and arrived at the beat-off clinic. It was part of the Truro Hospital complex, with the usual endless halls painted bureaucratic green, with signs that meant nothing unless you were a physician. Eventually we got to our destination, and it wasn't a beat-off clinic at all. It was the "Clinic for Reproductive Health," don't ya know.

I felt a little conspicuous striding into that room. Ten or twelve people were sitting against the walls, everybody trying to look at something else; a quick glance at me and then back to staring intently at nothing. So, I wondered, was everybody waiting to beat off? I wasn't sure, but judging from the ambience in the room I'm going to guess the answer was yes.

I walked over to the receptionist, gave my name and appointment time, and was handed a glass jar and informed that the "gents" was just down the hall.

Now, I'm not sure what I was expecting, but to be informed in front of twelve strangers where I was to beat off, and be handed a jar to gather my production — frankly, I found the whole thing rather off-putting. I've been in one or two sexual situations that I wouldn't necessarily want my mother to know about and I like to think I've discharged my duties reasonably well, but to walk down the hall with my little glass jar to a public washroom to beat my meat — especially after the morning we'd already had, with one leg still wet most of the way to the knee — well, suffice it to say that I wasn't feeling particularly horny. This is not to mention that there were at least ten people waiting for me to come. One or two are bad enough, if you get my drift.

But…time to man up, Peter, as they say. And I tried. God knows I tried. I pulled and pushed and thought of happier times and other situations (real and imagined) and…nothing happened. Of course, the longer it took, the more I thought of all those people sitting out here wondering how it could take so long.

Finally, I had to admit defeat. I charged back out to the waiting room and, with everyone looking expectantly (hopefully?) at me, grabbed the Englishwoman by the arm. I dragged her to the men's room and into a stall, pushed her to her knees, and said, "This is your problem. This is not my problem. Deal with it."

And she did.

CHAPTER 6

....

CARLOTTA'S LUCK

...any jackass can fuck a woman, but you goddamned well can't fuck a ship off a lee shore!
— Sterling Hayden

$\mathbf{A}$t some point during my relationship with *Carlotta* (I almost used the word "ownership"), and after I'd gotten her sailing, I came to understand that she was a lucky ship. I suppose I must have picked up the concept of lucky versus unlucky ships from reading Joseph Conrad. I couldn't help but notice that there were times when I would make the most disastrous failures of judgment and *Carlotta* would pull my ass out of the fire. This is not to say that I didn't have my share of embarrassments, some of which I note in these pages, but by and large I didn't suffer as much as I should have.

A quick example. In the very early days when I first got *Carlotta* sailing, I had Jane, the Englishwoman, on board with me, and no one else. I was determined to try to sail the boat by myself (what was wrong with me? — single-handing a boat with a 1,000-square-foot mains'l?), but was not confident enough to actually go alone. I explained the situation to Jane: she was to do nothing unless it was an emergency, and I would do all of the work. She accepted this without question and did exactly that for the next four years. It was not exactly what I'd meant, but what the hell.

On this particular day, we were having an afternoon sail to the Helford River from Falmouth. I had made the sail many times before on other boats, so didn't bother dragging out the chart for a short day sail in local waters. As we made our way around Black Rock, at the entrance to Falmouth Harbour, we came up on a friend on his boat, apparently also going to the Helford River. However, as we headed up for the river, he sagged well away to leeward, while I kept right on for the river. I had no idea what he was up to, but I've heard it said that you should "never judge your course by the course of another vessel; remember the man who followed the barge only to find it had gone to load sand."

We had an uneventful sail and anchored in the river, tired but happy. It was the next day while poring over the chart that I realized we had sailed directly over a major rock. I don't know how we could have missed it, but that was why our friend fell off to leeward. I had seen that rock on the chart a dozen times, but forgotten all about it.

A lucky ship.

. . . .

The following is an even better story about *Carlotta*'s luck. (By the way, I never spoke, or never in more than a whisper, of *Carlotta*'s luck while I owned her. I'm a great one for not tempting fate.)

This jumps ahead to my life in St. Barths, but the story seems to fit here. I had single-handed from St. Barths to St. Maarten, and remember writing in my log that it was "the final solution to the crew problem." The people I so often had on board detracted in such a big way from my early sailing experiences that it was a joy to discover the freedom of sailing alone. I didn't kid myself about my strength or about the boat, however, and I never did a big trip alone on *Carlotta*.

By chance, my friends Paul Johnson on *Venus* and the Frith Family on *Moon* were in St. Maarten too, and were also heading back to St. Barths. I had previously made a very bad mistake while sailing from St. Maarten to St. Barths (related in Chapter 10), but this time I knew the way. I went better to weather, so Paul and John had left a few hours ahead of me. After a while, as I came around the north side of Fourche, I could easily see them in the distance. The wind had freshened as I worked to windward up the channel, and by the time I could bear off for St. Barths I had a roll in the main and had dropped the stays'l.

One of the less endearing qualities of *Carlotta* was that, in order to sail and answer her helm, she required sail both fore and aft of the mast. In this case, I dropped the stays'l because I had most of the main still up, and she balanced better with the flying jib and a nearly full main.

I'm not sure whether it was due to a wind shift or my not being able to point as high as I'd hoped as we came around the north shore of the island of Fourche, but I became conscious that I was closer than I wanted to be to the lee shore. In fact, sailing a boat without an engine makes one extremely conscious of lee shores. I am often amazed at how differently others sail than myself, because they know they have that engine starter button under their finger.

Anyway, I was not happy with the shore so close, but Fourche is a small island and the lee shore would only be a lee shore for twenty minutes or so.

And then, into my head unbidden, came a thought: what would happen if the jib outhaul failed? The flying jib on *Carlotta* travels in and out on the bowsprit attached to a steel ring that is around the bowsprit. That ring is attached to the outhaul, a wire rope that pulls the ring out to the sheave in the end of the bowsprit. First you pull the jib out to the outboard end of the bowsprit, then haul it aloft with the halyard. When dousing, you just trip the outhaul and the ring shoots inboard; when the jib sags away into the lee of the stays'l, you drop the halyard and gather in the jib. Nothing could be simpler.

However, on this particular day I didn't have the stays'l up. Thus, if the outhaul failed, the jib would collapse and I would effectively have no sail forward of the mast; the boat would be unmanageable. But why would the outhaul fail? There wasn't much strain on it. Since I used it daily, I would have noticed if there were meathooks or any other signs of weakness. Still, I couldn't shake the thought: what if it failed?

The eastern end of Fourche was rapidly approaching. I could see Paul and John not far away and that was somewhat comforting (although what they could do to help if this disquieting premonition became reality I wasn't sure). Finally, we reached the end of Fourche, the lee shore ceased to exist, and…the outhaul broke.

The jib outhaul slammed back to the stemhead. The jib went mad, now being effectively half-lowered. The tiller became useless in my hand. Fortunately, with my now unlimited sea room, I fell off to leeward, strolled forward, and made repairs. But there had been perhaps thirty seconds between a minor repair at sea and a lost boat, or even death. *Carlotta*'s luck.

Paul Johnson and John Frith, I subsequently discovered, had no idea I was even there.

....

A final illustration of *Carlotta*'s luck (overcoming my stupidity) took place at the Maritime Museum in Vancouver, BC, when I'd first arrived with her in Canada. A friend of mine on the museum's board of directors had sailed on *Carlotta*, knew her history, and had arranged for me to have a space in the marina. However, I was living in Gibsons at the time and had never been in the docks with a boat.

Owing to the vicissitudes of owning an engineless vessel, it was about three in the morning when we prepared to enter the man-made bay that contains the museum's docks. I thought the entrance looked pretty straightforward: a breakwater formed one side of the very small bay and land formed the other two sides. I had a basic plan, but since I had never entered under sail before I took a few runs back and forth across the little bay until I was confident about my speed. Then I shot up into the wind. The breeze was light and everything went well.

Much to my surprise, when I arose the next morning I discovered that the whole bay was filled with mud, and just the smallest passage allowed access to the finger floats. I had gaily assumed there was deep water throughout the bay. It was only by the greatest of luck that we had arrived at the top of a big tide that enabled *Carlotta*'s eight feet of draft to clear the mud.

I'm here to tell you that it really is better to be lucky than good.

CHAPTER 7

·················

LEAVING FALMOUTH , ONCE, TWICE, THREE TIMES...

You don't heave-to in them ships unless you are waiting for something.
— John Reid Muir, *Messing About in Boats*

On a snowy afternoon in December working on this book, I sit looking over the logbook I started the day I departed Falmouth after four years of work on *Carlotta*. I see that the day of departure was September 21, 1976 — an auspicious day because it was my birthday, but made less so because of what took place.

If I remember correctly, I had five crew on board. They were friends with greater or lesser amounts of sailing experience, but all had some idea about what they were getting into. What none of us realized is that, despite having worked on *Carlotta* for four years, I actually knew very little about preparing a boat for sea. I had no idea how to make a skylight watertight. I had no idea about the strains imposed on a rig and boat by a 1,000-square-foot mains'l. I had no idea about lighting kerosene running lights in thirty knots of breeze. I had some idea that we were running into the infamous Bay of Biscay and what we could expect there, but except on the *Kanangoora* I had never had any true experience of bad weather at sea.

Good judgment comes from experience, and experience comes from bad judgment.
— Rita Mae Brown, *Alma Mater*

There have been countless changes since 1976 that make sailing a much safer proposition, and I would probably say the improvement in meteorology is the most significant of them. When we left Falmouth, we had no VHF radio, no radar, no electric bilge pump, no electric navigation lights, no loran, no GPS, no plotter and, most significantly, no roller reefing. Of course, this list is in no way exhaustive. We did have a Sailor radio direction finder that was quite helpful. We studied the weather before leaving Falmouth, but the forecasters of the day had no weather satellites so could only do their best (remember that this is just three years before the infamous Fastnet tragedy in which an appalling number of sailors were killed while racing to the Fastnet Rock off Ireland, not far from where we were headed. This happened because English forecasters had gotten it wrong, although apparently the French forecasters did much better).

So, though we left Falmouth with a good forecast, by the time we were approaching Ushant, three days later, that forecast was meaningless. We entered Biscay, and the boat that had taken almost four years to put together was taken apart in one night.

The log entries start off well, with the taffrail log streamed at Black Rock, then the bearing on the Manacles recorded. Soon the Lizard light was reported, and a bearing maintained on the Lizard and its loom, until the loom of the Ushant light could be seen. Past Ushant, the wind began to build. That's pretty much the last entry in the log until it reads "Returning Falmouth."

The list of damages reads as follows: "Broken or carried away off Ushant: gaff jaws, parrel bead line, topmast forestay (twice), mains'l lacing on mast, mains'l torn from gaff, lifelines torn off (both sides), log line and rotator lost, direction finder useless, main boom gooseneck and mast band rotated through 90 degrees, mast wedges falling out," etc.

I don't remember too much detail from that night, and it was not possible to make log entries given the motion of the boat and the volume of water finding its way below. We did get far enough into Biscay so that when it really started to blow we had some sea room. At first we hove-to and pulled down a couple of reefs. This sounds simple, but I had never taken any reefs in the boat in fresh winds. Although I had read how to do it and had practised at anchor and while day sailing, I had no idea what it was like in thirty-five knots of breeze. Later that night, we tore the reef cringles out of the leech line trying to pull down more reefs (and those are stainless steel cringles worked into 3/4-inch Dacron line).

As the wind increased, I finally decided to run off. This kept the boat a little drier, but meant we had to reduce sail even more. In the books of the period they always said that when it's time to reef, you just round up to get the wind out of the main…blah, blah, blah. I wonder if any of those authors had ever rounded up into the teeth of a full-blown Biscay gale. For one thing, the waves are incredibly steep. Steerage would be lost on the first wave, then you would be laying a-hull, not rounded up, and the sail would be going absolutely crazy. The motion would make working all but impossible, and the thirty-foot boom weighing several hundred pounds would be tearing the boat apart — as it pretty much did that night.

We managed to get the mainsail down altogether and secured on deck. We ran under bare poles and pumped and pumped and pumped; two people on watch, one steering and one pumping. Because God apparently loves morons, the gale lasted only twenty-four hours. After that, we did what repairs we could and made sail back to Ushant and then to Falmouth. Wet and demoralized, the crew departed and I was left with my wrecked plans and wrecked boat. For some time after that, as I remembered the water pouring unimpeded through the sky-lights, I liked to brag that we were the only boat with a rainbow in the saloon.

There is another memory from that night in Biscay that will be with me until I die. It was blacker than black at the time, with the wind howling and every moment the waves getting bigger and steeper. One of the crew was at the helm doing her best to keep the boat square to the approaching seas. I went forward to check the damage around the mast and, while there, happened to glance aft. There, towering over the boat, was the wave to end all waves. Its face was verti-cal and its top was already curling forward over the stern. This was the night-mare wave that every sailor dreams of at four in the morning; the wave from the hour of the wolf; the wave no boat could climb over. This was The Final Wave. I screamed at the helmswoman, "Hold on!" I jumped onto the mast band and wrapped my arms as tightly as I could around the mast, waiting to be dragged off a semi-submerged boat. Then the stern rose and rose, and then…nothing. A tiny trickle of water found its way along the deck. The woman at the helm looked at me quizzically.

I know what I saw that night, and somewhere deep in an important part of my brain it registered that this boat was really something. This was the reason pilot cutters were so famous.

As a well-known lover of pilot cutters (whose name escapes me) once said of them, "We shall be forgetting half their glory unless we recall that they were built by poor men for poor men, suffering from the two great spiritual evils of poverty — ignorance and prejudice. That they still produced fine boats is to the glory of natural man, who, living close to elemental things, develops an instinct for the earth or the sea that surpasses sophisticated understanding."

....

I'll digress here for a moment to remind the reader that *Carlotta* is one of the original Bristol Channel pilot cutters — arguably among the best sea boats ever built and which have withstood the rigours of the sea for hundreds of years — rigours that made our little gale look like a joke. The difference can be described thus: "It's not the boats, it's the men in them." The pilots went to sea at about age twelve and proceeded to eat, sleep and live at sea. To paraphrase Joshua Slocum, they knew the sea, and they *knew* they knew it. The boats were much better prepared, but that is not to say that these sailors' lives were anything but wet and tough. However, besides my ignorance, and my lack of experience and preparation, there was one other major difference between those boats and mine: every one of those pilot boats was equipped with Appledore roller reefing gear.

I knew about this reefing gear. I had sailed aboard the *Marguerite T* with it, and we had seen some tough weather and used it. However, I could not find it anywhere in England — believe me, I had searched throughout the U.K., to no avail. Finally, after our Biscay experience and an Atlantic crossing using traditional points reefing, I had Les Windley take pictures of his Appledore gear, and then I flew from St. Barths to the Lunenburg Foundry in Lunenburg, Nova Scotia, where I had it built. And I never used my adrenals again.

....

All of that occurred much later in the chronology of this story, of course. For now, I'm back in Falmouth, and the boat needs pressing repairs. If September in Biscay is tough, what will November be like? I scurried around Cornwall securing replacement gear for things that had broken, then refitting and refastening. By November 25, according to the log, I departed again.

This time, we didn't even make it as far as Ushant. Mother nature again took only hours to disassemble all my work. Once more, wet and disgusted, I returned to Falmouth. Once more, I ate humble pie in front of friends and detractors. But I was learning.

The next entry in the log is July 31, 1977 — one year later. For the third time, I streamed the log at Black Rock. And this time, we were in luck. A gentle crossing of Biscay, a nice run down the coast of Spain, and an uneventful entry into Vigo.

And it sure felt good.

Deck of the MV *Kanangoora* bound for Japan, circa 1967.

Kanangoora rolling home in better weather, circa 1967.

The author (right), aged 20, playing with a shipmate on *Kanangoora*'s deck. *Photographer unknown*

Left: Author and roommates at home on Ikaria, circa 1972. *Photographer unknown*

Below: *Carlotta* in Mashfords boatyard, with *Elsie* and a Colin Archer in the background, circa 1976.

Above and next page, top: Peter Divers and the author replacing a plank near the waterline between tides, circa 1974. The topmast is being used as a lever. *Photos by Kevin O'Shea*

Marguerite T in an Old
Gaffers Association race,
circa 1976.

The author's first race with *Carlotta*, Old Gaffers Association Race, Dartmouth, circa 1976.
Photographer unknown

CHAPTER 8

. . . .

ATLANTIC CROSSING

South till the butter melts — then west.
— Traditional instructions given to masters on the trade wind route to the Caribbean,
Conrad Dixon Basic Astro Navigation

I had brought *Carlotta* to the Canaries in the fall, in the knowledge that I would have to wait until the end of the hurricane season before I could cross the Atlantic. This strategy of being prepared to wait for weather has kept me safe for a great many years; even as a delivery skipper with owners getting upset with me, I will wait until I'm happy with the outlook.

Thus, it was in December that we departed for the new world. Two crew were on board with me: Paul, a young English waiter; and, Jane, the Englishwoman with whom I had been living for some time in Falmouth. It is still a source of wonder to me that women who have no affinity for the sea will nonetheless set off on quite impressive voyages just to — well, I'm not sure why. Is it, perhaps, to secure a meal ticket? Another story, and equally intriguing, is why we take these wholly inappropriate women to sea with us.

We got away to a good start after kedging out of the marina in Puerto Rico (Canary Islands). I doubt if many of the observing sailors had ever seen anyone kedge out of a harbour before and, in retrospect, I probably could have sailed her out. But these were still early days.

I remember I used to say (and I'm sure I stole the quote) that there were two things you could never know for sure: 1) Whether a woman would submit to your evil intentions; and 2) Where you would find the trade winds. We didn't find the trades for a long time, and, even when we did, we weren't sure we had.

There were only two events on this crossing that stand out clearly in my mind, and this is rather strange when you consider that William F. Buckley, Jr. got a book — and a good one — out of an uneventful Atlantic crossing in a much better fitted-out boat.

The first occurred on a beautiful, trade-wind day with 15–18 knots of wind, moderate seas, and me determined to get in a good day's run. Perhaps it happened because I carried the jib tops'ls longer than I should have. At any rate, the eyebolt that held the topmast backstays failed at the deck and the topmast went by the boards. This was not a very big deal except that it happened near dusk, so there was a certain amount of hustle to get the mess cleared away before dark. Working aloft at sea is never fun, and that broken mast was to plague me for years.

When I was rebuilding *Carlotta*, I had replaced everything that seemed to me likely to fail — anything that held even the slightest possibility of failing. Biscay had shown me how wrong I could get things, and the failure of this eyebolt let me know that I wasn't completely out of the woods. The eyebolt, of course, was located well aft on the counter. It was made of mild steel and passed through the teak deck and then through an oak deck beam. The acid in the oak had been eating away at the bolt for ages, something a more knowledgeable owner would have thought to check. On top of that, as Paul Johnson pointed out to me a year or so later, eyebolts are the strongest when the pull is in line with the shaft of the bolt, and get progressively weaker as the strain changes from tensile to sheer. In this case, the strain on the eye was also "out of plane," rendering it even weaker.

The second event was that, one fine sunny afternoon, I realized I hadn't seen Jane for quite a while. It was warm enough that we sometimes napped on deck, so I checked around and didn't see her; checked our bunk, which was the usual pile of bedclothes, and didn't see her; checked the foc'sle and didn't see her; and then seriously began to shit myself. I raced through the boat rechecking everywhere I had just checked, and finally threw the blankets off our own bunk. There she was, fast asleep but invisible, in the mess of duvets. It is a scare that lasts a lifetime, and a sensation I hope never to have again.

After twenty-nine days, we arrived in Carlyle Bay in the Barbados. I was extremely disappointed. To give you some idea, a good friend had done the identical trip the year before in the identical time, except that his boat had exactly one-half the waterline length of *Carlotta*. In my case, the topmast was broken, the trip was slow and the crew was slower, and I wished I had never started the whole mess. I wrote in the log "Wrong boat, wrong crew, wrong dream," or something to that effect.

One redeeming feature was being met upon arrival by my friend (Commander) Tom Blackwell, and being welcomed to the club of "those who broke spars." A great guy, Tom. He was then on his third single-handed circumnavigation, and personified the one great justification for the sailing life: the people you meet.

Many years before, I had hitchhiked across Canada and back during the summer of Expo '67. The hitchhiking was just about as awful as it could be, with every other college student alive doing the same thing. (Just as an example, we once waited at an intersection for three days before we got a ride, and that was on a freight train.) However, I learned an important lesson from that trip, which is that when things are really shitty, they are probably about to get better, and, when things are going fine…well, as our Japanese brothers say, "In the moment of victory, check your chin strap."

Looking back, it's hard to imagine being so unhappy after a successful crossing. We were young and we were in the tropics, but I was not a happy camper. I knew from my hitchhiking experience that things would soon get better, but alas, that was not to happen quite yet.

After the good friend (mentioned above) who had made the same trip in the same time in a much smaller boat arrived for a visit, it didn't take me long to figure out that he and the Englishwoman were doing things they ought not to have been doing. Bad, bad, bad.

As soon as the penny dropped, I suggested that, first thing the next morning, I would be very grateful if they took their sorry asses off my boat. I closed with a hackneyed but satisfyingly dismissive phrase: "If I never see either of you again, it'll be way too soon."

While my former friend tried to explain that it was only a small, coke-induced transgression that anyone should forgive, the Englishwoman headed straight for the hidey-hole where I normally hid our money. She was just a few minutes too late, as "I was born at night, but it wasn't last night."

So there I was, alone on *Carlotta* (except for Paul the Englishman, whom, it subsequently became clear, had also been transgressing with the lovely Jane; I swear, that woman should have been a park). All in all, I was not having a good time, but at least I had dealt with that little problem.

As noted earlier, some years before I had sailed from Puerto Rico to Bermuda with my good friend Freddie Roberts. I had learned a tremendous amount from him about sailing, and told him about my dream of one day getting an old wooden boat and sailing to the Caribbean. He mentioned in passing that if I ever did get it together, there was a small French island called St. Barths that was still pretty much unsullied by the great American invasion. I made up my mind to find out if it was somewhere I could leave the boat for a few months while I pulled myself together.

In the meantime, I hauled the boat in the careenage. That was a great experience, as it was one of only two screw jack boat (ship) lifts in the world; I believe the other is in Hong Kong. One engine at the head of the graving dock drove long horizontal axles that ran the whole length of the lift. Those axles turned a series of vertical threaded rods that in turn lifted the "floor" on which the ship — in this case, *Carlotta* — sat. A couple of employees were kept busy watching for smoke coming from any of the various gears. They would then run over with an oilcan, soak the offending gear, and then watch for the next wisp of smoke.

I painted the bottom (I was terrified of worms in the tropics) and glued the mast back together. In those days, we didn't have the great selection of glues available today. I think I used Cascophen, which by today's standards is something akin to flour and water. There was excellent glue made by Ciba Geigy called Aerodux that was used for airplanes, but for some reason I just used the natural scarph created by the break and used Cascophen. It was a decision I would regret for a very long time.

I spent some weeks after the haulout hanging out in Carlyle Bay. The only thing I remember about that time was the day that the 72-foot *Bolero* arrived from Europe and anchored directly upwind of *Carlotta*. She is a beautiful Sparkman & Stevens design, with that lovely, subtle sheer managed by only a few of the master design shops, among which are Fife and S&S. Designed to the old Cruising Club of America rule, it may be due to this boat that I now own a much more modest S&S-designed boat of similar heritage.

I admired *Bolero* daily, and couldn't help but also admire the bevy of young lovelies that the chubby, not-so-lovely Belgium owner had managed to gather around him. One day, he had the brilliant idea that he would treat his harem to some spinnaker flying. This is the sport of anchoring the boat by the stern, and then hauling the spinnaker aloft with the sheet and guy leading to a bosun's chair. A bikini-clad bit of fluff would sit in the chair and the spinnaker would rise and fall with the gusts, and everyone would think the chubby Belgium was even more wonderful than before.

It was plenty of amusement for me, too, as I went about my chores to the chorus of giggles coming from the other vessel. Glancing up, however, it seemed as if *Bolero* was just a bit closer than she had been before. Sure enough, my Belgian neighbour realized it at the same time. To his credit, he made what was probably the best response possible as the boat dragged, bow first, into *Carlotta*: he started the motor and slammed it into reverse.

He succeeded in stopping the vessel about three feet short of Carlotta's bowsprit, but not before the whole spinnaker dissolved — I think that's the only way to describe it — against *Carlotta*'s rig. I quickly rushed up the ratlines in an attempt to minimize the damage, pulling off bits of green spinnaker, but the sail had simply disintegrated. I don't think he recovered more than a square yard or so of material. As for me, I was still finding threads of green nylon years later whenever I worked aloft.

So that was the end of spinnaker flying. Oddly enough, although Chubby and I often passed one another on the dock, or in our dinghies, he never said hello, ahoy mate, kiss my ass, or anything else to me; I didn't exist, and it had never happened. This was a 72-foot boat, so the spinnaker (even in those days) probably cost $5,000–$10,000. If he had invited me over for pink gins on the poop deck, we could have compared stories about the imperative of public fuck-ups, but it was not to be.

I turned my attention elsewhere. Some friends were coming out from England to do some sailing with me, but first I needed to fly to St. Barths to see if I could leave the boat there safely.

This might seem strange to read, as it's quite strange to write, but at this point I was totally unhappy. The best-friend-screwing-the-girlfriend thing would have been upsetting enough, but, looking back on it, I think the true problem was that I was the sole energy behind the sailing. None of the women wanted to be there, and none of the various men knew anything about sailing, and I think the constant anxiety of being responsible for an old boat and everybody's safety had just worn me down. I wasn't exactly Éric Tabarly either, so there was a constant energy drain from all these people. I had to pay for everything and I had to know everything, and this when I was still just learning everything myself.

(I don't mean to whine these many years later. I'm just interested in trying to understand my own state of mind at the time. What you might like to hear is that it was just at that time that I finally outlasted my losing streak. I'm getting to that.)

I landed at the insane airstrip in St. Barths and found a small hotel in Gustavia. At the first meal, I struck up a conversation with a drop-dead gorgeous woman who took me under her wing. Things seemed to be looking up. The next day, I stopped by Lulu's Marine, as I thought I knew a woman who worked in the sail loft there. I was immediately greeted by, "Peter! Where did you come from? Where is *Carlotta*? You must be here for the wooden boat regatta next week."

I really had no idea who the rather large woman shouting all this was, but apparently she had been a student at the Falmouth School of Art. Of course, I had spent four years in Falmouth rebuilding the boat, and had "interacted" with the young women at the school whenever possible. The idea that I might have preyed on this particular one was a bit daunting, but apparently she knew both my boat and me.

This woman — Hurricane Jennifer, as we later came to know her — was living with Lulu Magras, a bit of an island institution. And there was indeed a wooden boat regatta taking place in a week or so. They thought it would be great if I could get my boat there in time.

I flew back to Barbados and returned to *Carlotta*. My English friends had arrived, and the world had changed. Suddenly I was sailing with friends — friends with energy. We were in the trades reeling off 180-mile days. They were impressed with the boat and I was impressed with the vitality of the people on *Carlotta*. Life was good again.

After three days of the most perfect sailing imaginable, we found ourselves at moonrise ghosting past Pain de Sucre into Gustavia Harbour. Barely a sound could be heard. There was just the occasional clunk of a block on deck and no outboards, and even whispered directions from me were almost a sacrilege. It was one of those magical moments that make it all worthwhile.

We anchored and, having been at sea for three days, my lubberly friends were keen to get a restaurant meal. Alas, we had no French francs or U.S. dollars, only ECC dollars and English pounds.

We piled into my old dinghy and made our way ashore. We found a restaurant — the only one open — and explained to the woman behind the reception desk our problem with currency. She didn't seem to grasp the issue. Her English was perfect, but we couldn't make her understand that her establishment actually didn't accept the only currency we had. Finally, looking befuddled, she said, "Look, there is no problem. You eat tonight and when you come to town tomorrow, you pay." That was St. Barths in 1979. Nobody dreamed of taking their keys out of their cars, for instance. Several times I left parties in drunken stupors only to discover that I had taken someone else's vehicle. At that time there were only two kinds of car on the island — Volkswagen bugs and Mini Mokes — so the mix-ups were understandable whether or not alcohol was a factor. Invariably, you'd pass your own car on the road, and everyone would stop and have a chat before setting off again in the appropriate vehicles.

We met many new people, and all the talk was about the upcoming regatta. I got to know Mad Man Murphy, still a good friend and sailing pal. Strangely, nobody thought of *Carlotta* as much of a threat in the races. It was true that, while I had painted her bottom only weeks before, I had not yet done the top sides, so there were a number of rust streaks remaining from the Atlantic crossing; in short, she wasn't looking her best. Also, when we were day sailing around the harbour, a local sailor by the name of Les Anderson (who had a New England pinky) tried to have a go at us. I whispered to the crew that they were not to trim the sails; he swept by us and, no doubt, reported at the bar (Le Select, of course) later that night that *Carlotta* was a dog and nothing to worry about.

The first day of the regatta turned out to be another beautiful trade-wind day. *Carlotta* won in many categories: first to finish; first on handicap; boat that travelled the farthest to attend the regatta; and oldest boat in the regatta. There were probably some others I can't remember. It was very gratifying to easily clean everybody else's clocks, and then we did it again the next day. After that, I won the single-handed 'round the island race.

Reading this, I hope you won't think I'm blowing my own horn (although "he who tooteth not his own horn, the same shall not be tooted"). This was just *Carlotta* at her best. Anyone could have held the tiller as I did, but give *Carlotta* fifteen knots of wind and some decent sails, and there were few gaff-rigged boats in the Caribbean in those days that would point as high or foot as fast. At the time I'm writing about, Antigua Race Week and Foxy's Wooden Boat Regatta were already well established, but *Carlotta* is an old workboat and not in the same class as the beautifully restored yachts that flock to the Caribbean every fall from the Med these days.

....

I can't help but give a further example of *Carlotta*'s capabilities. The time I'm thinking of, which I've never forgotten, occurred later that year. A few of us had organized some Wednesday evening races. This particular one involved only six or eight boats, but it stands out in my mind because my old pal, Freddie Roberts, had shown up from Bermuda. This time, however, we were on my boat.

We got a good start over the line near Gustavia. A buoy was set off Rockefeller's and we were to return back across the start line, but leaving Pain de Sucre to port. This gave the course some upwind, some downwind, and some reaching. There were no time allowances, spinnakers were permissible, and, obviously, it was just for fun. Still, everybody tried hard. Much rum and beer were consumed as well.

Of the race itself, the main thing I remember was that, as I prepared to tack to clear Pain de Sucre, Freddie said, "Hold it just a minute. There's always a big dead spot close to the rock." I did what he suggested, even though it would make the course slightly longer and was counter-intuitive given that the dead spot would have to be on the windward side of the rock. However, it did give us a close reach down to the line, a point of sail *Carlotta* loved.

We were barrelling toward the line on starboard and, for the first time since the start, could actually get a feel for our position. Since all of the other boats were flying spinnakers, we hadn't really given ourselves much of a chance, but here we could see that we were either in first place or very near it. Peter O'Keefe's Gallant 53 looked as if she might just nip us at the line. They were laughing and drinking beer, not paying much attention to the eighty-year-old pilot cutter lumbering along until it became very clear — dawning on the crews of both boats at the same instant — that although she could nearly nip us at the line, she was on the port tack.

There was a moment of absolute silence on Peter's boat. Then, to their eternal credit, they broke into a spontaneous cheer as we forced them over, tacked, and won the race. You could say this was just a Gallant 53 being sailed badly, but *Carlotta* also beat two Swan 41s in the race, with everybody except us using spinnakers. Of course, if we had raced the same boats the next night, the results might, although not necessarily, have been very different.

In the next year's regatta, the wind was much stronger — more like the famous "Christmas winds" (I would guess in the low- to mid-twenties). Paul Johnson was racing his boat, *Venus*, which just loved a storm. On the first day, Paul beat me by a few seconds on corrected time. It was in this race that the topmast failed. Although we didn't stop, it was enough to lose the use of the jib tops'l and give Paul get the win (obviously, we were well ahead, boat for boat). I skipped the next day's event — the single-handed 'round the island race — in order to repair the mast. And, quite frankly, I was glad of the excuse: I truly did not want to single-hand the boat in that type of wind. Having said that, I was surprised by how these regattas brought out a competitive streak in me that I genuinely hadn't known existed. After the races, I would virtually collapse in a heap, beat to hell.

On the last day of the regatta we had strong winds again. I managed to beat Paul both on corrected time and boat for boat. This is notable because Paul's boats are unstoppable in a hard breeze. Paul and I have shared many bottles of rum over the years, and a great book, *Memories From the Sea*, was published recently about him by some of his friends (see the reading list at the end of this book). He is extremely knowledgeable about the gaff rig, and was always generous with information, including helping me make some major changes to my rig.

I should note that Paul had also beat the *Marguerite T* in the Old Gaffers Regatta held in Cowes some years earlier (although Les Windley was sure he had won it). Paul's boats could carry sail forever.

Here are a couple of the many "Paulisms" I remember: "Never be afraid to be terrified," and "If it breaks, it's not strong enough."

CHAPTER 9

....

IN ST. BARTHS

There is a tide in the affairs of men, which, taken at the flood, leads on to fortune;
Omitted, all the voyage of their life is bound in shallows and in miseries.
— William Shakespeare, *Julius Caesar*

There is an inviolable rule of sailing that you will never make a complete fool of yourself until every person whose opinion you value is watching.

In St. Barths in 1979, I was courting a young Frenchwoman — Dany — whose many charms were both remarkable and unforgettable (doubly unforgettable because they reside to this day in my daughter, Sarah). Two of her most notable charms were on public display — in the manner of many Frenchwomen in the tropics — on Christmas Day that year, when all of the local layabouts, myself included, decided to sail to a beautiful bay on the west end of the island called Rockefeller's.

If memory serves, our excuse was that we were expecting Paul Johnson to arrive after one of his countless trans-Atlantic passages. In truth, it gave us something to do on Christmas Day, which, I suspect, always feels a little contrived to most northerners when it's 30 degrees Celsius.

Carlotta was anchored somewhat closer to shore than usual because there had been far fewer boats anchored at the time I arrived. With a 1,000-square-foot mainsail and no engine, I usually tried to be the most seaward of the anchored boats, and it paid to row a little further so as to be able to clear out at will. On this day — the first time the gorgeous Dany had ever set foot on my not-very-yachty pilot cutter, it would be necessary to raise the main, get the anchor "up and down," set the flying jib, back the jib to break out the anchor with the mainsheet slack, get the anchor on deck, harden up the main to skirt a few boats while slacking off the jib, then slacken off the main to bear away while getting the jib in. This was all pretty second nature to me, having sailed the boat almost daily for a few years. It actually takes more thought for me to describe it than to do it.

Naturally, with every sailor in the world whose opinion mattered to me there watching, I got the anchor over the bow roller, failed to slack off the main at the appropriate time, and sailed directly into the island. I was probably moving at about two knots, and since "tidal range" is almost an unknown concept in the Caribbean, I was in no danger. Also, after getting their full measure of enjoyment, I knew my friends would be glad to help me out.

In the meantime…

Following the best procedures, I dropped the sails and prepared to lay out a kedge. I got the dinghy alongside, anchor in the bottom, flaked the anchor line on deck ready to run and then, and then — did I mention before that this svelte, tanned, drunkard's dream of a woman spoke not a word of English? Being Canadian, my French was entirely adequate as long as the conversation revolved around "la plume de ma tante," which it didn't in this instance — with all of my very hip sailing friends watching, pantomimed to Dany how she was to pay out the line from the coil on deck. She seemed to understand.

I jumped in the dinghy and started to pull away from *Carlotta*. I got about six feet from her side and came to a stop. I couldn't see the line flaked out on deck because the dinghy was lower, but I assumed the line had tangled. Dany was looking at me expectantly, and it would probably be an appropriate time to mention that she had also never been on a boat before. Here we were, within the first three minutes, crashed onto the rocks. She was probably thinking the French equivalent of *Strange sport these fucking Englishmen enjoy*.

Of course, anxious to recover my dignity, I repeated my pantomime of paying out the line and began to row again. The dinghy still didn't move. I don't know which of my friends started grinning first, but I noticed they occasionally disappeared below deck where, presumably, they could give full vent to their mirth.

By now I was stage-whispering, "Please pay out the line," while continuing to demonstrate what I meant. She continued to fool around with said line. I continued to attempt to row away. Our audience continued to enjoy themselves.

Now, I know for a fact that I am the last honest man, and you will know this is true when I tell you that when I am getting tired, I will occasionally verbalize more enthusiastically than absolutely necessary. In this case, I had just gotten on board some 100 feet of half-inch chain and a sixty-five-pound CQR anchor, and then put up a 1,000-square-foot mains'l and a flying jib without the aid of any kind of winch. Then I had taken it all back down again, furled the main roughly, got the jib laid out in the scuppers, launched the dinghy, and got the 45-pound CQR kedge unstowed and in the dinghy. For context, at this time I probably weighed 175 pounds and was not an athlete.

And here was this woman who didn't seem able to simply pass the fucking line over the toerail so I could row out the goddamn kedge. Much to the pleasure of all assembled, I was now standing in the dinghy, acting out the paying-out of line while in a stage whisper that could be heard as far away as St. Maarten, saying, "Will you please, please, please pay out the fucking line NOW!" It wasn't long after this that I noticed the dinghy painter snaking up from under the stern of the dinghy, hidden among the coils of kedge line and fastened firmly around a stanchion.

Someone finally took pity on me and, with almost no effort or revs, pulled me off with their fifty-horsepower Boston Whaler. I then got all of the sails up, and sailed without incident to Rockefeller's, where I got it all back down again. After that I lay absolutely prone on deck for an hour (or perhaps two), far too exhausted to enjoy the festivities on the beach. Then, because this woman and I were not yet sleeping together, I repeated the whole thing to get her back to Gustavia.

But I did sleep very well that night.

CHAPTER 10

....

MORE ST. BARTHS

If you spend the night alone in an open boat in a thunderstorm, it will bring you closer to God than going to church forty Sundays. — L. Francis Herreshoff

I want to tell just a couple of more stories before leaving St. Barths. I wasn't born with the happy gene, but, looking back on the two years I spent there, they were probably as close as I'll get to that elusive state in this lifetime. After all the years I had spent working on *Carlotta*, people finally appreciated her. I remember having a chat with Jimmy Buffet after one of the regattas. He said, "Peter, no matter how long you worked on this boat, and no matter how hard it was, it was worth it." Jimmy was not a great sailor as far as I could see, but it's nice when someone gets it.

It should be easy to see the mood change I had gone through from Barbados to St. Barths. The problem, as I was to discover ultimately, is that life is like real estate, or perhaps, more accurately, the stock market: you go into the stock market and make a lot of money. The first thought that occurs to you is, gee, I'm pretty good at this. In fact, you happened to stumble over a bull market and really don't know a thing. I suspect this is what happened to me in St. Barths. But it was the bull market of happiness.

"There is a tide in the affairs of men, which, when taken at the flood…"

And so, to continue…

One day, John Frith and his family, Paul Johnson and I decided to sail to St. Maarten for the day. John and Paul had sister ships, built alongside one another in Bermuda, and we were all close friends. I was going to make the trip single-handed. Since I hadn't actually done any single-handed cruising, I was glad to be in company. At this point, I still didn't have a VHF radio on the boat (although a few months later I did buy a used one from Jimmy Buffet for $800; the cheap prick).

The sail over to St. Maarten was uneventful, and we anchored off Philipsburg. On our return, they left long before me and began tacking upwind through the channel between Fourche and St. Maarten. I did not understand their thinking at all, as I could see our destination, St. Barths, clearly. I took a much more direct route, heading straight for Gustavia. It was now late afternoon and I soon realized that I was being swept away from the island by a strong current. As the wind lightened, I had no hope of reaching St. Barths before dark. In fact, tack as I might, I was soon closer to the islands to leeward than to St. Barths. There was nothing to do but keep sailing. Tack after tack, I tried vainly to make some headway against the current. Night fell and I managed to get some semblance of a meal together, but the tacking was endless.

It wasn't long after dark that I noticed the stars to windward disappearing under an oncoming blanket of cloud. The wind picked up a bit, but not enough to roll in a reef. It was probably about 2100 hours when the first bolt of lightning ripped the sky apart with a crack. Another followed in a few seconds, and another to port, then to starboard, then from ahead again. The thunder was continuous, unrelenting.

(Note: At the time of this writing I am sixty-six years old. With the exception of one other time, I have never seen lightning like this again in all my life. It was non-stop all around me. Sometimes it seemed only yards away and sometimes a mile or more, but for hours and hours it never stopped. The thunder was uninterrupted. It was impossible to tell which roll of thunder was associated with which lightning strike. And the rain: I can't even describe the torrents. There was no ocean surface, just rain and sea in collision.)

Like everyone caught in lightning at sea, I felt vulnerable. I had no lightning conductor — or rather, *I* was the lightning conductor, as I was obviously the highest point for miles around. I couldn't make out the outline of the island, lost as it was in the black night and teeming rain. I don't remember actual fear, but I did have an overwhelming feeling of *Holy fucking Christ; what now?*

By about four in the morning, I could finally make out the odd light on St. Barths. Then, in a particularly brilliant flash of lightning, I could see the outline of the hills behind Gustavia. Of course, now that I was approaching safety, the sky cleared and the thunderstorm abated. The wind lightened as I came into the lee of the island.

Although I was tired beyond imagination, having just spent the last twelve hours tacking with my asshole puckered absolutely tight, a wave of peace descended on me like a cloak. There was relief combined with the knowledge that I was safe and would soon be heaving-to in Blanket Bay. I'm not a spiritual person, but I experienced an awesome feeling of almost transcendental calm in that pre-dawn early morning.

At one point I drifted close under the stern of one of the large passenger schooners that dragged cheap tourists around the Caribbean. A seriously inebriated American escapee leaned over the rail, looking down at me, and yelled back at his companion, "Hey Fred, c'mere and look at this crazy motherfucker!" That served to terminate my few hard-earned moments of spirituality.

Some years later I became skipper of a ship called *Legacy* that was the pride of the fleet of the same cattleboat line carrying this drunk. I did all I could to discourage drunken yelling at sailboats whose skippers were having a cosmic moment, and hope to be rewarded for that in my next life.

....

On a side note, my old friend, Mad Man Murphy, sailed around the Caribbean with me quite a bit, and at that time we had the habit of drinking very light drinks of rum and water almost all day long. This kept us hydrated and reasonably sober, and was a little more interesting than drinking plain water.

On St. Barths, I was known as Peter Carlotta to distinguish me from other Peters on the island (Peter O'Keefe, to name just one). We came to call these very light rum drinks "Peter Carlottas," a play on piña coladas.

Years after I left St. Barths, I was visiting with Murphy and some other old St. Barths hands in New York City. Walking down the street one day, Murphy thought it was time for a drink and, without telling me we were in his local, he walked into the nearest pub, moseyed up to the bar, and ordered a couple of Peter Carlottas. Without a moment's hesitation, the bartender turned around and mixed up two very light rum and waters. It was my fifteen minutes of fame.

CHAPTER 11

....

ST. BARTHS TO PANAMA

I made a plan to leave St. Barths for Panama with Dany, the Frenchwoman, as crew. When we awoke on the morning of departure, we realized we were hemmed in by other boats. Having no motor, this could have been a problem. Fortunately, the night before, Jimmy had volunteered himself and his Boston Whaler, and he soon had us towed clear.

The trip was, for the most part, pleasant downwind sailing in the tropics. Two young people on a beautiful boat. I'll touch on some the highlights.

....

One of our first stops was the island of Anguilla, where we spent hours snorkelling naked on Sandy Key (the most postcard-perfect islet, with sand, three palm trees and nothing else, and which apparently exists no more due to one of the more serious hurricanes). Later that same night, we went ashore to have a drink. Of course, the Anguilla of 1980 was not the Anguilla of today. At that time, I opened the door of a tin-roofed shack with music blasting out of it, and the bad vibe I encountered nearly loosened my teeth. It seemed clear that white folk were not welcome in this particular establishment. Before I could turn and stop Dany from coming in, there she was at my shoulder. She had a very dark complexion and a large afro, and suddenly the atmosphere in the bar was all sweetness and light, as they assumed I was with a "sister" and, consequently, cool. After a few drinks, one of our new pals actually asked her if she had some "blood," but by then, luckily, we were all friends and it didn't matter.

A few days later, we set off for the British Virgins. Using only dead reckoning, we were somewhat unsure of our position as we approached land. A sailboat was closing in on a reciprocal course, so as we passed we asked our position. It turned out that it was Hank and Charlie from St. Barths, so we had a quick gam and found out we were exactly where we had thought we were.

We had *Carlotta* hauled out in Nanny Key, a boatyard that had not been in existence for very long. I was always nervous about travel lifts, and I think this was the first one on which *Carlotta* had been hoisted. Because she looks fast and light, people never believe she actually displaces thirty tons. After the usual argument about how many straps were needed, they began to lift her out of the water — without enough straps, naturally. Just as she cleared the surface of the water and the straps were singing like a castrato, a rain squall came through and all the yard workers ran for shelter. Five tense minutes passed until the weather suited the workers enough to come back, and until I could change my underwear.

The other thing of note during our time at Nanny Key occurred while we were motoring back to *Carlotta* one night, slightly the worse for wear. We heard calls of help coming from outside the harbour. At that time, I used a British Seagull outboard (the motor with only one moving part: the guy pulling on the string), so the fact that I heard them over the din of this ancient machine was itself a miracle. I altered course to try to find the problem, and soon discovered that one of the charter boats from Nanny Key had attempted to re-enter the harbour at night and gotten herself onto the fringing reef. The wind was light, as was the swell, but naturally this family was fairly tense given that they were on a lee shore with kids on board and in a rented boat. Anyway, I laid out their kedge and helped get them off the reef, then towed them into Nanny Key. They fell all over themselves with gratitude, which I enjoyed (being half cut as I was). I accepted their proffered bottle of wine, and went back to *Carlotta* to sleep.

The next day, my daring rescue was all the talk of Nanny Key, except for deafening silence from the management of the yard. No, "Thanks, Peter…great job…yada, yada." Nothing at all. When one of my pals finally asked them why they didn't at least thank me for saving one of their boats, they replied that doing so would imply liability. Ah. America spreading its greatness around the world.

The days rolled by, as did the islands. After the Virgins, we found ourselves in Puerto Rico. The eastern end had a good boatyard, but it was at Isla Grande, every mariner's nightmare from the point of view of the surrounding reefs. Of course, we were under sail only, but I was still young and brave enough to manage to get her in and anchored.

This was the only place in which we ever experienced people with evil intentions boarding the boat while we were asleep. In the dead of night, Dany shook me awake, gasping the broken-English equivalent of "Someone's on board!"

Normally, given the heat, we slept naked. Upon being awakened from a deep sleep on this night, I reacted by charging up the companionway, bare as the day I was born. Imagine a naked, long-haired hippy, waving his arms and screaming, "Get the fuck off my boat, you fucking assholes. I'll fucking kill you!" It was a clear case of naked aggression, and not normally how I greeted visitors (contrary to what some of the women I have lived with might tell you). I was halfway down the deck when it started to dawn on me that there were three fully clothed boarders, all rather large, and one was holding something that appeared to be a handgun.

Perhaps the appearance of a screaming, dishevelled hippy with flying genitals held some religious overtones for these gentlemen, or perhaps these intruders were not used to blind aggression from a half-asleep dimwit. In any case, by the time I was awakening to my own predicament and trying to execute a graceful retreat, they were mumbling apologies and making to climb back into their skiff.

By now I was backing down the companionway and Dany, having much more presence of mind, was piling artillery on the top step. By the time I had my loaded .45 in my hand, the poor robbers were pulling with a will for distant shores.

It hath been truly said that a special providence protects children, fools and drunken men.

....

After Puerto Rico, we left for the Dominican Republic and a little adventure in Samana Bay. This bay is several miles wide, with a narrow entrance into the actual harbour at the head. At this time, no lights were displayed in the bay. Although there were lighthouses, the government had turned them off in the belief they might assist insurgents arriving by sea. We weren't insurgents, of course, but we arrived in the early evening, and a coast without lights is a lonely coast — think back to the days of no plotters, no GPS, and only celestial navigation and dead reckoning to guide you.

The sunset was an oily yellow as we approached the bay after a day of normal trade-wind sailing. I knew there were no navigational aids in the bay, and the sunset made me nervous. The bay itself, although wide, was surrounded on the west by cliffs, and on the east and south by the most daunting ring of ugly, breaking reefs I have ever seen. I don't remember the width of this band of reefs, but I would suspect at least three-quarters of a mile in most places. Therefore, if for some reason you were washed up, it would be impossible to survive the surf and make it to the beach.

I told Dany we wouldn't be attempting the inner harbour that evening. She may have looked longingly at the harbour entrance, but she agreed.

As soon as the sun set, the wind backed to the northwest west and commenced to blow onshore and onto the reefs. My plan had been to heave-to and work our way back and forth across the bay. I wound in more and more reefs (God bless Les Windley for copying the design of the Appledore roller reefing gear from the *Marguerite T*, and God bless the Lunenburg foundry for making it so well), dropped the stays'l, left the jib up, and hovered over the tiller as night fell and the wind grew. Then the rain came and the wind continued to blow harder and harder until it was just stupid.

I stood in the lazarette hatch, seeking what shelter I could get from the horizontal rain and a solid wall of wind. When I felt we were approaching the reefs too closely on one tack, I would let the jib draw to get some way on, tack, and be already hove-to on the other tack for the return crossing. These boats were made to heave-to, and this was one of many times *Carlotta*'s ability saved my bacon. I have no idea how many times we crossed the bay that night, but twenty would not be an unreasonable estimate.

It continued like this for the entire night. I found a discarded cup in the lazarette that I used to pee in. It wasn't terribly rough, just a wind gone mad, but at some point Dany tried mightily to get me a cup of tea that mostly ended up to leeward. And then there was this dreaded thought that was never far from my mind (a premonition I'd had before, you might remember): what if something failed? Those boat-destroying, man-eating reefs, half a mile to leeward, were nothing other than certain death.

Whether you're dealing with certain death on a lee shore, or just normal 0400 "hour of the wolf" blues, everything improves with the sunrise. So naturally, at dawn, the wind fell right away to a normal breeze, allowing us to make our way into the harbour proper. We soon learned that twenty-two local fisherman had died that night. These are men that go to sea in very rough boats, as that is their only option to feed their families. The government had a splendid patrol vessel tied at the wharf, yet, despite the pleading of widows and priests, would not put it to sea. It was armed, of course, but the government trusted no one, not even their own Coast Guard.

(Note: The trip from St. Barths to Panama was done with just Dany and me on board, as mentioned, and I'm writing all of this without the benefit of having the log of the various voyages in front of me. But I do remember that in all of our sailing together, Dany made only one entry in the log. After this night in Samana Bay, she wrote, "I am so affraid [sic]." Looking back on it, I'm kind of impressed that we did all of that together.)

....

From the Dominican Republic, we made our way, relatively uneventfully, to Haiti, and then on to Panama.

During our time in Haiti, we enjoyed a tour of the citadel, a fantastic fortress built on a mountaintop by mad King Henri Christophe. Arranging for massive stone blocks to be carried up the mountainside, he had prepared the citadel to defend Haiti against the return of Napoleon, from whom he had liberated the country. (Napoleon probably couldn't remember where Haiti was, but such are the joys of madness.) Mad King Christophe's labour relations were interesting to read about, as it is certain the people dragging the gigantic building blocks up the almost-vertical cliffs to build the citadel would have been somewhat less en-thusiastic about the project than their leader. As history tells it, whenever one of these great granite blocks got stuck on the tow up the hillside, the guards would shoot a few of the workers to motivate the others; then, lo and behold, the block would somehow get moving again. Modern Haitians are incredibly proud of their mad monarch. Go figure.

It is said that, in modern times, the French tried to get some of the beauti-ful bronze cannons down from the citadel to a museum in the capitol. Despite having all of the modern gear and technology, they were unable to get any of the cannons *down* the hill.

I remember leaving Haiti on Christmas day after a very enjoyable stay. The Haitians at that time were incredibly poor, but, in the countryside at least, were a happy and welcoming people.

We sailed for three or four days until we approached Panama. The number of ships was increasing radically, necessitating more vigilant watches. I remember being very tired by this point, and then a rare thing happened: thick fog appeared in the tropics. Of course, it was just what we didn't need on the approach to Panama, with deep-sea vessel after deep-sea vessel converging on the canal.

Fortunately, we did have some reliable radio beacons, so we somehow found our way into the anchorage. At that time, the canal was controlled by the Americans. (If you don't know the history, the U.S. created Panama so they could build and control the canal without having to bother with the Colombians, who held Panama as part of their country.) We were met by a launch that guided us to the anchorage and took the information necessary for our transit.

One of the questions many people asked me at the time was how we planned to transit the canal without an engine. Although I knew it could be done from my reading of Hiscock's *Voyaging Under Sail*, I didn't know exactly how.

Fate, as Goethe promised, took a hand. While lying at the anchorage, who should turn up but my friend Wolfe from St. Barths, delivering the beautiful *Mistral* (a restored Herreshoff owned by a famous rock and roll star whose name I forget). We rafted up to them at the anchorage, and Wolfe said, "Hell, don't worry, I'll tow you through the canal."

I thought of Wolfe as a friend, but really, the offer was beyond anything that friendship alone could expect: this was an overwhelming demonstration of generosity. As I said, we were rafted up together. Of course, it being the tropics, we all had our skylights and hatches open, and I couldn't avoid hearing the owner of this pristine masterpiece of nautical art saying to Wolfe, in no uncertain terms, "We are not towing that piece-of-shit boat through the canal. End of discussion."

I was cringing in my bunk. The last thing I wanted was to be responsible for acrimony between Wolfe and his employer. To my surprise, instead of caving (as any reasonable person might have done), Wolfe replied, "Look, I have brought your boat from Maine to Florida, through a refit in Florida and then on to Panama, without a scratch. I'm towing my friend through the canal. If this doesn't work for you, find yourself another skipper."

This was not what I wanted to happen. I was sure I could find an alternate tow — I'd never heard of anyone stuck on one side of the canal without an engine dying of old age — but, after a long silence, the owner said, "Okay, but there'd better not be a fuckup."

It went generally well.

There was one moment with which every experienced skipper will sympathize: *Mistral* had *Carlotta* tied alongside entering one of the locks, and not yet secure, with the water boiling around as the lock filled. The boats got sideways and we were steaming directly toward the wall of the lock at full throttle. You come to a point when you must decide whether to keep the power on and wait for the rudders to grip, or bail and hit reverse. Wolfe kept the power on, and we had both rudders hard over. After agonizing seconds that seemed like minutes, they finally answered — in just enough time to avoid driving both bowsprits into the concrete of the lock.

Whew.

CHAPTER 12

....

PACIFIC CROSSING

We (Dany and I) had been held up in Panama because we couldn't find any crew to accompany us on our long voyage to Hawaii. Many people don't realize that Panama is on the same longitude as Florida, and consequently it is almost exactly the same distance from Panama to Hawaii as it is from San Francisco to Japan: five thousand miles. Perhaps it is no surprise that no one wanted to do the trip with us in an old gaff-rigged pilot cutter with no engine, no instruments, and no means of long-range communication.

Finally, though, we found a young Swiss couple who agreed to come with us. In retrospect, I suppose I can say they worked out fine. The man was a world-class competitive kayaker and a wonderful athlete. His girlfriend was neither. As so many Swiss seem to be, they were both polyglots. That made life in Panama easy.

Before heading out, we took them for a sail around the Perlas Islands to be sure we would all get along. In those days, the islands were primitive, with no doctors, no electricity — not much of anything at all except the villages of the native Cuna Indians. The exception was Contadora, the island to which the Shah of Iran had been exiled.

We had been exploring the islands and enjoying the exotic wildlife; I still have a picture somewhere of a bird sitting on my head. We regularly had to chase birds out of the accommodations and unhook pelicans from our fishing gear, and it was not unusual to see three or four massive manta rays leaping through the air at once. Anyway, we pulled into a tiny village and the first person to come alongside in his small dugout canoe had a terrible burn on his arm. These people knew from experience that yachts carried extensive first aid kits. Since my crew was fluent in Spanish, we were able to sort him out with appropriate antibiotics.

The second dugout alongside wanted to sell us a pound of pot. I asked how much this would cost and he named a price of US$10. My response: "Sure, we'll take a pound." Naturally, he asked for the $10 and promised to return with the pot. I know you've all had this conversation. I was about to reply that I had seen that movie before and didn't like the ending, but then I hesitated. Here we were, miles from civilization in a tiny village — why not risk ten bucks to find out what kind of people we were dealing with?

And, voilà, he came back in an hour with a grocery bag full of Panama Red.

(A few weeks later, back in the Canal Zone, we were chatting with old friends and we told them this story. They were more than curious about the great pot connection, and ended up making their fortune from this small village in the islands. But that was their destiny, not mine.)

We decided to go ashore and visit the village. In Balboa, I had bought a new inflatable dinghy. Since I already had a good outboard motor, we had quite an efficient tender set-up. We ran the boat up on the beach and started toward the various shacks that made up the town. As we approached, there were three men standing on a small grassy knoll.

Let me digress here for a moment to point out that most Cuna Indians are not small people. In fact, the men can be decidedly large. Furthermore, they generally have very high cheekbones that give them, at least to me, a forbidding (if not actually threatening) appearance.

We moved to pass these three gentlemen, trying to be as inconspicuous as possible (weak smiles, much bowing and scraping, etc.). The last thing we want-ed was to be offensive, or even noticed. Just as we were abeam of the knoll, one of these large, very unfriendly looking men shot out his arm and beckoned us with his fingers.

We all looked at each other with "who, me?" expressions on our faces. Again, this giant shot out his hand and beckoned us. And believe me, he was not smil-ing. I couldn't imagine what we'd done wrong. Had his wife seen us peeing over the side of the boat? Had we broken some cultural taboo by landing on the beach without permission? We had no idea, and no options. We approached the men, emitting our strongest supplication and apology vibes.

What a surprise when he handed us the biggest super bomber joint I've ever seen. And things only got better from then on. We enjoyed the village, people were friendly (although they didn't look it), and we had a very good time being immersed in a radically different and quite primitive culture.

....

I mentioned earlier that I'd purchased a new inflatable dinghy in Balboa. It was expensive and I really didn't want to lose it. Unfortunately, it had come with a polypropylene painter that was extremely slippery, and I'd already found the dinghy almost escaping a couple of times as our various knots worked loose. A couple of days after meeting the welcome party mentioned above, I went up on deck to brush my teeth before bed and discovered that both the dinghy and outboard were gone.

I was more than upset. I screamed at the crew until it was pointed out that I was the one who had tied it up last; obviously, I had a bad case of Dinghy Fever. I immediately launched our old, raunchy, hard-bottomed dinghy, which I had planned on getting rid of. I needed the language skills of my crew, so we all went ashore.

It was probably after eleven at night and the village, with no electricity, was pitch black. What was more eerie was that there were no people to be found anywhere, and I needed help if I were to have any chance of recovering the dinghy. We searched everywhere for assistance, but it was a complete ghost town. Then we heard music — not some ethereal, primitive flute played by a half-naked native, but serious hard rock. We followed the sound to a dimly lit basement and inside found the whole village, stoned as rats, with a ghetto blaster turned up to nine. We had to corral one of the men from the grassy knoll and get him outside to make ourselves heard.

My crew explained what had happened and our new friend got to work immediately. Summoning appropriate helpers from the basement, one guy ran to get his outboard motor, another knew where to get some gas, and three others ran to the beach to launch the biggest Cayuga on the shore: a long, narrow native canoe hollowed out of one log and, as I was to discover, extremely fast.

It was only moments before everything was assembled. With about six natives in the boat and me, we went screaming down the coast. It was a dark night, with lots of stars but no moon. Fortunately for me, these Indians had operated in these waters for generations and knew every rock and shallow place. Occasionally, I would hear the propeller just wing something on the bottom, but without apparent damage. They knew the coast *that* well.

Now, it's not every dark night that I find myself in a dugout canoe with six Indians, racing through warm tropical waters, just inches outside the surf line and with a brilliant canopy of stars overhead. Was I thinking about my dinghy? Nope. I was thinking, Christ, even if the dinghy is lost it's worth it for this amazing experience. I just sat and soaked it up, and hoped I'd never forget these great people and this great night.

In fact, my hope for the dinghy was fading. It is a rough, rocky shore with probably three feet of surf breaking on the lee shore, and no dinghy could survive that for long. However, as we swung around a low point of land, we saw a tiny sand beach, perhaps thirty feet wide, in which sat my dinghy, unharmed, bumping gently on the sand.

They dropped me on the shore, waited to make sure the dinghy started, and then headed back to enjoy Exile on Main Street. I trailed after them, going as fast as I could but with no hope of catching their hollowed-out log.

....

We had one other experience worth noting in this village. We wanted to give *Carlotta* a scrub before heading out across the Pacific, but were afraid to go in the water. This was because of what happened to a friend of ours on another boat, a guy who lived only to snorkel and scuba dive. A few days earlier, he'd jumped into the water at his anchorage for a swim, gone out about twenty yards, and then reversed direction and bee-lined back to his boat a damn sight quicker than he'd left it, three fins rapidly closing in behind him. The islands are called the Perlas Islands because there was once a pearl industry there. The natives had dived for oysters, and, I suspect, had come to some accommodation with brother shark.

At any rate, we went ashore and my Spanish-speaking crew tried to solicit someone to clean the boat. No luck. These were poor people, so we were a bit surprised. Finally, one particularly healthy-looking specimen said he would do it, but only if we moved the boat right up close to the beach.

We did this and he paddled out in his small Cayuga. He climbed on deck, took off his shirt, and had a good look all around the bay. We couldn't help noticing a tremendous scar that circled his shoulder, obviously the work of a shark. He made it clear we were to stand watch and bang on the side of the boat if a shark approached. We could do better than that. We had a 30/30 rifle on board, as well as a .45 semi-automatic pistol.

Without hesitation, he dove in and began to work. It wasn't more than three minutes before we saw a fin cutting its way toward us. I grabbed the rifle while the others hollered and banged on the hull. Our new pal came to the surface slowly. Looking carefully at the approaching shark fin, he shook his head, mumbled something, and returned to scrubbing. I guess he knew his sharks, because nothing happened and the boat was cleaned without further trouble.

....

We departed Panama and carried a nice breeze out into the gulf, where we were promptly becalmed. You can imagine the preparations we had gone through, as this could be a very long voyage — and we were without an engine, not to mention refrigeration or water-making capabilities. Water was our primary concern, and I went to great lengths to make sure that, not only were all our tanks full, but also that the crew clearly understood how careful we had to be with the precious 135 gallons we could carry.

The calm in the Gulf of Panama is legendary, and we didn't escape unscathed. With no engine, we drifted for days that turned into well over a week. After a week had passed, I sounded our main water tank and nearly fainted to discover that it was only one-third full. I checked the hoses and couldn't find any leaks. To this day, my only explanation is that the hose we'd used to fill the tank had had such strong pressure that the air in the tank couldn't escape fast enough and a bubble was formed. The bubble forced water out the intake pipe and I, or whomever was doing the filling, interpreted that as a full tank. I have never been able to determine if that is the correct explanation.

But now we had a pressing question: what do we do? Try to sail back to Panama? Try to make it to Hawaii with much less water than we'd planned on having? We pondered for an hour or so, and then, when it was time for our noon sight, I climbed on deck. There, sitting a mile or so away, was a 150-foot tuna boat. I now had Jimmy Buffet's old VHF so I thought, what the hell, and called them up. To my surprise, they responded, and after a discussion agreed to give us all the water we wanted as long as we could sail alongside them. That didn't bother me at all: with the amount of breeze we had, we couldn't have damaged either vessel if we'd tried. And so it was, after discovering we had a critical water shortage on a 5,000-mile voyage, that within an hour we had full tanks plus a case of cold Coke and a case of cold beer. The tuna fishery is not one I'm very fond of, for a lot of reasons, but God bless those folks.

After the better part of two weeks, we finally eased our way out of the Gulf of Panama and started to pick up the trades. It was decision time. Follow the Great Circle route and head northwest? Or follow directions from *Ocean Passages* and head southwest across the Equator? I made the decision to go with the pilot charts, which describe the winds and currents, have been compiled over a great many years, and are relatively up-to-date. *Ocean Passages*, on the other hand, while compiled over many years, ceased being concerned with sailing vessels in the 1930s. This decision turned out to be a good one.

A great circle is any circle whose circumference is on the surface of the earth and whose centre is at the centre of the earth. The equator, for example, is a great circle, while lines of latitude are not. A great circle is the shortest distance between two points on the surface of the earth. Our great circle route would parallel the coast of Central America, and then gradually turn westward until we would be running west, fully in the trade winds.

Off Costa Rica about three hundred miles, we were beam reaching in a gentle breeze and all was right with the world — that is, until about 1500 hours, when we were approached by a Costa Rican gunboat of about seventy feet in length. The ship launched a Zodiac and the captain and a half-dozen young men drove up on our stern to ask for our papers. The fact that I'm a private school reject who loathes all forms of authority aside, I knew we were three hundred miles offshore and therefore well into international waters. You won't be surprised to learn that I suggested the captain "go take a flying fuck at the moon."

He didn't reply to my rudeness. They returned to the mother ship, went forward, and took the cover off this Jesus great gun they had mounted there. By now, my crew were exhorting me: "Please, please, be cool!" They didn't have to, as I was already beginning to understand that the Costa Ricans were not messing around.

They reboarded their Zodiac, only this time everyone was armed with M-16 rifles. I got very polite. They proceeded to search *Carlotta* carefully, from stem to gudgeon, with special emphasis placed on the garbage for some reason. The kids doing the searching were slightly embarrassed, but the officer was there to make them do a thorough job. They didn't find anything because, thankfully, they didn't have a dog. If they had…well, I'd probably have Costa Rican citizenship by now.

The reason they carried out this act of piracy was because I'm a moron. In fact, Costa Rica lays claim to the Cocos Islands, which are four hundred miles offshore in this neighbourhood. If you draw a 200-mile circle around the Cocos, and a 200-mile line off Costa Rico, we were well within their territorial waters and should have produced our papers. My next book will be about how private school turned me into a radical, anarchist dipshit.

When we had first left Panama, I naturally began taking sun sights. The young Swiss guy got very curious about this and asked if I would teach him celestial navigation. I was happy to, as it made us safer to have two people who knew how to navigate by the sun. On the first day of our lessons, I showed him how to use the sextant. On the second day, I showed him how to do the computations. On the third day, we both did the sights and computations. I should explain that I am functionally innumerate. I can add and subtract if I pay close attention. I like to say that, in the first grade, I had to pee one day during arithmetic class, and while I was gone the teacher gave out the secret to mathematics; it was never repeated for the next twenty years I was in school. At any rate, on the fourth day, the Swiss guy pointed out to me what I had been doing wrong, and I don't think I took another sight between there and Hawaii.

Once we got out from under the central American wind shadow, the trades really kicked in and we had more wind than we wanted all the way to Hawaii. Pilot cutters love to run, so only prudence kept us from getting any really great mileage days. Regardless of our focus on prudence, however, one day the topmast snapped just above the masthead.

Of course, if it had broken off cleanly, our job would only have been to coil up wire rope stays and shrouds and put away the various halyards, tops'l sheet, leader, downhaul, etc. But the damn thing didn't fall down; it was held up by about four inches of wood that was broken, but not sufficiently — due to the tough nature of spruce — to actually separate. The only solution was to go aloft and cut it away.

Carlotta is equipped with ratlines, so climbing the mast wasn't a big problem. However, to work above the top of the main mast in those sea conditions made holding on very difficult. I went first. We had some crude harnesses to prevent us actually falling to the deck, but it was still necessary to hold on with one arm while sawing with the other. Climbing the ratlines was straightforward once you got the rhythm: hold on as the boat rolled toward you and the rigging went slack, then climb as the boat rolled away. When you reached the spreaders, you needed to rest for a few seconds, then use the mains'l crane and various peak halyard eyebolts as a ladder until you were sufficiently high to begin sawing. The sawing occurred while holding your other arm in a death grip around the masthead as the boat rolled toward you and you were suspended far over the sea.

My problem was that although we had been at sea for about five weeks, when I arrived at the masthead the motion was so exaggerated that I became seasick almost instantly. I managed a few strokes with the saw and didn't vomit, but I only made it down to the deck in time to avoid the big spit. The Swiss fellow said he would give it a try. Happily, I surrendered the saw and could tell right away that he was a natural — strong enough to literally swarm up the rigging, able to hold on easily with one arm, and immune to seasickness. The one small problem he had was that he had never held a saw before. The saw bent, twanged and jammed, but little wood was removed.

By now I felt better, so he came down and I went up until I started to vomit again, and then he went up. We alternated like this until the mast finally gave way. It couldn't fall to the deck with all the lines still attached, but we managed to get it down by successively slacking off the lines. No real harm done, no injuries, and no time lost.

The trip took forty-nine days, and that seems like a lot for a boat that's about forty-two feet on the water line. It should be remembered, however, that we spent weeks in the Gulf of Panama before getting any wind at all, and weeks after that in the wind shadow of Central America. When we arrived in Hawaii, the two couples had had quite enough of each other (although, looking back on it, we didn't get along that badly). I found out that the Swiss girl had stopped doing her watches after a while. Her boyfriend had started doing them for her, and I had been none the wiser. And thus we parted ways.

At the beginning of this story, I mentioned how I had made the decision to take the Great Circle route. In the Keehi Lagoon boatyard, in Honolulu, we met a gentleman from Maine who had done the same trip at the same time of year but had gone with the *Ocean Passages for the World*. It took him 117 days to do the same trip. He was single-handing, however, and in a replica of Slocum's *Spray*. When I expressed my awe at a journey of such length, and being alone for so long, he just smiled and replied in his strong New England accent, "Well, I guess everybody has to be somewhere."

CHAPTER 13

....

HAWAII TO VANCOUVER

During our sojourn in Hawaii, Dany miraculously found herself with child. She decided to fly to Vancouver rather than risk morning sickness at sea, so we began a search for new crew. I soon discovered that everyone was anxious to sail to the South Seas, but no one wanted to come to Canada. Go figure.

After weeks of searching, I had only two candidates and no option but to accept them.

The first was a young Dutch fellow. He looked very fit and was a parachutist by inclination. Now, it has always been my opinion that anyone who wants to jump out of an airplane ought to be allowed to do that, but I did like the idea that he had some jam. Furthermore, I have spent lots of wonderful time in Holland and, if I can generalize wildly, I seem to get along well with my Dutch friends and Dutch people in general. I was happy to have him on board.

The other young man who presented himself was a somewhat different story. Thin, long-haired, guitar by his side wherever he went, Pat originated from South Carolina and — as I discovered when I informed him that *Carlotta* was a dry ship when at sea — had a serious drinking problem. In fact, he said he could go only if he was permitted to have two beers every day. He swore he would never have three. Since I was in no position to argue, I agreed to let Pat accompany us as well. But I was nervous.

We left Keehi Lagoon early one morning. The only excitement was nearly running aground in the very narrow channel by the boatyard as the wind failed and *Carlotta* wouldn't pay off. With much backing of jibs and rowing with the tiller, we finally got her around and off we went.

This was the first of many trips I have made on this route; since this inaugural journey, I've brought seven or eight boats from Hawaii to Vancouver. Even so, I never fail to debate with myself about which way to go around Oahu. Although going around Diamond Head is the shorter route, it's upwind into pretty fierce trade winds and ends up with the island as a lee shore for a day or so. Going the other way about leaves one in the lee of the island with little or no wind, and gives up some ground to windward that will have to be made up on subsequent days. My choice has always been to go around Diamond Head and I have found it much more benign than anticipated. This time — my first, remember — gave us the almost unique experience of bashing into some strong trade winds, but with the wave period fitting the boat's length perfectly. There was, in fact, no bashing at all. We slid beautifully to windward for a day with almost dry decks, before bearing off so that we could close reach comfortably north until hitting the westerlies.

It wasn't long before the crew began to sort themselves out. The crucible of a small wooden boat crashing to windward soon forges either great friendships or great animosities. I was required, once more, to come to terms with my total failure as a judge of character.

The young hippie, Pat, was a truly delightful companion. He was always willing to do more than his share, whether cooking or sail-changing, and was forever amusing us with great stories of his extremely interesting life. The Dutch guy, on the other hand, did nothing unless it would result in some moronic, self-inflating story he could recite at a later date. Pat and I calculated later that, of the seventy-two meals cooked on the trip, perhaps two had been prepared by him.

Pat wanted very much to become a writer and faithfully spent an hour each day at his journal. He would drink his two beers every evening and, good to his word, never three. Out would come his guitar, then, and he would play the most beautiful bluegrass music for half an hour. But that was it. He'd put the guitar away, and wouldn't play again until the next day no matter how much we begged.

In a nice variation on an old theme, he had been the only white student at a black university and told a great story about his days as a starving student. One day, he decided to try to write a pornographic novel in order to earn some tuition money for himself and his girlfriend. He ran down to the local bookshop and bought a half-dozen dirty books to see how it was done. Then, locked in his room, he began to type. For days he emerged only to ask his girlfriend, "What does it feel like when…?" then back to the typewriter. After five days, he sent it off to a publisher and, in time, received five hundred dollars by mail. Pat was yet another example of some of the great people you meet at sea. I hope he's doing well.

In fact, that trip turned out to be one of the best sea voyages I've ever made. Great wind (I believe we averaged 150 miles a day as far as Tofino), great fishing, great music. Sailing the way it's supposed to be.

As we approached home, we made landfall somewhere near Tofino, and not long afterward were enveloped in a heavy fog. We weren't sure of our position, so we felt our way slowly southward against significant northbound coastal traffic that was revealed to us only by the deep, steady thrumming of big diesel engines as they worked their way past us. We couldn't see a thing.

During this time, there didn't seem to be any radio beacons on which we could get good bearings, so after three days of dead reckoning we were hopelessly out of touch with our position. The rule for sailing vessels in foggy conditions has always been to head for shallow water and anchor, but I challenge anyone to do that on the west coast of Vancouver Island.

Finally, one morning, the fog was slightly lighter and we found ourselves sailing at daybreak through a fleet of anchored trollers (I subsequently learned that we were on a bank the fishermen called "12 Mile"; it's a place I would end up fishing years later with my own fishboat). Anyway, when I cut close to the stern of a vessel just ahead of us, I interrupted a young man having his morning pee. The sudden sound of my voice and the forbidding appearance of our 1,000-foot mains'l almost sweeping his deck could not have failed to wake him up fast, and it's a sure bet that not all of his pee made it over the side.

"We've just arrived from Hawaii. Could you give us our position?" one of us hollered.

"Hold on," he yelled back, ducking into his wheelhouse (in those days, the trollers used Loran-A).

Before he could get the position, we had drifted out of sight into the fog. We were wondering what to do next when we heard a diesel firing up and someone recovering their anchor chain. Moments later, the same boat slid expertly alongside. The fisherman tossed us a big coho, yelled out our exact position and said, "Welcome to Canada."

We were chased down Juan de Fuca by a rather impressive gale of wind accompanied by great rolling thunderclouds. The Appledore roller reefing gear had never had such a workout as we watched that mess chase us down. We let our Dutch friend sleep through it to reduce the subsequent bragging (petty, you may be saying, but trust me when I tell you that being trapped in a small boat with an asshole tends to bring out the petty). We tried entering the country officially at Bedwell Harbour on South Pender Island, but were told we couldn't enter because of the fact that I was importing *Carlotta* to Canada. We would have to go to Vancouver.

I asked if my crew could go ashore for a walk, as they had been at sea for seventeen days. Of course, the answer was no; it's a favourite word of bureaucrats). (Here's more of the petty: I hope those shitty little people continued to waste their lives sucking away at the public tit and now have a lovely big pension to enjoy, with plenty of time to watch game shows on a big-screen TV, and lots of time to regret their stupid, wasted lives.)

Oddly enough, the remaining thirty-two miles to Vancouver became the most memorable of the trip. There was no wind — and I mean *no wind*, as there can only be no wind in the Pacific Northwest. No afternoon sea breezes. No morning land breezes. Nothing. We managed to get around East Point into Georgia Strait and then drifted with the tide for one…two…three…four…*five* days.

I can't imagine what the ferry crews thought as they left work for the day, watching us drift across their path. Then, coming to work the next day, there we'd be, drifting across their path again. They watched us drift up and down the Georgia Strait for five solid days.

Finally, on the fifth day, we were approached by the Canadian Coast Guard. They ranged alongside to ask if everything was all right. Apparently, they'd been watching us on radar for almost the entire time.

We were fine. Bored and anxious for the trip to end, of course. And I was worried that I wouldn't make it for my wedding date. (Ha! If only I could have read the future, I would still be contentedly drifting back and forth.)

As it happened, the Coast Guard vessel was heading to Vancouver later that day and would give us a pull in if we wanted. I agreed readily, for all of the above reasons, and off they went about their Coast Guard business, planning to come back for us later. I hadn't thought to ask about the feelings of my crew, having just assumed we all wanted to get ashore. Pat rounded on me: "Goddammit Peter, you've just sailed 12,000 miles without an engine and you're going to be pulled by the nose the last 15 miles?!"

He was so incontrovertibly correct that I hung my head in shame. I agreed I would not accept the tow. It was the right decision: within minutes, a light southeasterly developed, and we were able to slide home to Vancouver. Thirty-two miles in five days. The end of the voyage.

CHAPTER 14

....

A NIGHT AND DAY ON
THE WATER TAXI

Now that we were back in Canada with *Carlotta*, it became necessary for me to earn a living. I wanted, above all things, to work on the water. To that end, I bought a small water taxi company in Gibsons Landing, just northwest of Vancouver. My wife, Dany, thought this was just about the dumbest idea I had ever had. What can I say? She was right.

About fifteen minutes after buying the company, the great recession of '81 struck and business immediately fell to almost zero. A lot of the cash business done by the company involved people going to their vacation homes, and they just weren't going. I also worked with a number of companies that continued to use my services, but they were also cutting back their usage. Among these were BC Ferries, BC Hydro, the BC Ambulance Service and Canada Post. BC Ferries gave me a lot of lucrative work whenever their small, inter-island ferry broke down (thankfully, it was a mechanical disaster and broke down often). BC Hydro was also lucrative, but usually only after a big storm when power was out on the islands. The post office was a regular client, but represented a small source of income.

The upshot was that I was really struggling, and this is without even taking into consideration that my boats, acquired with the business, were in very rough condition. I had assumed I would be able to afford improvements, but this proved difficult given the abrupt drop-off in business. I had two boats, both originally intended as pleasure vessels, both gas-powered, and both showing their age.

Eventually, I decided to change the larger of the two boats to diesel power. This would increase reliability while lowering my fuel bills drastically. The downside was that I would be operating only my smaller boat for the few weeks the changeover to diesel would require. The smaller boat had just one engine and was limited to eight passengers. To get the timing right, I checked with all my main customers to make sure I knew about any projects they had in the offing. That didn't include the ambulance service, of course, which couldn't anticipate its needs.

Things proceeded well. The new diesel engine was ready at the dealership with the rebuilt clutch. A welder friend was standing by ready to build the struts and shaft, and a prop was on order. When all the ducks were in a row, my large taxi was hauled out and the smaller one put into service.

Right away, I began having difficulties with the smaller boat. Doing normal work around Gibsons, I found the engine suddenly quitting. I knew it was a fuel problem, and an examination of the fuel filter/water separator found it full of water. Fortunately, it was a small thing to drain the water and roll the engine over a few times; it would fire up and run fine until, after an hour or two of running, the separator would be full once again. Eventually, I got in the habit of draining the bowl regularly and all was well. I spoke to the fuel supplier and they checked their tanks, swearing that their fuel was clean. It was a bit of a mystery that was never cleared up, but life went on.

Well…life went on until it didn't.

I knew by now that I had made a terrible mistake buying this company. I had paid too much, having based the purchase on financial statements that had been produced in a much better economic climate. I stayed afloat, but only through constant infusions of personal cash. I couldn't afford an employee, so I was on call twenty-four hours a day. When the boats had mechanical problems, I worked all night to fix them and then ran the service all day. Add to this the fact that we had a new baby at home and my marriage was turning to shit. I cursed the previous owner who had sold me the garbage boats and an economy that was forcing me closer to the abyss every day.

It was in this climate (of joy and happiness) that one night, at around midnight, the company phone rang. It was the ambulance service. My relationship with BC Ambulance had always been very good. If someone was injured on one of the nearby islands, a call would be made to the ambulance service, and then they would call me; I would go down to the dock and get the boat warmed up and ready to go. They also had a human touch: either the dispatcher or the attendants would always give me clear information, and invariably reassure me by saying, "Relax, Peter, don't rush. Everything will be fine."

But this night was different. This time the dispatcher said, "This is a serious one, Peter, touch and go. Get the guys to the island absolutely as quickly as you can." Moving as fast as I could, I got down to the boat. The ambulance arrived seconds later, siren screaming. No question, this was a Code 3.

I got the two attendants on board with their clamshell stretcher, flashed up the engine, cast off the lines and headed out. We had exactly one mile to go across to Keats Island. It was probably only at about this time that I remembered my fuel problem. When had I last drained the bowl? For the life of me, I couldn't remember. Well, there was nothing to be done about it now; when we tied up at the dock on the island, I would have plenty of time to drain it while the attendants were stabilizing the patient. But alarm bells were still going off in my head.

We arrived at the government dock and the first thing I noticed was that the tide was extremely low. In the area I'm talking about, sixteen-foot tides are not unusual, so the ramp running from dock to wharf was at an extreme angle. As I pulled alongside, the ambulance guys jumped for shore and one of them shouted over his shoulder, "Leave it running, Peter — we'll need you to help us get him down the ramp."

What could I do? I secured the boat and left it idling, then chased after the attendants. It was a black, dirty night and the patient lay on a stretcher in the eerie glow of the orange, incandescent dock lights, rain falling gently on his face. I haven't seen many people near death, but one look at the grey, contorted face convinced me that this person was very close to the edge. His wife hovered over him, supported by neighbours, some still in housecoats and pajamas in spite of the weather.

And what was I thinking about? My fuel filter, of course.

All this time, the bowl was filling up with water. What would happen if the boat stopped on the return trip? I went through the procedure in my mind. Open the engine hatches, have a flashlight ready, drain the bowl but don't worry about catching the water; as long as the water level was reduced, the engine should fire. I was nervous, but figured it would take only a couple of minutes.

By now, the attendants had oxygen on the patient. His wife stood beside him, her hand on his shoulder. He spoke, but couldn't be heard through the oxygen mask. As I watched, he struggled to speak again and she leaned in close, putting her ear right up to his mouth. Then she staggered back, convulsed in laughter. Whatever he'd said had put a big smile on her face. I thought it must take a special kind of man to laugh while staring into the dragon's mouth.

One, two, three…we heaved the stretcher up to shoulder height and struggled toward the ramp down to the boat. He was much heavier than I'd thought possible even with all the neighbours helping (there was literally no more room on the circumference of the stretcher for more people to lift). The ramp angle was stupidly steep, and one side was studded with wood cleats to prevent slipping. The other side was just slick wood. Somehow we got him down without mishap.

At this point, I ran ahead to open the doors to the interior of the boat. I'd never had a stretcher patient on this smaller boat before, but was pretty sure the stretcher could rest on the seatbacks and still give the ambulance guys access to the patient. We manhandled the load onto the aft deck, then got everyone aboard and sent a couple of people inside to receive the stretcher as we passed it through.

Except…it wouldn't fit through the doors. We tried different angles, but unless we turned the whole thing on its side and dumped the patient, the stretcher was not going through those doors. All this screwing around was taking time and I could tell the attendants wanted to get moving. And I was thinking about the fuel situation. "Never mind," one of them said, "we'll ride out here."

So two ambulance attendants, the patient and his wife were now on the aft deck of my little twenty-five-foot (piece of crap) water taxi. Not only that, but their weight aft raised the bow to such an angle that the boat could reach a speed of only eight or ten knots. Oh, you think that's a problem? The problem was that all of these people and the patient were now standing on, or supported by, the engine hatches. In the event the fuel system failed, there was no way to get at the filter to drain the bowl, short of putting the patient overboard.

I was at the helm inside, thinking, how long has the engine been running without draining the filter? Had I drained it after lunch or before I went home for dinner? I simply couldn't remember. And how long had the boat been running at the dock while the patient was examined, then lifted and carried down the ramp, then all the time trying to get him inside? That filter bowl had to be very, very full by this time.

Am I the only atheist who has conversations with God when in a tight spot? I mean to say that I am a truly profane atheist and yet, when things get sketchy, I still engage God in some interesting dialogue. That night it went something like this: "God, if this boat stops and this guy dies, when I finally do get to Gibsons I am tying up this piece-of-shit boat, getting in my car, driving home, getting my family out of bed and putting them in the car, leaving this fucking town and this fucking water taxi, and never coming back again!"

The boat didn't stop. We arrived in Gibsons and got the patient up to the ambulance. It roared away into the night.

....

I was home in bed by three a.m. The alarm was set for six so I could spend an hour working on the fuel system before I had to get the boat down to the ferry terminal for the morning run to Keats and Gambier islands. I made it, but I was still in my coveralls plastered with grease and filth. I don't know what the passengers thought, but at this point I didn't care.

It was Saturday and the weather had cleared up nicely. There were lots of recreational boats around, as Gibsons is one of the first waterholes up the coast from Vancouver. The morning went well aside from my own total exhaustion. The boat ran fine, even though I wasn't sure that all of my mechanical issues were resolved. Finally, at about one o'clock in the afternoon, I got the opportunity for a couple of hours off. It was time to get home and out of my coveralls and, with any luck, grab an hour or two of sleep before the afternoon ferry runs.

I kept the boats at the government dock in Gibsons, and the harbour master had been kind enough to assign me a designated spot with the bull rail on the dock painted yellow, with large black letters that read "WATER TAXI ONLY." This was necessary because Gibsons gets terribly crowded with low-rent boaters who want to go boating…but only as far as the first bar out of Vancouver.

I pull into the docks, dreams of sleep and a hot shower dancing in my head. Naturally, there was some moron tied up in my berth. Pulling alongside, I could see there were three twenty-something-aged kids, half-drunk and boiling with testosterone. Trying to be polite through my exhaustion, I ask them to shift their boat, as this was my spot by arrangement with the harbour master.

Immediately, they started giving me grief.

"You can't have a reserved spot at a government dock. We'll park wherever we want and there is fuck-all you can do about it."

Oh, Jesus, I did not need this right now. I needed a shower and sleep, not these muscle-bound twits making my life miserable. I moved the boat to an open spot, tied her up, and walked back to the jerkoffs. In situations like this, I have some testosterone of my own.

"Listen, you stupid assholes: get your piece-of-shit boat out of my berth now. I'm tired and I do not want to fuck around."

I must have looked a pitiful sight standing there in my filthy coveralls, face and hands covered in grease, eyes red with sleeplessness, but that didn't stop the biggest of the dunderheads. Without a second's hesitation, he leapt from the flying bridge of his boat onto the dock and charged me. Even in the state I was in I was pretty impressed with this jump, and I recognized the look in his eyes.

His plan was clearly to show off for his buddies by throwing me in the water. He was twice my size, so my only defence was to grab hold of him and let his momentum pull both of us into the water. This worked, but now I was in secondary danger of having him drown me rather than just throwing me in the ocean. Luckily, I was able to swim away from his grasp and climb back onto the dock.

But there was no comeback. He was bigger and had two friends. Some days you chase the bear, and some days the bear chases you.

After this pleasant interlude, I went home and interrupted a nice lunch my wife was giving for friends. You can only imagine the looks on their faces when I dragged my sorry, bedraggled ass through the door, dripping wet, filthy, and with smoke coming out of my ears.

Lunch and a hot shower put me partly to rights, but I wasn't finished with my three friends yet. I called my pal Gary, who was younger than me, huskier than me, and, best of all, really liked to mix it up. I described the situation. Gary said, "I'm out the door, meet you at the dock."

We met at the head of the dock next to the pub. Gary was positively bursting with excitement at the chance of a brawl. I was a bit more circumspect, as there were still three of them to our two, and they were fairly large. However, before we could even get down the car ramp to the dock, the door to the adjacent pub burst open and out came my three "friends." We turned to face the younger guys, ready to fight. To my surprise, the one who had thrown me into the water came on all conciliatory, with his hands down, obviously placating us.

"Lookit, "he said, "I'm really sorry, that was just stupid and I feel like a god-damn bully. We've moved the boat. We understand that you're just trying to earn a living and I never should've done what I did. I'm really, really sorry."

And that was that — just another night and day on the water taxi. A few days later, a dispatcher from BC Ambulance called to let me know that the guy on the stretcher hadn't made it. I took consolation in the fact that the last words the man ever spoke in this life gave his wife a big, big laugh. What a man.

CHAPTER 15

....

RACING *CARLOTTA* IN THE PACIFIC NORTHWEST

Sometime after arriving in Canada with *Carlotta* — before we started going to Port Townsend, which I talk about later in this chapter — it occurred to me that I missed racing the old girl. This had been tremendous fun in St. Barths and it didn't matter that the boats were old and relatively slow. All sailboat racing is idiotic, in truth, as it's not possible to find a slower or more expensive way to get from one place to another.

I contacted the Old Gaffers Association in England and said I wanted to open a branch in Vancouver; they enthusiastically agreed. At the time, I was living aboard *Carlotta* at the Vancouver Maritime Museum, so I had a venue. After that, it wasn't long before I'd organized what I believe was the first wooden boat regatta in Vancouver (I forget the exact year, but it was around 1985 or 1986).

For handicapping, I used the same rules we had used in St. Barths. I divided the classes into gaff or Marconi (something they still fail to do in Port Townsend, being so hopelessly wrapped up in their devotion to schooners). I had a great poster made up, laminated, and hung around the various yacht clubs and other locations. Of course, people immediately stole all the posters, as I had not yet learned that you must slash visually appealing posters diagonally to make them less desirable to steal. Another lesson learned.

On regatta day, it was blowing a nice, fresh westerly. There were lots of other wooden boats at the museum, as I was holding my regatta in association with a wooden boat show. Naturally, *Carlotta* was still engineless, so one of the wooden powerboaters offered me a tow out of the museum and up toward the starting area.

It was at that point that I made a very amateurish mistake. I assumed, because this person had restored his boat — it was the oldest tugboat in British Columbia, vintage 1886 or thereabouts, though not large — that he knew something about its operation. Leaving the museum, we were travelling into a stiff westerly, with Kitsilano Beach park close on the port side — *too* close, I should say. We had no VHF communication and I could see that he was preparing to toss off the tow line. That would be fine if we paid off to starboard; however, if we paid off to port we would be in deep shit, and on the beach in seconds. It was then that I realized he knew nothing about sailing.

Although we were on a relatively short tow, it was long enough — and the noise of the wind loud enough — that communication was nearly impossible. So, in sufficiently raised voices, we made him understand that he must tow us further, to where the land turned away to the south, so that we would be safe if we fell off the wrong way. I had my guard up by that time. Finally, when we were well clear of land, the skipper of the tug took his boat out of gear, came out of the wheelhouse, and tossed off our line. The tug, wheelhouse forward, immediately swung broadside to the fresh west wind. *Carlotta*, displacing thirty tons, continued forward with her speed unchecked; her bowsprit, which extends approximately eight feet beyond her bow, slipped neatly through one of the tug's portholes. There we were, tug firmly harpooned on the bowsprit like a speared fish. *Carlotta* was still driving forward and the tug was being blown ever more firmly onto the sprit. There was considerable slop aggravating the problem, and only the bobstay and bowsprit shrouds prevented the long proboscis from driving even deeper into the tug's interior, potentially ripping the cabin roof right off.

With good luck and significant effort by the crew of both boats, we managed to separate the vessels and went on to enjoy a very fine race and successful regatta. However, throughout it all I was worried that we would be held responsible for serious damage to the tug, when I felt strongly that it was the other fellow's lack of skill that had caused the problem. When we arrived back at the dock, the tug was there and appeared relatively undamaged except for the mouldings surrounding the assaulted porthole. My longtime pal, Jim, owned a successful millwork shop at this time. Without telling a soul, he quietly took some measurements, snuck away to his shop, and an hour or so later showed up and installed brand new moulding. All's well that ends well.

....

I lived at the museum for a couple of years. It was a beautiful situation. Moorage was free, but we were encouraged to be good to the members of the public who flooded the docks every weekend. We had free parking and were located in what is absolutely one of the finest locations for a boat in Vancouver.

What is often overlooked, in speaking of the advantages of the facility, is that in Vancouver the wind blows in only one of two directions: either from the west or from the southeast (experienced as east in the museum area). The designer had installed the docks so that the fingers ran in an east–west direction. The significant advantage of this for an engineless thirty-ton pilot cutter was that, if the wind was blowing from the west, I could get the boat more or less parallel to the docks, with her head canted slightly toward them, and then, by just giving an occasional encouraging touch of the main or jib sheet as necessary, crab sideways onto the finger with little or no forward motion. When the wind was from the east, I could sail further into False Creek, drop all sails, and sail under bare poles and at very slow speed onto the same finger. From my time at the museum, I gained a somewhat undeserved reputation as a wonderful boat handler for regularly sailing *Carlotta* into the docks single-handed. With her extremely long keel, the boat was docile, yet her cut-away forefoot (relative to other pilot cutters) gave her just enough maneuverability. Credit really goes to her.

One day I nearly did have some serious trouble, though. It was a beautiful, sunny summer day, and the docks were crowded with people. I was gliding into the dock single-handed under bare poles, something I'd done many times. Since the dock formed a T, it was important that *Carlotta* be stopped before she crashed into the top of the T. I had judged things nicely, except perhaps that I had a bit too much speed; this, you will understand, is hard to control when you're already down to bare poles. I could partially control this by using the rudder as a brake and sweeping the tiller back and forth across the cockpit.

I had a tied a bowline in the stern line so that if the loop was passed over the cleat on the dock, the boat would come to a nice stop alongside, at which time I could hop ashore and secure the bow. Unfortunately, the sweeping of the tiller had moved the stern just far enough away from the dock that I wasn't happy throwing the loop. So, spotting a likely looking young man standing next to the cleat, I tossed him the line and, in my calmest voice said, "Would you mind just dropping that line over that cleat by your foot?"

The young man caught the line, and, as he looked down to locate the cleat, his girlfriend reached across his chest, grabbed the line and, in an insistent whisper, said, "Don't get involved." Then she threw the line back to me.

Ah, well…it was a minor crash and hardly damaged the dock at all.

....

After bringing *Carlotta* to Canada, one of my other great pleasures was taking her down to Port Townsend for the wooden boat regatta in June and the wooden boat festival in the fall. When I'd begun rebuilding her around 1975, it was not long after the inception of *WoodenBoat* magazine in Maine. (Why wooden boats should suddenly become such a big part of the hippy cultural imperative, I'm not sure.)

Port Townsend is doubly blessed in its location for sailing and racing. First, it is located at the eastern end of the Strait of Juan de Fuca, ensuring much more reliable wind than is common elsewhere in the Pacific Northwest. The second blessing is that the town itself is located behind a long spit of land, so, while the wind finds its way onto the race course, the waves don't.

The racing was a big thrill for me. My first time there, I remember looking over the other boats as I tried to identify the serious competition. Somebody pointed out that *Passing Cloud* was an exceedingly fast boat, but I took one look at her and secretly laughed. She looked more like a motor sailor and was dragging a massive fixed propeller. Needless to say, it was not long after the start of the first race that I stopped laughing. She was designed by Roue, the same person who designed the *Bluenose*; she was very fast indeed, and comfortable too. Her owners eventually spent a ton of money to set her up for Category 1 offshore racing against modern boats (for the Victoria–Maui race). I'm not entirely clear about how she fared, but I don't believe it was all that well.

Up until the Port Townsend races, no schooner had ever crossed the finish line ahead of *Carlotta* (under my ownership, at least). That was to change when *Barlovento* appeared at the starting line. Designed by Burgess in the thirties, I had never thought her a particularly pretty boat, with almost no sheer, but Christ, was she fast, and certainly in a whole different league than *Carlotta*.

I should note that *Carlotta*'s sails were now getting very old and had many miles on them. Mr. Williams, who'd made them, certainly had nothing to be ashamed of. However, the boat did get noticeably slower from year to year, especially after the North Sails loft in Vancouver absolutely destroyed the leech of the main.

At any rate, there were some amusing moments related to my Port Townsend trips, so I'll mention a few here briefly.

One year, we left the festival and headed home across the Strait of Juan de Fuca. It was absolutely flat calm, as it often gets in the Northwest. A boat motored up astern — I think it was called *Moonglow* — and offered us a tow. We gratefully accepted. This family I hardly knew happily towed us right across the Strait. I mention this only because some years later, under a different owner, *Moonglow* was sunk at the other end of the Strait by a submerged submarine of the Chilean Navy. The conning tower sliced her in two one evening while the owner was drifting along, single-handed, under a full moon. One moment he was on board (perhaps contemplating the folly of all human endeavour), and the next moment he was swimming like hell.

Another year, during the really long and awful recession of the '80s, I decided to splurge — despite imminent impoverishment — and take my family on a trip to Port Townsend. At the last moment, some art student friends of mine asked if I would take their instructors (a married couple) along, as they had recently purchased a wooden boat and wanted to see how it was done. First, I surreptitiously checked out their boat and found out that it was, indeed, a very pretty one. Since it met my approval, I happily agreed to take them along.

They were not bad people, as it turned out, but we couldn't help noticing that they had no interest in contributing to the groceries or booze. Although *Carlotta* was fairly crude by yachting standards, I had noticed over the years that most people with an interest in wooden boats appreciated her provenance as well as her beauty, and were consequently grateful to have a ride on such an historic vessel. These folks, however, apparently felt we should feed and house them, provide great sailing, and then get lost. When we entered Canada Customs in Bedwell Harbour on the way home, they went ashore to look at real estate, leaving us to wonder — as we did in those days — where our next meal was coming from. Apparently finding nothing to their liking, they decided to charter a plane back to Vancouver; it turns out the sailing had been rather *too* exciting for the wife. We continued home, eating turnip greens or something like that, pleased to see the end of them.

Amusingly, we later heard from the art students about the "severe storm" this couple had "barely survived" aboard *Carlotta*, only just escaping with their lives. Perhaps it was a gastronomic typhoon they experienced, caused by our meagre onboard offerings.

．．．．．．．．．．．．．．．．．．

During our many trips to Port Townsend, I especially loved racing against *Alcyon*, the beautiful Frank Prothero schooner. I don't think I've ever seen a boat designed by Prothero that is anything less than gorgeous.

One race stands out in my mind. On this particularly beautiful day, we had sailed a good race, managing to stay ahead of *Alcyon* (although in the gusts, her greater waterline length almost let her pull up to our stern). The powers that be in festival race committee were always careful to arrange the finish line directly off the town, so that everybody attending the festival, as well as the townspeople, had a spectacular view of the finish.

We were quite pleased to be beam reaching along the waterfront, tops'ls set, rail down, sun shining, just beating *Alcyon* by a couple of boat lengths. Literally thousands of people thronged the piers and beaches as we crossed the finish line and…yup, here it comes…the pin rail to which all of the halyard tails were secured split in half. All the sails — main, gaff tops'l, stays'l, jib tops'l jib — came exactly halfway down, and stuck there. It was a pretty humbling picture at the time, although fun to laugh about later.

On another memorable day, a competitor failed to give way to *Carlotta* when we were the starboard tack boat. At the time, we were beating up to the weather mark that lay just off the big power station, and I could see that the boat we were crossing would just about bisect us if she failed to give way. As they got closer, I could hear a perfect stage whisper as someone on board repeatedly told the helmsman to bear off. Perhaps this made us let down our guard, as it was clear they knew we had the right of way — at least, someone on their boat did. The wind was in the neighbourhood of ten to twelve knots, so both boats had plenty of way on. As we got closer, I hollered, "Starboard!" at the top of my lungs, but nothing changed. The boat was close to *Carlotta* in size, and it suddenly dawned on everyone that there was going to be a Jesus-awful collision. While they could still bear off, there was little *Carlotta* could do. Heading up would reduce the impact, but, since the impact was going to take place about one-third of the waterline forward of the stern, we couldn't avoid it entirely.

One of my crew — my friend Charlie Cook, who had not done much sailing but is smart and athletic (he later crewed for me in the Pacific Cup race to Hawaii) — grabbed the opposing boat's bowsprit as it crossed over our toerail at about shoulder height, and heaved it aft. Realizing what he was doing, I put the helm up instead of down. This pushed our stern to weather, while Charlie had the strength and leverage to force their bow to leeward. They missed us only by inches. We could hear grumblings coming from their boat, but no apologies. Later, as we drifted without wind into the inner harbour, they motored smartly passed us. I hollered over to them asking if they could take a line to get us around the dogleg into the marina. They yelled back that they wouldn't help anyone who'd come so close to colliding with them, and left us to bounce off the dolphins. Go figure. It had been the most simple port/starboard crossing, with no extenuating circumstances. It always stupefies me to find out that someone can own a big, powerful boat like that and not have the foggiest idea of the rules of the road.

CHAPTER 16

....

CARLOTTA AND THE
LITTLE CRIMINALS

Adapted from an article previously published in *Pacific Yachting* magazine.

After the water taxi fiasco, I turned my thoughts once again to figuring out a way to earn a living from *Carlotta*. Earning a living with a boat presents many problems, not the least of which is the unromantic problem of marketing.

This is not a story about marketing.

I had successfully used my boat as a "head boat" in the Caribbean charter trade for several years. The boat had some obvious shortcomings for charter work, in that it had neither an engine nor a head. In doing day-charter work in the Caribbean, however, neither of these items was of any great importance, for the simple reason that there is nearly always a breeze in the Caribbean, and because people were on board for only a day. All but the most fastidious could manage with the bucket-and-chuck-it method I employed.

On my arrival in Canada, however, I gave up the notion of earning a living with the old girl because of the strong currents and generally light winds. In fact, as I noted in Chapter 13, on our arrival from Hawaii we entered at Bedwell Harbour and then took five days to cover the remaining thirty miles to

Vancouver; this was after having taken just eighteen days from Hawaii to Tofino. I certainly can't blame the boat.

The obvious solution would have been to install an engine. There are many reasons why I wouldn't do that, however, the foremost being that the boat was built in 1899 as a Bristol Channel pilot boat — without an engine — and I was pigheaded enough to want to see her stay that way. Underlying this amorphous (but nonetheless strong) inclination was the knowledge that engine installations as afterthoughts are never very satisfactory. The propeller must necessarily be under the quarter, so maneuvering is seriously compromised. I also knew perfectly well that, if I had an engine, I'd probably end up using the damn thing.

The lack of a head follows directly from the lack of an engine. Without an engine, the boat has no underwater through-hulls, and it seems a shame to violate this most seaworthy characteristic for the dubious pleasure of the cantankerous porcelain throne. I would be curious to know whether boats have been lost more frequently over the years due to stress of weather or plumbing failures. I have always suspected the latter.

My own bucket had a private compartment and a nice, varnished mahogany seat, so was not at all uncivilized. In thirty-five years, it never let me down (well, there was that one time I sat down and did my business and there was no splash. I spent the next half-hour chasing turds around the bilge with a wooden cooking spoon in hand — but you can hardly blame that on the bucket).

For several years after arriving in Canada, I had really given up hope of earning a living with *Carlotta*. I didn't stop chewing the problem over, of course, and I continued to rent myself out as a skipper and sailing instructor. However, as long as I perceived the problem as a physical one, i.e., of strong currents and light winds, and not as a marketing problem, I could get no further.

The realization that there was a solution to my problem of earning a living under sail came from a chance meeting with an old friend from my university days. He was working with the Department of Corrections and suggested I get in touch with the people running the high-risk wilderness program for young offenders.

And it is here our story really begins.

The high-risk wilderness program is patterned on the Outward Bound organization. Suitably trained adults take eight to ten juvenile delinquents into the bush for a three- to four-week period to teach them survival skills, as well as rock-climbing, canoeing and, generally, how to overcome difficult and dangerous situations by relying on themselves and each other. Although there has been one death in the program and some minor injuries, it has persisted in the face of bureaucratic trepidation and government cutbacks.

It was my good fortune that the program had recently been privatized, and consequently the company I dealt with was very keen to try new ideas. Further, I had discovered that these programs were already having success using traditional vessels in Denmark and Finland. We soon came to a satisfactory agreement, and I was once more earning my living, under sail, aboard my own boat.

Now it was my turn for trepidation. I had visions of "For a good time call Mary at..." being carved an inch deep into my beautiful teak skylights. Who exactly was it that took the risks in the "high-risk" program? It had been many years since I'd been a juvenile delinquent, and I wasn't sure what they were like these days.

The first group boarded for a five-day trip, and I had only a vague understanding of what was to be achieved. I was a sailing instructor, so I felt confident I could keep them busy, but surely something more was to be accomplished than teaching bowlines to car thieves. It took me a long time to ferret out the thinking behind the program, and I believe this is because the staff had been in the program for so long that they'd developed a slight case of tunnel vision. In short, they had taken for granted the premise of the program for so long that it was no longer easy for them to elucidate its specific goals.

A look at the history of the youngsters channelled into this program almost always reveals not only such commonplace things as a broken home, but also desertion, abuse and all manner of unpleasantness. I am not a social worker, but it was clear to me that the majority of these kids had been dealt a bad hand.

The program itself lasts for four weeks, and until I came along was spent entirely in the bush. The final three days are spent "solo" — that is to say, each youngster spends those last three days entirely alone in the bush with a sleeping bag, a tent and an oxo cube, practising the skills acquired in the preceding twenty-five days.

At the conclusion, there is a graduation ceremony and the child is released to his parents, foster parents or guardians. The youngsters have entered the program voluntarily, usually as an alternative to incarceration, and can leave whenever they want (although this sometimes results in a warrant being issued).

There is no simple way to put a value on this program. One social worker with whom I spoke could only describe the other side of the coin this way: "We pick these kids up off the street. They're hooking, and buying, selling and ingesting all kinds of drugs. They are constantly on the lookout for the police. It's a fast, hard, exciting life. Then I pick them up and take them…roller skating."

Another person I spoke with thought the best thing the program did was get them away from their peer groups and break the cycle of Saturday night trouble. He also believed it was important to give the immediate community a break from the kids, and offer them have a chance to develop a relationship with a father figure who was both caring and firm, something many of them had never experienced.

From an economic point of view, it might be said that it costs $36,000 per year to incarcerate a juvenile, so this program is very cost-effective even if just a few kids are turned around. Of course, such a dollar figure fails to take into account the social costs of the crimes themselves. The recidivism rate, though forever being studied, remains indeterminate.

After operating my boat during several of these programs, and spending many hours after "lights out" yarning with the counsellors, I think the rationale behind the program is as follows: the kids are basically losers in their own minds, they have failed in their families (as they see it), they have failed at school, and they have failed at special schools. Collectively and individually, they suffer from poor self-image. Probation officers or the courts encourage them to enter the program. And it is *hard*. They climb ropes forty feet in the air. They dangle above rivers supported by a single cable. It's not a joke. The work is exhausting, dirty and, to some extent, genuinely dangerous. And they survive.

Put more succinctly, if you accept that the way the world reacts to you is in large measure determined by what you think about yourself, then success through self-reliance can do nothing but good. In this type of program, failure is not an option.

The kids themselves did not seem particularly bad to me, but perhaps they just don't make juvenile delinquents the way they used to. Of course, there were those who shirked, and one or two who stole food. However, for every instance of this kind of behaviour, there was another instance of the kids doing some nasty job voluntarily — like the time they cleaned the galley so well that I was no longer afraid to stick my hand down behind the stove.

For the same reasons that *Carlotta* is not appropriate for the "pink gins on the poop deck" set, she is a most appropriate training vessel. And that, of course, is the marketing difference between chartering and sail training.

Everything on board is done by the "Armstrong patent method" — handraulics to those who know it. The gaff mainsail is 1,000 square feet, plus there are the stays'l, gaff tops'l, flying jib and yankee. The anchors range from a 35-pound CQR to a 120-pound fisherman.

The beauty of this is that, while I often single-handed the boat, it was also possible to keep ten people busy sailing her. Of course, one of the truths of sailing must be that the confusion level increases as a square of the number of people on board.

The Pacific Northwest is an area plagued by light winds and strong currents. On our cruises, we covered mile after mile, towed behind a pulling boat. So, if nothing else was accomplished, there were eighteen kids out there who really knew how to row. We were probably the first boat in 150 years to be towed by pulling boat entirely around Texada Island. And we didn't always reach an anchorage in the evening. Thus, within days of coming on board, boys who had never seen the ocean found themselves standing watch alone on an 87-year-old boat, entirely responsible for the lives of their shipmates.

Once, when we ran out of fresh water, we sent four boys ashore by dinghy to a nearby island, where they found a stream. They ferried out the water while we stood on and off with *Carlotta* — a real problem, a real solution, and the kids responsible for both.

There were humorous moments as well. Once, when a counsellor was giving a lecture on manners (developing social skills is part of the program), he was illustrating the utility of good manners when dealing with the police: "If you are rude and being a wise-ass when a policeman asks your name and address, you know he'll drag you down to the police station. But if you are polite —" At this point he was interrupted by a raggedy young kid who looked just like a young Pete Townsend: "He'll know I'm stoned as a rat and drag me down to the police station anyway!"

The long and short of it is that it's not all exciting on board. The crew stands anchor watches, scrubs decks, learns knots, and memorizes all the parts of the boat and gear. They cook and wash dishes. There's a fair bit of tedious work, but the opportunity for these city kids to sail, rail down, at midnight into a strange anchorage of their own choosing — with the phosphorescence exploding along the lee deck and the sky electric with northern lights — is not a bad alternative to the vicarious thrill of watching television, or the rush of some strange, potentially deadly chemical pulsing through their veins.

My own evaluation of the program does not rest on a matter of dollars and cents. Sure, I know some people will say that initiatives like this can be rationalized on the basis of money alone, but I can't help feeling that it is an agreeably benevolent society that pays this kind of attention to troubled kids. The counsellors genuinely care about these boys (which didn't stop them from handing out 250 pushups as a punishment when they found someone asleep on anchor watch). Years of private school had made me very suspicious of highly authoritarian situations, so for the first week I leapt to attention every time a counsellor hollered at one of the boys. But it was clear the youngsters revelled in it.

At a certain point, the future of *Carlotta*'s involvement with the program was put into limbo. We hear so much said about cost-effectiveness in this type of situation, and usually with very little understanding of the true cost-to-benefit ratio. At the time, I responded by pursuing recidivism information from the Danish and Finnish authorities to lend weight to my intuitive belief that "we done good."

Also this: what a satisfying way to keep old boats working.

CHAPTER 17

....

THE DISMASTING

But I got to stop wishing, got to go fishing
Down to rock bottom again... — Jimmy Buffet, "A Pirate Looks at Forty"

I've always had a dread of dismasting. Whenever the wind is screaming in the rigging and water is washing along the lee deck, I can't help thinking about the load on the weather shrouds and wondering if the mast can stand the strain. So, ignoring the many times I lost the topmast on *Carlotta*, the only time I can remember being dismasted, I was not on a sailboat at all, but rather on a fishboat.

I had been going through a very rough patch and the recession was well and truly established. No jobs were available, I lived in a single room with the toilet one floor down in the basement, and I had two hundred dollars left in the world.

My friend Jim (mentioned throughout this writing) had a struggling business at the time and, just as he had many times before (and since), pulled my proverbial chestnuts out of the fire by offering me a job. I was grateful beyond measure, but it was a job working as a cabinetmaker. Since I am naturally messy and almost innumerate, it was not a great fit. The job continued for six months and our friendship was seriously strained (but not broken), when another friend suggested I buy a fishboat and join him killing salmon on the west coast of the Queen Charlotte Islands. It seemed like a great idea: no more cabinetmaking, and rescue a friendship at the same time.

This pal, Ron Fowler, was an established fisherman and promised to teach me all he knew about fishing — at least for a couple of years until I was established. He even knew a good boat that was for sale, the *Two Sisters*. On the one hand, I had never been on a fishboat before and, even as a sport fisherman, I was demonstrably inept. On the other hand, it couldn't be worse than trying to be a cabinetmaker and taking shit from Jim every day.

In no time, I had found a co-signer and had a bank loan. A little bit of dickering, a $45,000 cheque, and I was a fisherman. Next, I needed a deckhand.

The single room I lived in was in a large revenue property in Kitsilano. We called it "Fowler's Rest home" because it was owned by Ron Fowler, because there were a lot of rest homes at that time in the area, and, ironically, because the only thing guaranteed was that if you lived there you were sure never to get any rest.

I was in my forties by that time, and the drug-crazed, alcohol-soaked hippy days in the house were pretty much over. The occupants were now mostly students from the Emily Carr College of Art (as it was then called) on Granville Island. As with all housing for poor students, the population was fairly transient, but they seemed quite happy with six to a bed.

One morning when I went down to have my shower, I found someone's diaphragm drying on the shower taps. Because I'm a considerate neighbour, I placed it on the counter with a note that read, "This bathing cap doesn't fit very well and now my head smells funny."

It remained there, giving everyone a laugh, until its owner happened to use the toilet the next day. Her name was Sarah.

When she knocked on my door to make her own comments about my note, I ended up with my first deckhand. She was twenty-two, cute and athletic. I was forty or so and wondering the same thing you're wondering . But hey, who's into motives?

I worked like hell to get the boat ready for the season — I knew a bit about boats, but not fishboats — and headed north to join up with Ron on the northwest coast of the Queen Charlotte Islands. Learning to fish was a real struggle (normally, a person would be a deckhand for a number of years and then graduate to owning a boat). Just getting the gear in and out of the water without incredible tangles was a major accomplishment, and catching fish only complicated matters.

Our favourite fishing hotspot was near Frederick Island on the west side of Graham Island. This was a few miles south of Dixon Entrance — the Canada/Alaska border. This story takes place in June, when the days were very long: the sky was still light at 2300 hours and light again by 0400 hours. Exhaustion was the norm. It took me years to get used to the long hours: get up at 0345, almost vomiting with tiredness, eat some breakfast, then up-anchor. With the wind pushing up a big lump, adrenaline was also the norm rather than the exception. The boat, I should not fail to mention, was one of the smallest boats fishing on the west coast, so on windy days fishing right out in the north Pacific was a pretty tough ride. The joke went like this: "You can listen to the weather and starve, or don't listen to the weather and drown. Take your pick."

The day of our dismasting was a month or so into my first season. I could now run the gear in and out; the tangles, if not eliminated — they were never eliminated — were at least reduced. We were catching fish and it looked as if I was probably going to be able to make the boat payment. The weather was not terribly bad and the sun actually broke through occasionally, an almost un-heard-of event in the "misty isles."

A modern sailboat usually has one or two masts. A trolling fishboat has a mast that is somewhat shorter than a sailboat's, plus two trolling poles about the same length proportionally as a sailboat mast, a boom fixed permanently amid-ships, and, in the case of my boat, two pecker poles that extended horizontally forward from the trolling poles. The trolling poles were attached to the bulwarks approximately amidships, and when fishing they were lowered to form an angle of about forty-five degrees from the vertical. In addition, there were two stabiliz-ers that streamed from the trolling poles to a depth of around fifteen feet.

The trolling poles and pecker poles towed three steel trolling lines on each side. They were encouraged to hang downward in the water by heavy weights on the ends (usually between thirty and sixty pounds each) called cannonballs. From each of these trolling wires streamed anywhere from fifteen to thirty pieces of gear. That is, each piece of gear was a Purlon (monofilament nylon) fishing line with a snap hook on one end and a flasher and hoochie, spoon or plug on the other. If you think you have a mess when your sailboat mast goes by the board, try to imagine cleaning up after your fishboat mast goes over, remember-ing that attached to the gear will be a number of twenty-, thirty- or forty-pound fish that are not having a good time.

We were fishing just north of Frederick Island, trolling very slowly into a six-foot sea. Directly downwind of us was La Pérouse Reef — a very ugly half-tide rock with water exploding fifteen or twenty feet in the air with every wave, and which we all took great care to avoid. With no warning at all, I heard a sudden groan as the boat lurched off the top of a wave. I was in the cockpit aft and I thought I saw the mast shift. Sarah was just coming out of the wheelhouse. "Get back!" I shouted, and for once she obeyed. On the next wave, the mast crashed sideways and down. The foot of the mast jumped out of the partners and slid across the deck to become wedged under the bulwarks on the port side, while the starboard bulwark supported the whole length of the mast that extended out over the sea. The trolling poles and pecker poles, which were fashioned out of wood, were immediately smashed to kindling.

I slammed the clutch into neutral and ran to the wheelhouse to kill the engine. This was to prevent the twisted mass of steel wire, fishing gear, stabilizers, shrouds and stays from getting into the prop. My next move was to turn on the one radio that had a wheelhouse-mounted antenna (for just such an eventuality; all other antennae were located on the mast). There were probably fifteen or more boats in the immediate vicinity, and, to my great relief, when I put out a call on 78a, the general fisheries calling channel, six or seven of them picked up their gear and started to circle us.

I had no time to chat, though. Normally, all this gear is handled hydraulically through two sets of three gurdies (reels) for the wire rope; these depended on a series of blocks whose position on the trolling poles and davits had been carefully refined over the last hundred years. With the trolling poles broken into small pieces and tangled beneath the boat, recovering the gear hydraulically was not an option. It would have to be the Armstrong method.

I began randomly pulling on the wire trolling lines — first on the "heavies," which had a sixty-pound cannonball on the bottom. Soon my gloves were sliced through and discarded, then it was just skin and blood. As a piece of gear came up, Sarah would try to land the fish and save the gear. The gear was expensive, and critical if we wanted to fish again that season. The mess on deck grew as we recovered more and more gear. Fish that were usually handled with extreme care flopped, jumped and beat themselves to death amid the mess, adding blood and slime into the mix.

The boats circling us were having their own discussions as we drifted slowly closer to La Pérouse Reef. Finally, Billy DeGrief, on the largest of the trollers, sent everyone but himself back fishing, saying, "I'm the biggest. I'll tow him up to Parry Pass and get him anchored." We were not yet ready to go, as there was still a big mess under the boat. However, when we were finally only yards off the tremendous rollers smashing on the reef, Billy came on the radio again, "This is as close as I go, so if you want a tow you've got to take it now." With that, we cut loose the rest of our gear and passed Billy's deckhand our towline. In minutes we were away from the reef and knew we'd be safe.

The seven-mile ride up to the shelter of Parry Pass won't soon be forgotten. With the mast and poles down, and no stabilizers in the water, we rolled our guts out, but there was no time to go into the wheelhouse and hold on. The fish still needed to be dressed and sent down to the hold, where they had to be iced and stacked with care. The gear needed to be cut from the Purlon and stored neatly according to type. All the hundreds of bits and pieces that made the gear work properly and smoothly had to be salvaged and stored in some kind of order.

For every minute Billy had his gear out of the water, he was losing money, so he towed fast and hard. With each passing wave, our mast would roll ten or twelve feet under the water and then, as we rolled the other way, arc skyward as the rail on the other side was dragged under. It was a big relief to enter Parry Pass and get into the lee of Langara Island. Billy found a good place for us to anchor, dropped our line, and headed back to *Freddie*, adding on the VHF, "You owe me a drink. Good luck." The exercise had probably cost him five hundred bucks in lost revenue. Not everyone on the coast likes Billy, but I do.

Now the work really started. Ron showed up, and he had a bigger boat and a hydraulic winch on his mast. We soon had the heavier pieces of gear shifted around and the mast on board, secured fore and aft against the wheelhouse. With Ron and his deckhand helping, it all went quickly, but it was way after dark by now. With everything on deck and out of the water, we could now use our own power. Ron slipped away into the night and we got our heads down. At first light, we were up and on our way to the Masset Slough to begin repairs.

I always like to describe Masset as a dirty little Mexican town — but cold, wet, and with no sun. There were, however, good fishing and hardware supplies to be found in Masset in those days, as it was the centre of the northern fishing fleet (which included trollers, seiners and crabbers). The biggest problem was getting trolling poles. In the old days, it had been just a matter of heading into the bush and finding a couple of young, suitably straight trees. But I had a better idea. There was a sunken fishing boat in the slough that had two aluminum poles. I asked around until I discovered that the owner was on a six-year bender, and met someone who assured me I could pay him and he would make sure the owner got the money. "Two hundred bucks sound good?" He agreed.

I unbolted the poles without a backward glance, used them as a couple of sheer poles to lift the newly rigged mast into position, and was then able to lift the trolling poles into place. I think I bought every wire clamp in Masset. At some point, one of the poles gave Sarah a boink on the head, but she recovered after a quick trip to the hospital. In three days we headed out of the slough and back to *Freddie*. When we got there, we learned that the weather that had threatened to put us up on La Pérouse Reef had gotten so bad that no one was able to fish for two days. So, relative to everyone else, we had missed only one day of fishing.

And that's dismasting, fishing-boat style.

CHAPTER 18

....

THE FIRE THIS TIME

Note: This story originally appeared in *WestCoast Fisherman* magazine. The title when the article was published was "The Fire is Out...This Time." The title here is as I intended it originally, and is a play on the title of James Baldwin's book *The Fire Next Time*.

We hadn't taken the usual pounding heading west out of Masset. By 2330 hours, the pick was out on the south side of Parry Pass. The weather was thick and cold, but calm.

At 0230 I awoke, choking and unable to breathe. I leapt out of the upper fo'c'sle bunk, hollering at the deckhand, "Get out, get out. Fire! Fire!" The flames were clearly visible through the various cracks in the engine room bulkhead. The thick, oily smoke of burning diesel was rapidly filling our living space.

Hamish Lloyd, my deckhand, awoke and got on deck a damn sight quicker than usual. [Note: In the published article, the previous sentence was trying to follow a narrative line that implied Hamish was not a willing deckhand. So, just let me say that Hamish was a *great* deckhand — so good that after this season of training with me he soon moved up to bigger and much more successful boats.] I followed as fast as I could, but took time to throw various fire extinguishers into the wheelhouse and rip away the stairs to give access to the fire. There was no question of fighting the fire from the fo'c'sle, as there was no breathable air and this would have left the fire between the exit and me.

Once outside, I could breathe, and I knew my deckhand and I were safe. However, when I removed the stairs, the deckhouse filled immediately with smoke, forcing us out on deck and making it impossible to fight the fire (or send a mayday). Hamish discovered that he could operate the VHF through the wheelhouse window, and I found I could fight the fire by dashing inside and firing off the extinguisher from on my knees underneath the cabin sole, then rushing out when I needed air.

While the Coast Guard was inquiring about the colour of the boat and whether the gumwood was painted or varnished, I managed to extinguish the fire. Our relief lasted only seconds as, with a dull "thwump," the flames reignited.

This scenario was to be repeated a half-dozen times as we rushed in, extinguished the flames, then crawled out to get air. Each time, before we could catch our breath, the flames erupted once more. At last we had only one large extinguisher left. We were reasonably calm by this time, and I realized we were going to lose the boat: we could put out the flames, but we weren't eliminating the source of heat. I ordered Hamish to get the dinghy into the water while I blew off the last extinguisher.

Gulping air, I charged for a final time into the black void that was now the wheelhouse. This time, however, I noticed a different sound coming from the engine room. Of course, the crackling of the flames could still be heard, but above that was another sound. It took a few moments to realize that the starter had engaged and was turning over the engine. My first reaction was to reach for the fuel shutoff…but I hesitated. And therein lay our salvation.

If it hadn't happened to me, I don't suppose I would believe it. The wires going to the starter motor and solenoid had melted, shorted and started the engine. It was then a simple matter to reach through the wheelhouse window, flick on the hydraulics, and have untold gallons of water gushing from the hydraulically driven washdown pump. Turning this hose into the engine room reduced the flames — albeit to a stinking sodden mess, but at least the fire was out.

Most people I've told this story to find it interesting and almost unbelievable. However, unless there are some lessons to be learned, hearing this story is about as valuable as hearing about somebody else's drug trip.

Before I relate the dumb things I did or didn't do, let me say that I care a great deal about safety on my boat. I'm with Mutual Marine Insurance, and they had inspected the boat weeks — not months — before the fire. Its origin was most likely electrical (we never did discover the source), and yet I'd had the entire boat rewired three years previously. I'd even taken firefighting courses when getting my "ticket."

Now on with the humiliation. You may notice that in the above story there is no mention made of halon. I had a halon system on board, and it failed to discharge automatically (although it was located approximately two feet above the source of the fire). Why, then, didn't I pull the manual release? Well, I apparently had what a radioman might call "a short between the headphones." It just never occurred to me. And there's an even worse confession I have to make, just on the off chance that anyone on the coast is as dumb as me. After having had the halon system inspected a few weeks earlier, I had reinstalled it using gangion (a Dacron fishing cord) for the manual release cable. That cord had melted, obviously, so even if I'd thought of that it wouldn't have worked. It was not much consolation that, while visiting recently on a friend's much larger fishing vessel, I glanced at his halon system and discovered that, indeed, all men are brothers.

I have some doubts about whether halon would have been any more effective than the ABC fire extinguishers I was using. Only water (or better, foam and water) would have cooled the area and prevented reignition.

Another dumb thing I did was to waste precious time trying to awaken people on the next troller with my horn. In the first place, my horn sounds like an elderly asthmatic breathing in your ear. In the second place, after twenty hours of fishing, people can reasonably be expected to sleep through a major fire right in their bunk, never mind on a neighbouring vessel. VHFs that automatically turn on for maydays may go some way toward solving this problem.

Why didn't I start the engine in the first place? In retrospect, it is clear I should have. But somehow, with the engine engulfed in flames, the last thing that would have occurred to me was to start it. Who can say whether a melted fuel return line would have made the situation worse by spraying diesel all over the fire? A wiser man than me once said, "No matter what trouble you get into at sea, and no matter how you solve the problem, there will be some smart SOB on shore who will know exactly what you should have done."

One aspect of the whole episode that wasn't important (but could have been) was our clothing. (Yes, I know you're all wondering what the well-dressed fisherman was wearing that season as firefighting attire.) The fact is, I slept in the upper bunk, and it's hot, so I wear bugger all. The deckhand slept in the lower bunk and, either because it's cooler or because he saw me wearing bugger all, kept his long johns on. I fought the whole fire buck-naked. At the conclusion, both of us looked as if we'd taken part in some strange Tongan fertility ritual. If we'd ended up having to take to the dinghy, however, my deckhand would have been better off than me.

"What started the fire?" and "What put the fire out?" are the two most important questions here.

I don't know the answer to the first one, except that the apex of the charred, inverted triangle on the bulkhead pointed directly at a new battery. This was the type with the external "live" straps between cells. I don't think I'd have that type again.

It's easy to say what put out the fire. Shithouse luck put out the fire.

CHAPTER 19

....

THE *TWO SISTERS* CONTINUED

Fishing as an industry runs very hot and cold. A great many people have gotten rich fishing, and some continue to do well. But for me, as we entered the '90s, things were getting decidedly tough. Each season was worse than the last, and predictions for the future were worse still.

Naturally, you take what action you can. Some people bought halibut licences and prospered. Others bought shrimp or prawn licences and did well too, although not for a number of years. I took the least expensive option and decided to add a drum to the stern of the boat and go gillnetting (drift netting). The expense involved was only for equipment, as my salmon licence covered both troll (hook and line) and gillnetting.

The advantage was that I could carry on trolling for the season and then, at the end of the troll season (say, sometime in September), "put on the rag" and gillnet for another month or two — well into November — as the last salmon arrived back on the coast. It seemed like a good idea at the time.

I found an old drum and rollers for sale and reworked my hydraulics to accommodate the new equipment. I didn't have a net, but the local marine college had a net-mending course. I took that, figuring I'd learn something. By the greatest good luck, I became friends with a young guy who owned a seine boat but who'd been gillnetting for years. He talked me into buying the materials to build a net, and we built it at lunchtime and during coffee breaks. I ended up with a brand new net for the cost of the materials. I was very saddened to hear a few years later that he was killed in the rip that forms off Cape Mudge when a screaming southeasterly meets a strong flood. He was a kind and generous man, and one of three or four people I knew who died fishing.

Around the fall of 1993, it all came together. I returned home after another disastrous troll season hoping I could make something out of the remaining gillnet season. I spent a few days installing the gear, then waited for an "opening." (It should be remembered that I had no idea what I was doing. Practising is prohibited: if you're found with your net in the water and there is no opening, you're arrested. Thus, just as when I had begun trolling, I was heading out with no clue what to do.)

It's the nature of salmon that they go deeper during the day and rise closer to the surface at night. The nets were two hundred yards long, with a lead line to hold the net down about thirty feet below the surface and "corks" to hold the top of the net on the surface. When you wanted to set the net, you cast one end into the water and drove away from it at speed, and then the rest of the net unrolled off the drum. The bitter end of the net usually remained attached to the drum and, using hydraulics, you reversed the process to wind the whole thing back onto the drum.

Night fishing was the norm, as that's when the fish would not be passing under the net but would swim into it. Attempting to escape, they would entangle their gills and drown, and, when they did so, the "cork" or float above them would be drawn under water to indicate there was a fish in the net.

Now you know as much as I did when Smiling Tom and I headed out for our first night of fishing.

Fortunately, it was calm, and we were fishing in a large area. Usually it is just the opposite, with people fighting over the best spots, but for now, with the sun just going down, we ran out the net. Much to my surprise, it ran out as advertised. There we were, hanging onto the net by the stern. The lesson was about to begin.

One of the constant problems for the new gillnetter is getting the net caught in the wheel (prop). I had been warned about this, and had built a primitive net guard that I lowered into the water to guide the net away from the wheel. What I didn't understand was that the clutch in my fishboat did not have a positive neutral; therefore, even though the boat was in neutral, the wheel kept turning slowly.

It took about fifteen minutes for me to realize that my brand new net was thoroughly wrapped around the wheel and shaft.

So there we were, adrift, hanging off the net and unable to recover it or drive the boat. Fortuitously, I'd had the foresight to bring a wetsuit and mask along. I struggled into the suit and, with Tom's help and my biggest, sharpest knife in my hand, slipped into the freezing water. Twilight was well advanced and I will always remember the ethereal green-black water. It was only about six feet down to the wheel, and I could easily swim down and inspect the mess. What was more difficult to see was the slack, almost invisible gillnet wafting back and forth and all around me. It suddenly occurred to me that I was holding my breath, surrounded by a net cleverly designed to be invisible so as to ensnare and drown anything that came into contact with it.

With the greatest possible care, I made my way back to the surface and took a very large breath. Tom helped drag me over the side and we proceeded to hack and chop and pull at my new net from the safety of the deck until I was free. Then we recovered the rest of the net and an incidental few fish, and headed home. First round to the fish.

Oddly enough, although I'm sure I was the least experienced fisherman out there that night, I didn't have the worst luck. Another guy fishing about a mile from us got his entire net filled with dogfish (small sharks). They sounded simultaneously, and before he could cut his net free the entire boat was dragged by the stern underwater and sunk (at least, that's what I heard).

Once at home, and with my humour on the mend, I took another look at the enterprise. There wasn't much I could do about the net guard. I hoped that being forewarned was to be forearmed. I installed some engine shutoffs around the boat so that if I felt myself drifting back into the net I could obtain a positive neutral by shutting off the engine. I put my net-mending skills to work and got the net functioning. Then I waited for the next opening.

This time, the opening was in Johnstone Strait just above Seymour Narrows. Seymour Narrows has one of the fastest tidal flows in British Columbia; countless fishboats, tugs, and even small freighters had been sunk there. But, what the hell. If others could do it, I probably could too.

This time, for reasons I can't recall, I was fishing by myself. When I arrived in the Strait it was well after dark and the fleet was already fishing. I had been instructed that the way to set your net was to watch your radar until you saw an open space and set in there. In this case, there were up to a hundred boats all vying for such a space. If you set your net just upstream of someone else, you would effectively be "corking" them, which meant it was unlikely any fish would get into their net as they would be intercepted by yours. There can be lots of aggro and fights over this issue, and because I was the new guy in town all I wanted to do was get my net in the water and try not to piss anyone off too much. Catching fish would be nice, but I had to learn first.

I set the net a couple of times, and each time, some pissed-off fisherman would pull alongside and scream that I had corked him and tell me to fuck off. This I did, with much bowing and scraping and apology.

I knew there was a tide change coming up, and I thought that would get the fleet jostling around. Perhaps there would be some room for me then. It was completely dark — no moon — and all of my strategizing took place on the radar screen. On the screen you could see the boats, but you could not always figure out which way the nets were streamed. I spent a long time running around trying to find a place to set.

Finally, it was slack water and the biggest, most beautiful vacancy appeared on my radar screen. It is important to note that we were fishing at the confluence of two major channels: Johnstone Strait, which, as you might expect, was straight; and Okisollo Channel, which bisected it. The vacancy I'd just spotted was where Okisollo ran into Johnstone, and I didn't hesitate. I ran right into the middle of the large, empty black hole on my radar screen. For once, the net ran smoothly off the stern. There I was, fishing with no mess and nothing around my wheel.

I did wonder (just the slightest bit) why, when everybody else was packed together fighting over every available inch of space, I had about three acres to myself. Never one to look a gift horse in the mouth, though, I drifted happily for an hour or so and then thought I should recover the net and count my fish.

I recovered about six feet of net before I came across the first of the logs. It was nearly impossible to work it free, as the net caught on every bit of bark, every twig, and every branch. I managed to free it after a half-hour struggle, using my pike pole. Each time the log rolled, though, it hooked itself back into the net until the net was draped all around it, working its way tighter all the time. As I say, I did get it out, but every foot of net now had sticks and leaves, branches and plastic garbage tangled up in it.

I had to work out another plan. I had a very small dinghy on board — it was about seven feet long and made of aluminum, without flotation of any kind. I figured that if I launched the dinghy, I could row alongside the net with my pike pole and work the logs out and push them away.

I launched the dinghy and got into it, thinking, by Christ, it's dark out here. I also thought about the fact that I was now in a seven-foot dinghy in the middle of one of the most dangerous stretches of water on the coast at two in the morning, with no life jacket and no lights, and, if successful, at some point I would be two hundred yards from *Two Sisters*. Then I thought, the smart money does not do this, and I got back on board.

By now I was drifting along, with three-quarters of the slash produced by the BC logging industry in the last ten years attached to me by my net, and not a fucking hope in hell of ever getting clear. What to do?

Well, when all else fails…beg. This was a real shit-eater, but I got on VHF channel 78a and basically said this: "…I've never fished before, I'm totally fucked up with logs and trash in my net, and if anyone could help me I would be really grateful for about the next ten lifetimes."

And, to my surprise, I got an almost instant answer. Another fisherman called his son who was fishing on his own boat and said, "We should probably go over and help this guy."

And they did. They knew exactly what had happened, why, and how to deal with it.

I think that was the last time I ever went gillnetting.

CHAPTER 20

....

MAYDAY

I've been fortunate over my many years at sea to have had to send off a mayday only once (I related that story in Chapter 18, "The Fire this Time"). It did no good, even though there was a government vessel with appropriate firefighting gear only a mile or so away. It was a Department of Fisheries and Oceans vessel, and no doubt the idea of having to stop sucking on the public tit in the middle of the night and actually do something irked them. They launched their Zodiac with various hoses, pumps and fire extinguishers, but the night was thick and they got lost trying to find us; any other mariner could have fallen over twice and found us. At any rate, we ended up saving ourselves, so I suppose it all worked out in the end.

Of the other two stories of mayday calls I'm going to relate here, in the first one I was the mayday relay, and thus only peripherally involved. In the second story, I was merely a listening bystander, but it is such a riveting tale that I'll pass it on for your edification and entertainment.

Toward the end of my career as a commercial fisherman, I took to fishing by myself. Normally, a deckhand was paid ten or fifteen percent of the gross, but as the fishing fell off it got to the point (at least on my boat) where ten or fifteen percent wouldn't support anyone. In addition, with less production, there was less need for another person to handle the work. The final reason was that it was great to have my own space and not have to put up with a deckhand/stranger who lived with me cheek by jowl, but was (in truth) just another farting, stinking, burping, eating-with-his-mouth-open male who was in my face twenty-four hours a day for ten days at a stretch.

During the time I'm writing about, I was fishing out of Winter Harbour, located near the top end of Vancouver Island just south of Cape Scott. If you've ever wondered where it is they make the wind, I'm here to tell you that it's Cape Scott.

When fishing out of Winter Harbour, you can sometimes (depending on the wind direction) anchor just behind the lighthouse on Kains Island. The advantage to this is that there is less distance to the fishing grounds, and therefore you can get a half-hour more sleep every morning.

When the wind doesn't serve, however, it is necessary to travel to the next anchorage inland, in Browning Inlet. This means a longer run every morning and evening, but the anchorage is totally snug and safe from any wind. On this particular night, we'd been forced by a particularly persistent southeasterly to use the Browning Inlet anchorage. This meant getting up at 0400 instead of 0445, and heading down the channel. Except for losing precious sleep (nobody who hasn't fished for a living can ever appreciate just how precious), I kind of enjoyed it. There was something romantic about pouring down the channel in the pitch dark with twenty or so other boats, running lights all around you, the squealing of blocks as the trolling poles are lowered, the occasional insult on the radio because somebody isn't watching where they're going, etc.

Because I was fishing alone, it was a little trickier in the crowd of boats. I would get the boat on course, click on the autopilot, then quickly jump out of the wheelhouse, undo the halyard for the particular pole I was lowering, hold the halyard in one hand and place my back against the wheelhouse, then force the pole out of its bracket with my feet. When it was out of its bracket, gravity would take over and my hold on the halyard would control its descent. Once it was fully down, I could reach up with my other arm and pull down the "grasshopper" (a bisected steel rod that held the trolling pole down, resembling a grasshopper's back leg) into position. Then it was just a matter of pulling the halyard to raise the tip of the pole slightly so it was "in column," and that was one pole done. The only caveat was that all this had to be done in one operation: if the pole was not secured in either the up or down position, it was very vulnerable should you encounter a big wake or bash another boat — and the trolling pole is a fisherman's living. After this, I would dash back into the wheelhouse to make sure I wasn't crashing into any of the other boats doing the same thing.

Radios play a major role in every fisherman's life. In fact, the first thing you do after getting out of your bunk in the morning is click on the radio. Normally you fish in a group so that information can be shared with your group but not with anyone else. We went to such lengths that we had "chips" installed in our VHF radios so that we could talk on a special frequency and nobody, including us, would know what frequency it was; this was so that no one in the group could share the frequency with someone outside the group. Later on, we got scramblers in order to scramble communication on a frequency we didn't know. This gives you some idea of the importance of information.

However, when fishing alone, as I was doing, all this changed. I would get up in the morning, turn on the radio, and set it to scan. This simply meant that the radio passed over all the channels. If there was talk on one channel, it would stop on there until the conversation was over, then return to scanning. The hope, of course, was that the radio would stop scanning on someone's conversation and they would inadvertently give out some good fishing information. It never happened, but I still picked up the odd bit of gossip; fishing alone week after week, that had some entertainment value.

On the morning in question, I had the anchor on board and was steaming down the narrow channel toward the open ocean. Checking radar, I could see no other boats crowding me, so I clicked on the autopilot and ran out of the wheelhouse. Just when I had the pole out of its bracket, I heard on the aft deck speaker of the radio, "Bill, Bill, can you hear me?"

Now, fishermen and people who work on the water have a way of talking on the radio that is abbreviated and not at all proper, but it works and we all do it; it's not at all like they teach you at the Power Squadron. The voice I heard on the radio now was different, for several reasons. First, it was a woman's voice — not unheard of, but rare. Second, the plaintive, pleading tone was completely unusual. Third, a fisherman would have said, "Hey, ya on this one, Bill?" or some close variant.

Unfortunately, it is the nature of the scanning function on the radio that, by the time I had my pole secured, and while the woman was waiting for Bill to reply, the radio had begun scanning again. When I returned to the wheelhouse, I was unable to see what channel she was standing by on.

I waited a bit before going out to lower the other pole, because it sounded a lot like someone was in trouble. After a few minutes of not hearing anything, I went back out to do the second pole and, just as you'd guess, I got the pole half down just in time to hear the same voice, "Bill, Bill, please, please come back." Now there was no doubt in my mind that someone was in trouble, but again I had to finish doing the pole. When I got back inside, the scanner was merrily scanning around, with no indication of what channel (there are about ninety) the woman was calling on.

However, this time at least my outside work was finished for a while, so I could attend to the radio. Sure enough, a few minutes later: "Bill, Bill, please come back, we're in trouble." I spotted the channel she was calling on, got rid of the scanning function and called her back, asking, "Is there someone on this channel in trouble?"

"Oh, yes, yes, my husband went out to pull up the anchor and collapsed on the foredeck."

"Is he still breathing?"

"No, we're sure he's dead."

"Where are you located?"

"I don't know. Somewhere near Kains Island."

"Are you alone on the boat?"

"No, we have a deckhand."

"Can the deckhand run the boat?"

Long silence, then, "He says he thinks he can."

"Can he get the anchor up?"

Long silence, then, "He thinks he can."

"Are you fishing with other boats?"

"Yes, but they are all unloading in Winter Harbour for the day."

"Okay, listen carefully: stay on this channel. I'm going to contact the Coast Guard and either they or I will get back to you on this channel. I'm going to get in touch with your guys in Winter Harbour. Tell the deckhand to get the anchor up and start heading toward Winter Harbour. When you leave the bay, you are to turn slowly north. You are now in the channel to Winter Harbour. Stay in the middle of the channel except when you make your last swing toward the docks, then stay a bit wide as there is a shoal there. Is this clear? You must stay on this channel for now."

"Yes, we've got all that. The deckhand is working on the winch already."

"Okay, stand by on this channel. I will be back to you shortly."

At this point I switched to channel 16, the calling/emergency channel.

"Mayday relay, mayday relay, mayday relay. This is the *Two Sisters* on one six."

I won't drag you through all the radio nonsense. The Comox Coast Guard came back on channel 16 and I described what had happened and what was happening. They, of course, took over in that very authoritative way the Coast Guard has, even though Canada has virtually no search and rescue capability due to budget cuts and the government morons failing to realize that we are a maritime nation (and that's a totally unbiased opinion, as you might guess).

They had me get the woman to switch to 16. This I did, and then I managed to raise some of her fishing group in Winter Harbour. I explained the situation and relayed that the boat would be entering the docks at Winter Harbour and the poor kid at the wheel had never run a boat before.

Then I switched back to 16 to see how the Coast Guard and the woman were making out. They had gotten her to describe the boat, then asked how many people were on board, how they had voted in the last election, and whether their taxes were up-to-date. I'm exaggerating, of course, but anyone who has listened to one of these calls knows exactly what I'm talking about.

Just then the strangest thing happened. The Coast Guard, after gathering all of this information, said, "Stand by, we'll get back to you in a minute." And then…nothing. Believe it or not, the Coast Guard never got back to this woman, who had her dead husband on the foredeck and a youngster running the boat — a youngster who had never run a boat before. I sat by my radio and waited. Finally, I called the woman back and checked to make sure she was doing all right and that they were making their way to Winter Harbour. Then I called her pals who were now waiting in Winter Harbour. This pretty much finished my involvement.

In late September, I wrote the Coast Guard and described the above incident. I told them how incredibly badly they had dropped the ball. First of all, nobody had ascertained that the person was actually dead, and I also failed in this regard. The first rule I'd learned in my First Aid and CPR classes is this: "They are not dead until they are cold and dead." The Coast Guard should have had the kid on the foredeck roll over the body and begin CPR. Two people who knew no first aid thought he was dead, which he probably was, but "probably" just isn't good enough. Second, the Coast Guard should have summoned medical help from Port Hardy or Comox (I think the other fishermen did this). The Coast

Guard should have been on the radio following the boat's progress into Winter Harbour, as it's a narrow, winding inlet, and, although not difficult at all for someone who knows the way, in the dark with someone at the helm who almost certainly doesn't know how to adjust the radar or plotter…well, it could have been another disaster. And yet the Coast Guard never spoke again. Must have been coffee time.

They wrote back to me and explained how difficult it is for someone in my position, listening on the radio, to understand everything going on behind the scenes. This, of course, was total bureaucratic bafflegab. I knew exactly what the woman was experiencing, and what was going on was this: no Coast Guard assistance with a death on board. I didn't pursue the matter further, although I believe someone should have been publicly horsewhipped for their total stupidity and lack of compassion.

. . . .

One of my introductory quotes, located in the very first chapter of this book, reads, "We are all scared balls of puke." This was suggested to me by an eighteen-year-old drunk at a very drunken party in 1967. It has stuck in my mind because (at least to some degree) it's probably true for most of us. This next story will make you doubt that truth, however.

At the time the following events took place, I had been fishing for four or five years. By this time I was an "okay" fisherman, in the sense that I could do everything I needed to do in order to catch fish, but I didn't have the magic that differentiates a journeyman from a master. I knew this, so I tried to make up for my lack of talent by working harder and longer: first boat out of the anchorage in the morning, last boat into the anchorage at night.

In Canada, the Department of Fisheries and Oceans determines when and where fishermen are allowed to fish. Very occasionally, they will call for an early spring opening. The good troll fishermen usually ignore these openings, because there are seldom many fish and it costs a lot in fuel and grub to get to the outer coast where these openings invariably take place. I, on the other hand, had no choice, as the only thing standing between me and failure was my work ethic.

It was due to all of the above that my pal Smiling Tom and I found ourselves in Port Hardy on the northeastern corner of Vancouver Island, getting ready to make the jump around to Winter Harbour. Navigationally, it's straightforward, but care must be taken. This is because it's necessary to cross the Nahwitti Bar, which can be pretty ugly at the wrong state of the tide and/or wind. Further along, you must round Cape Scott, where more often than not there's a gale of wind blowing. With all this in mind, we decided we would head up to Bull Harbour early one evening. Bull Harbour is a completely landlocked small bay, safe from any winds and located immediately south of the Nahwitti Bar, so we could sit happily and securely at anchor until we had an appropriate tide, then be over the bar in short order.

To be honest, I was not looking forward to the four- to five-hour run up Goletas Channel from Hardy to Bull Harbour. It would be dark, and, with a bit of a lump running, boring. Little did I know that I was in for one of the most fascinating stories I had ever heard — live, and available on a VHF radio near you.

We were not even out of Hardy Bay when we heard the first mayday. There was no mistaking the tone of voice: the person calling was terrified.

"Mayday, mayday, mayday, this is the 110-foot American packer [I can't remember the name of the vessel in question, so I'll just call it the packer]. We are on the rocks and breaking up! Mayday, mayday."

"This is Comox Coast Guard Radio. What is the nature of your distress and your location?"

"We're on the rocks in big surf and breaking up. I'm not sure where we are; I was off watch sleeping and can't find my glasses. Somewhere between Cape Caution and Cape Calvert."

(As an aside, since those words were spoken some years ago, I never go to sea without a pair of reading glasses wired to my nav area. I also have a pair packed in my life raft.)

"Roger, packer. How many people on board? Are they wearing life jackets?"

"There are six people on board. You've got to send the helos. The vessel is breaking up under us."

"Roger that, packer. We have launched aircraft. Prepare to set off some flares."

That was kind of interesting, because the Canadian Coast Guard has very few helicopters, and none anywhere near this incident, but I think the guy on the radio was too embarrassed to admit it. It is a fact that there have been a large number of nautical mishaps in Canadian waters in which the mariners involved have been saved by the U.S. Coast Guard flying in with appropriate aircraft from Washington or Alaska.

"Man, you've got to send helicopters now! The boat is breaking up in the surf! You've got to send them now!"

We were riveted to our seats at this point, listening to these people who, from all we could understand, were about to die; certainly, if they were depending on Canadian helicopters, they were going to die. We thought, given the very clear radio reception, that we might be able to help. What happened next is something I'll never forget. But first, some geography.

Due to the nature of the Inside Passage, all American fishboats travelling from Washington to Alaska travel in the passage and not out at sea. This pretty much guarantees they will have a passage unimpeded by weather. There are only two places between Olympia, Washington and Sitka, Alaska where there is exposure to the open ocean and — that's right, folks — one of them is between Cape Caution and Cape Calvert.

This area, known as Queen Charlotte Sound, can have some pretty tough weather, but on the night we are talking about there was little wind and about a four-foot swell — enough that your boat would not last long if it were up on the rocks. Passing Cape Caution or Pine Island on the way north, there are well-defined passages, but there are also hundreds of "rock piles," beginning with Egg Island, that you're not likely to hit due to its big lighthouse. However, as you approach Calvert Island, there is an absolute minefield of rocks just waiting to snare the mariner whose attention wanders.

At about this time, the generators on the packer failed as the water level rose in the engine room. All lights were then extinguished, although there was still emergency power for the radio. Following instructions from the Coast Guard, the packer started firing off flares as the fixed-wing aircraft from Comox Airforce Base entered the area. In a short time, the aircraft had located the vessel in the area of "The Virgins" — arguably one of the ugliest of the rock piles in an area famous for ugly rock piles.

The aircraft dropped a parachute flare of incredible intensity. We could clearly see its loom from our position, which I would guess was thirty miles away.

Also at this time, the Coast Guard issued a mayday relay asking assistance from any mariners in the area. Of course, the poor guy in the packer was still pleading with him: "Send the helos, send the helos!"

Two boats — I think they were returning from a herring opening in the Queen Charlottes — responded. These were both vessels in the fifty-foot range, and both were towing "super skiffs" (mostly open, aluminum, flat-bottomed boats that are grossly overpowered, with large inboard diesels and equipped with their own radios, GPS plotters, depth sounders, etc.).

Both these boats diverted to the position relayed by the aircraft despite the fact that they were approaching an area that is a navigational minefield. There were no further flares from the packer. The occasional radio transmission let us know they were still alive and, seemingly, getting more terrified as time passed.

The search vessels spent perhaps forty-five minutes searching for the packer, with no results; we could hear them talking to one another as they coordinated their efforts. Finally, when the tension was almost unbearable, we heard one say, "I can see him." Another five minutes of silence followed, and then the same voice came back, saying, "I can see him, but it's impossible for him to be where he is. I'm just south of him, and there are a hundred yards of breaking waves between us and him. It's not possible for him to have gotten to where he is before hitting."

At this point, the two boats made a plan. They would each work their way around the rock pile on which the packer was lodged. Every few yards they would head into the pile until either the surf conditions or their sounders forced them back. This probing continued for about half an hour, then finally one of the boats broke the silence: "I think I can see what happened. Just in front of me there's a long narrow channel with no surf. He must have inadvertently run down the channel, and didn't strike until he was about a hundred yards in. But it's crazy out here, with big, breaking surf and no light."

At this point, the Coast Guard came on, "Break, break, this is Comox Coast Guard Radio, Comox Coast Guard Radio. Are you able to go to the assistance of the packer?"

A long pause took place. Then the skipper of the herring boat came back in a very hesitant voice, saying, "I don't know if I can ask my guys to get in the skiff tonight. Standby one."

Another even longer pause ensued. We were miles away and even the tension on our boat was almost unbearable.

Finally, "They want to give it a try. I'll be off the 'phone' for a bit."

At this point, they would have been donning life jackets, getting the skiff alongside, flashing up the diesel, and getting the various instruments up and running. From this point forward, the communication was all between the VHF in the skiff and the VHF in the mothership. We could hear both sides perfectly.

Another long silence, then from the skiff, "Radio check on one six."

"Five by five."

"Okay, we're going to try to head up that channel."

"Roger that."

Another long silence occurred — although, given the tension, it was hard to know if it was really as long as it seemed. Then: "Well, we got pretty close. We could see them all huddled up on the bow. The rest of the boat is pretty much gone. The waves are actually breaking against the bow, so I'm not sure how we're going to do this. Stand by."

More silence then, and us wondering if these guys were out there dying trying to save six strangers. Finally, after what seemed like an hour (but was more likely three or four minutes): "We got one!"

Another agonizing wait. "Got another one! What we're doing is riding the wave in against the bow, having a guy jump down into the skiff, then backing out like hell before the next wave."

At this point, the skipper of the herring boat came back on, saying, "Christ, be careful."

Six times we endured the silence, then after each the terse phrase, "Got another one."

Six times we wondered if just one out-of-phase wave or a wave bigger than the rest would kill them all. Until finally: "Got 'em all. We're outta here!"

Man, Tom and I hugged each other, slapped each other on the back, and practically danced with relief and joy. The radio erupted in congratulations from the bystanders all around the area, who, like us, had spent the last three hours glued to their radio sets listening to the potential tragedy unfold.

And that was our "boring" run up to Bull Harbour. In fact, we were just turning into the dogleg before the harbour when we heard that everybody was safe aboard the mothership.

Now, I don't regularly read newspapers, but that next winter I was in the laundromat, idly thumbing through a paper someone had left, and I saw an article about a handful of fishermen who had been flown to Ottawa and presented with some kind of medal for bravery. I hadn't even gotten partway into the article when I knew it was our boys. And Christ, they deserved it.

Carlotta racing in St. Barths, just
seconds before the topmast snapped.
Dany standing at the stern, Freddie
Roberts at the foot of the mast, and
the author steering, circa 1979.
Photographer unknown

Left: *Carlotta* in Gustavia,
St. Barths, circa 1979.

Left: The author repairing the topmast in Barbados, 1979.
Photographer unknown

Below: The author's daughter, Sarah, instructing how to tie a Turk's Head on the deck of *Carlotta*, Gibsons Landing, BC, 1984.
Photographer unknown

The *Two Sisters* fishboat anchored in Gorge Harbour, Cortes Island, BC, circa 1992.
Photo by Smiling Tom

Right after the dismasting of *Two Sisters*. *Photo by Ron Fowler*

Skippering in Tracy Arm, AK for Bluewater Adventures, circa 1998. *Photo by Chris Tulloch*

Lunge-feeding whales in southeastern Alaska, 1998.

CHAPTER 21

....

THE GREAT CHAINSAW MASSACRE

The tigers of wrath are wiser than the horses of instruction. — William Blake

Toward the end of my fishing career, I had taken my Fish Master IV certificate (100-ton). I did this only because my role in our fishing organization was to produce the newsletter and, since the Department of Transport was threatening to make us all have licences, I thought I would get mine so I could elucidate for all of our members the process involved. However, with the end of fishing, this became moot and I applied for work with Bluewater Adventures, an eco-touring company. The owner was very interested in hiring me, but running their boat required a 350-ton commercial licence; with my 100-ton fishing license, it would seem I was out of luck. However, through the good offices of the owner, we obtained an exemption from the Coast Guard on the understanding that I would complete the 350-ton licence over the course of the next couple of years. This I did, and the licence fed me and mine over the rest of my working life. For many reasons, I truly struggled to get this licence, and the year after I did they invented a 60-ton version. The boat I ran was 59.6 tons, so it was absolutely the best of luck that forced me to get the greater licence, enabling my family to eat a lot better for many years.

Working for Bluewater Adventures was in many ways a dream job. Travelling the length of the northwest coast and exploring every inlet, trail and abandoned native village, as well as having a front-row seat for mind-blowing natural events: lunge-feeding humpbacks in Alaska, calving glaciers, grizzlies close enough to touch, etc. There was a downside, though. The company, for reasons of economy, required back-to-back trips. This meant twenty-two days on board at the beck and call of passengers, with no privacy and no timeouts.

The crew usually became a real team and gave each other whatever privacy could be offered, but the fact was that we all slept outside in the large enclosed cockpit — two on the sole and two on the bench seats, men and women tossed in together. Waking at 0600 hours, the females would be struggling out of their sleeping bags, trying to arrange their T-shirts appropriately; the younger males had issues of their own. We all found somewhere else to look out of respect.

The point I'm trying to make is this: great job, great people...but God, after twenty-two days of not one moment to yourself, getting home was wonderful. I used to joke that it was the only time I found solitude erotic.

During the time I'm talking about, I was living in Gorge Harbour on Cortes Island. This was post-divorce, and I had nearly lost the house in the acrimony. I was holding on by my teeth financially, as I knew what a gem I had: large house, eighty-foot dock, gardens, etc. In order to be able to afford the place, I had taken in roommates. With my job on the water, I was away much of the time, so it generally worked well. However, after twenty-two days on an Alaska trip spent with people in my face every second, being watched to struggle in and then out of my sleeping bag every evening and the next morning...well, when I came home I needed space. Space, and peace.

Although it is not the case today, at that time Gorge Harbour was extraordinarily peaceful: quiet and serene, with very few boats and very little noise. As the sun set, I could sit on my dock and experience the peace as something almost tangible. The silence lay on the place like a warm blanket, almost daring some errant seabird to break it.

I'd just arrived home after a particularly intense Alaskan cruise. Roommates filled my house, so I took a glass and my bottle of wine and headed down to the dock. It was a gorgeous late afternoon. The light was perfect and the wine was good. My only problem was a Zodiac with a particularly loud two-stroke motor that was doing doughnuts almost directly in front of my property. It didn't worry me all that much, though; how long could a person turn circles in a noisy boat? I did notice there were a lot of sailboats rafted up not far away, but I was content to drink my wine and wait for the offending cretin to get bored and leave. I waited and I waited…and I waited some more. This moron continued to go around and around and around in the water just off my dock.

Around and around and around and around.

By the time an hour had gone by, my wine had gone by too and I was seriously bent out of shape. I worked hard for my peace. I paid for it and I needed it. I wanted my goddamn quiet and I wanted it now. Still this idiot went 'round.

I climbed back up to my house. Everyone was in a good humour, having dinner and laughing, but I was seething. "This is not right," I announced. "This cannot go on." I pulled the cork on another bottle of wine and watched him out the window until, as the sun set around 2200 hours, the noise ceased and the Zodiac returned to the rafted sailboats.

"They will pay," I announced to no one in particular.

Perhaps more wine was consumed; I'm not sure. At around midnight, I saw the last light go out on the last of the rafted yachts. Apparently, they were unaware of how loud their two-stroke outboard was, while I, on the other hand, had a full understanding of, and great confidence in, the noise made by my old Stihl 090 chainsaw.

One of the guys from the house walked down to the dock with me and helped me launch my skiff. I loaded in the chainsaw and a couple of seal bombs saved from my days as a fisherman; these are something like cherry bombs, and are used to discourage seals that come after your catch.

I headed out. Locating the anchor line of the offending yachts, I secured my painter, lit the fuses of the two seal bombs, and jerked my mufflerless chainsaw to life.

I think I saw house lights go on at the other end of the harbour, well over a mile away. I know for sure that the folks at the head of the Gorge, half a mile away, heard me as they phoned the cops, and I have no doubt I got the attention of the offending party. Within thirty seconds, every man, woman, child and screaming baby was on deck shitting themselves.

They had been generous with their noise, so I felt I should be generous with mine. I could see them shouting and gesticulating, but I couldn't hear a thing. An unmuffled Stihl 090 is a dominating influence in the aural environment. After a few minutes, I shut down the saw and let them vent. To my great surprise, they didn't get it. The world was their playground, they had done nothing wrong, and so on and so on.

Where to begin? I decided to start the saw for a few moments to regain their attention; this set a few babies to screaming once more. Then I explained, "It is difficult to live on Cortes. To go to a supermarket involves two ferries and quite a bit of money. Friends from Vancouver can't visit for a weekend if they have normal jobs because it takes three ferries and a whole day to get here, and three ferries and a whole day to get back. When there is a storm, we often lose power for a couple of days, and up to a week is not unusual. When we do lose power, we have no water because our water comes from wells that use electrically powered pumps. We lose all of the food in our freezers. High school kids have to board with families two ferries away and get to go home only on weekends. So why do we live here? For peace. For neighbourliness. To raise our kids in a calm, safe environment. And then here come the Royal Vancouver Yacht Club storm troopers. Most people on the Gorge raise oysters for a living, so you take your dogs ashore to shit on the oysters [some intelligence I had received during the evening]. You destroy the peace of the anchorage that I have just worked hard for twenty-two days to earn. In short, you're a bunch of citified, insensitive pukes who should leave and return after another ten thousand years of evolution."

Well, they started to rant again until they saw me reach for the saw. One bulky guy suggested I was just a coward, but shut up when I proposed that we should go ashore and discuss that issue further.

There was nothing more I could do, so I rowed home and went to bed. I woke up the next morning with a major headache, wondering what the fuck I had done. Everything I'd said about the small community of Cortes Island was true. (As an example, our local school had a drive-by *shouting* once and it was all anyone talked about for weeks.) I felt what I did was personally justified, but how would the community deal with my random act of insanity?

The next day, the yachts all swooped by my dock, where I was working, and screamed, "We'll never come here again!!" That's the plan, I mumbled to myself. That's the plan.

After that, with a serious hangover, I took my old chainsaw and headed out to get some firewood. Running that old saw with my eyeballs bleeding from alcohol abuse was not going to be a ton of fun, but there was a long, cold winter ahead. This is an annual chore; for wood to be dry enough to burn in the winter, it was necessary to get it in during the spring or early summer. On Cortes, there was plenty of Crown land, so, although you were technically stealing the wood, there was nobody to complain. Over the course of an hour or so, I loaded up my old truck.

When I turned into my driveway, the "heat" was parked in front of my home. I was not sure whether I was being arrested for stealing firewood or for driving the morons out of the Gorge. The cop read me my rights and then started asking questions. You should understand that, in the madness of my life, whatever he was here for was pretty small beer, so almost immediately I interrupted him to point out, "If you're going to arrest me anyway, why in the world would I answer your questions?"

"If you answer my questions, maybe I won't have to arrest you," he replied.

We carried on sparring like this for a few minutes until I finally said, "You go ahead and ask your questions and I will tell you what I think might have happened if I had been there."

It turned out that the cops had been told that someone had been firing a gun; I offered a guess that perhaps someone had set off seal bombs. Finally, after about ten minutes of verbal tennis, I suggested that no laws had been broken so I couldn't see the problem. He asked, "What about disturbing the peace?"

"Where were you when some moron turned circles in front of my house for four hours in the loudest Zodiac in the eastern Pacific?"

It was clear we were at a stalemate, so he departed. And that was the end of the great chainsaw massacre. The whole incident was later editorialized in a regional yachting magazine, and at some point lawyers were sniffing around, but nobody ever said anything to me. Well…unless you count every single person on Cortes who had an opinion and shared it with me.

Fuck 'em if they can't take a joke.

CHAPTER 22

....

A FEBRUARY DELIVERY

Anyone in their right mind is afraid of ... [the] next leg. — Paul Cayard

Working for Bluewater Adventures, it was always a bit difficult to get through the winter financially. So, during the winter of 1997, I was pleased to be asked to deliver an Ocean 71 from Cabo San Lucas to Vancouver.

It is notoriously difficult to sail northward along the west coast of North America in the summer months. The Pacific High hangs around off the coast, and the circulating breezes tend to blow parallel to the beach in a southerly flow. In winter, the low-pressure systems that originate on the west side of the Pacific march across the ocean with almost military precision and reliability. These lows tend to curve northward into the Gulf of Alaska as they reach the eastern Pacific and are responsible for the predominantly southeasterly winds experienced in coastal areas during the winter.

I bother mentioning the meteorology of the coast just to make the simple point that, difficult as it may be to believe, you are actually smarter to transit the coast north of San Francisco in the winter. It does take some patience, but if you can hide out until a low passes, and then pick up the last (and hopefully least) of the accompanying southeasterlies, you can have following winds until the low has completely disappeared to the north. Then you just need to find a port in which to hide out until the next system passes.

I first heard this theory when I was preparing *Carlotta* for her passage from Hawaii to Vancouver in 1980. I had the boat out of the water at the Keehi Marine boatyard, managed by John Slattebo. John, besides being a great guy (both then and now), was a thousand times more knowledgeable than me about things nautical. *Carlotta*'s lack of an engine was the reason I was in Hawaii, and I believed a northbound trip up the coast of North America verged on the impossible.

I never regretted the trip from Panama to Hawaii and then north, but it was very educational to speak to John and I never forgot what he told me. It was thus, in the late '90s when the possibility of this delivery came up, that I was not as intimidated as some others I will mention, all due to John's instructive lessons. I did, however, make it very clear to the boat's owner that I would be proceeding at my own speed and would not be pressured to hurry.

The owner of the boat chose the crew, so I didn't even meet them until the day before we took the plane south to Cabo. As I recall, there were four and myself; some had sailing experience and some had none at all, but everyone had something to contribute. One of them, Marco, was great with engines; I'm pleased to report that he remains a good friend to this day. The names of the others escape me, but we generally got along well.

Since this was an El Niño year, apparently it meant that it was going to blow like hell all the way to Vancouver. In situations like this, I find that, after the general plan is hatched, it's best not to dwell too much on what's going to happen in two weeks. Instead, it's advisable to pay a lot of attention to what's going to happen tomorrow.

We arrived at the Cabo airport and grabbed a taxi to the marina downtown. The cab driver got his vehicle up to just over a hundred miles per hour, and I thought this was a great opportunity to let the crew know that I was safety-conscious and also in charge. After a big argument, I managed to get the driver to slow down to about eighty-five. As far as the crew went, I had made my point. Or at least I felt I had.

We found the boat, and what a boat she was! Seventy-one feet and a real beauty. We pored over her — not with the owner but with the skipper who was leaving. While a bit tired-looking, she definitely looked strong. At this time, she was named *The Big O* and had been bought from the owner of the nautical magazine *Latitude 38*. To this day, I'm still amused when he pontificates about nautical safety in the magazine, because I know what terrible condition his boat was in when he was through with it. Nevertheless, we were in Cabo with a job to do. The boat may have been rough, but she was strong.

We spent a day or two getting supplies and acquainting ourselves with the various systems. The next morning, we got up at five sharp and prepared to depart. Just as we were casting off the last line, a man came running (yes, running) down the dock, waving his arms and shouting, "You mustn't leave, you mustn't leave! Every harbour from here to Alaska is closed. The weather is totally out of control. If you leave here, there is not another harbour that will let you in! I am watching the weather on the entire coast. You can't leave!"

I looked at him, looked at my crew, looked at the fat, puffy, white cumulous clouds floating overhead, and said, "Let that goddamn line go and let's get out of here."

As I have found many times over the years, when the weather sounds dire it is sometimes a good idea to go outside and have a look. This is what we did and, as often happens, the weather was perfectly benign. In fact, instead of the usual Baja Bash north to Turtle Bay, we had to motor some of the way. What sailing we did do helped to convince us that this was a very safe boat.

The trip north to San Francisco was not terribly eventful. We did have some fresh breezes. I remember once coming on watch and glancing at the anemometer and seeing it momentarily touching fifty-four knots (fortunately, the breeze was from astern). We discovered that the boat was hard to control downwind at twelve knots — as were many of the boats of its era given that the sterns were too narrow and the rudders too small. To my understanding, this was in emulation of the twelve-metre boats of the period that tried to reduce wetted area by reducing rudder size; although it might be fine for an afternoon bash around the cans, it was not so good for surfing down ocean swells at speed (I know this very well now from my current boat, *Scaramouche*). Interestingly, fifteen years after this delivery, *The Big O*, now called *Ocean Light 2*, is moored twenty feet from *Scaramouche* in the small harbour of Gibsons Landing where I reside.

We spent some time in San Diego getting a few technical problems worked out and letting an impressively awful front go through. We enjoyed watching the golfers on shore walking around in the horizontal rain with inverted umbrellas, all the time thinking, Christ, they're crazier than sailors.

One thing that struck me then, and seems to ring true to this day, is that port police are total assholes. I don't know if they are bred to be like pit bulls or if it's just a great training program, but believe me, they excel.

I had never entered San Diego before. Since we were coming from Mexico, we had to report to the port police and U.S. Customs at the police dock behind Shelter Island. There is a buoy that, I've since learned, must be left to starboard when turning into the channel that makes Shelter Island an island. However, it was four in the morning and I could not figure out which side to leave the buoy on. I don't remember now if we didn't have the correct chart (the owner had promised many things — and many things weren't as promised — but it's probably my fault for not checking more carefully if he was being truthful), but we certainly didn't have a plotter or any modern aids. I called the police dock, which was about two hundred yards away, to ask directions. In the snidest voice possible came the reply: "It's not our job to give navigational advice. Over and out." When I typed the above, I made a typo that said "over and pout," and that pretty much sums it up.

I've been back to San Diego more times than I can count since this trip, and am glad to report that they are still total assholes. They have become an institution like the Customs agents in English Harbour, Antigua — where you brace yourself in anticipation of dealing with them, waiting to see if they are still jerkoffs. It is an inside joke with sailors because you know just what to expect. Of course, you pretend to take them completely seriously in the interests of furthering your own plans.

While at San Diego, we made repairs to the boat and waited for the weather to improve. In due time, the front passed and we made the leap to San Francisco. The trip from Cabo to that point, we expected, would constitute the easy part of the voyage — including Point Conception, which has a bad reputation but which we found to be not unpleasant. I read recently that Point Conception is called "the Cape Horn of the north…but not by anybody who has been to Cape Horn"; that certainly sums up my experience of it (but maybe it'll get me next time). At any rate, the temperatures had been fairly mild up to that stage — although they didn't seem "mild" at four in the morning. Either way, the dropping temperatures and northerly latitudes led us to view San Francisco as the beginning of the potentially dangerous part of the trip.

By now, the boat was in good shape following the repairs we'd carried out. She leaked badly, but only over the bunks, so we felt quite safe despite suffering the usual Chinese water torture blues. All we really had to do in San Francisco was wait out the weather. I had already decided that our next stop would be Crescent City, if possible, and it wasn't long before I was able to announce to the crew that we would be refuelling the next morning and leaving.

We all went ashore for a final dinner before the big push. After dinner, everybody got on the phone to say goodbye to girlfriends, etc., then it was back to the boat. That is, it was back to the boat for everyone but one guy we could not pry out of a telephone booth. It was important to me that the crew get a good night's sleep and, since we were anchored out and had only one dinghy, we couldn't leave without the entire group. But this guy simply wouldn't get off the phone. As the other four of us stood around kicking our heels for forty-five minutes, it stopped being a joke. Love is great, but we had a voyage to complete. We finally dragged him kicking and screaming down to the dinghy and returned to the boat to hit the sack.

Just as I was dozing off, I heard a light tapping at my cabin door. In came Mr. Telephone Booth. "Jesus, what is it now?" I blurted. "Well, Peter, I have to tell you that I won't be going on with you. I've got to get off the boat. It's just too dangerous to try to do this trip in February." His leaving would sure as hell not make it any safer for the rest of the crew, and I told him so in pretty explicit language. But he was resolved: he wasn't coming with us. There was nothing I could do, so I asked him to let the rest of the crew know and I went back to bed.

I began to doze off again and, just as I was gratefully entering the arms of Morpheus, was disturbed a second time. Some scuffling on deck was responsible. Being in a big city, I thought I'd better check it out, so I wearily put on some pants and climbed on deck. Who should I see but Mr. Telephone Booth sitting on the toerail in his underwear with his sea bag by his side, in the process of slipping over the side into the water.

"Are you fucking nuts?!" I asked him calmly (you could hear my voice only as far as Sausalito). "What the fuck do you think you're doing?!!"

"I'm going to swim ashore," he replied.

"Oh, for Christ's sake! What do you think this is, a prison ship? If you want to get off, I'll put you ashore when we refuel. Now, for Christ's sake, can you please let me sleep? It's February in San Francisco; you'll fucking freeze to death, you dumb fuck!"

Fuck.

After we put him ashore the next morning, the rest of the crew rallied, as often happens when faced with this kind of adversity, and became a much tighter unit (albeit a much tighter unit that ate less well, as Mr. Telephone Booth had been rather a good cook). We never saw him again. Marco tried to contact him in Canada, but he wouldn't return calls. I can only assume he was ashamed of himself for leaving the rest of us in the shit.

The shit that never was, I should add.

We made it past Mendocino without incident (if I'd known then what I know now about Mendocino, I'd have remembered to take a moment to give serious thanks).

Crescent City was next, and the entrance, although always requiring full attention due to outlying rocks, can be entered in just about any weather. I should probably amend that to say "in any weather I've experienced there"; while there, we discovered that the local crab fleet had not been out of the harbour for a month or more because of the weather. However, we snuck in without any problems. We could receive only daily VHF weather on board, and had no weatherfax or means of obtaining GRIBs, so I decided it was best to stop and get a longer-range forecast. There is not much to recommend Crescent City, I must say. As far as I know, it exists only to support a large prison and a small fishing fleet, and is otherwise (sorry) a dump.

What Crescent City does have is a harbour master's office on the dock. Every morning, the harbour master printed a large weather map of the North Pacific and posted it on the public notice board. Every morning I would walk over and check out the map. We had grub on board and were fuelled up, so all we had to do was wait. And we didn't wait too long before the map revealed the biggest high-pressure area anyone had ever seen in February in the North Pacific, centered right over the coast. These were *not* the southeasterlies John had instructed me about earlier.

We were off like a bride's pajamas.

And we proceeded to motor — yup, motor — all the way up the coast of Oregon and Washington. This was the "hellish" weather we'd been dreading, at the worst time of year in the worst year on record, and we motored in flat calm through it all. Providence.

CHAPTER 23

·················

YACHTING,
AS IT WAS DONE

The working class can kiss my ass,
I've got the foreman's job at last.
— Ron & The Rude Boys, "Red Flag"

Like many other individuals and companies here in the Northwest, I've had to move from work on commercial vessels to yacht work. From being the skipper of fishboats and tugs, making the shift to touring vessels, cruise ships and, finally, yachts, now seems to have been almost inevitable. Thus, when I got the nod to be skipper of *Exodus*, a ninety-foot American yacht, I didn't even hesitate. Anything was better than starving on the beach.

I could tell right from the start that the owners, who were quite a bit younger than me, got a kick out of having a grizzled old tugboat skipper in their employ. At first I took exception to this characterization. Old? Well, maybe. Grizzled? Seldom after ten or eleven in the morning and my fourth cup of tea. But what they really valued was the fact that, over the years, I'd skinned the occasional knuckle in the engine room. That, and the fact that I could balance all of the peas on my knife while eating with their guests, made me ideal for their yacht. They weren't going to have an engineer, so they needed someone who understood the "round and round and up and down," which I assured them I did.

Work progressed much as you might imagine for the first month or so. Trips to the Gulf Islands, trips to the San Juan Islands — nothing at all challenging. Engine room work was not much more than checking fluid levels in the morning and trying to figure out the various systems that were, for the most part, still in pre-breakdown mode.

When I took the job, I didn't lie to these nice people. I told them that I wasn't an engineer but had some familiarity with Cat engines. (I never actually lie, although a friend once accused me of "loving the truth so much [I] spend the whole day embellishing it.")

The last tug I'd worked on, the *Service IX*, did have a Cat in it. You could say I kept it going, but really it kept itself going. Its engine room was a mess, littered with buckets of dirty filters and filthy rags pushed into various corners. Where valve handles had broken off, vice grips were applied, and broken and grease-clogged tools were strewn everywhere. For changing the oil, there was a little rotary pump hose-clamped to the side of the engine. The other skipper, who was my boss, valued neatness and safety equally. There was no CSI (Canadian Steamship Inspection) certificate, the life raft was years out of date, and at one point the deckhand — accidentally and without knowing he had done it — set off the EPIRB.

We learned later that the EPIRB had been stolen from another boat. I'll just say here for the non-mariner that an EPIRB or "emergency position-indicating radio beacon," when set off, sends a signal to a satellite. That signal gives the position of the vessel in distress, as well as communicating the name and type of vessel. The satellite then sends the information to the appropriate ground station so that a search can be initiated for the vessel. The first clue we had was when we were contacted by the Coast Guard and "tasked" with searching for a boat in trouble in our area. They gave us a description of the boat in question (read: the boat whose EPIRB had been stolen). We searched diligently for several hours without any luck until it dawned on me that *we* had set off the EPIRB; then we realized that we were, in fact, searching for ourselves. (You do what you have to do when you have mouths to feed, but I left that job at the earliest opportunity.)

My new engine room was carpeted. The engines — all four of them — were white. We regularly took up the carpets and washed the bilges, although I don't know why given that they were spotless.

On the day this tale begins, the owners had to leave the area on business, no doubt to wring the lifeblood from my proletarian brothers in some third world country so they could afford to pay my rather excellent salary. (Ah, well, my devotion to socialism seems to wax and wane with my bank account.) Before they left, we discussed the work that should be done in their absence, the main job being to change the oil and filters in all four engines and service intermediate bearings, stuffing boxes, and the usual nautical minutiae — all things with which I was thoroughly familiar. In fact, it was easier on this yacht because the clean oil was kept in a large internal tank. The dirty oil was stored in a large, dirty oil tank. The dirty oil was moved from the engine to the tank by a pneumatic pump that was operated by a compressor. The same pump then pumped new oil into the engine. This meant no more searching the garbage for discarded five-gallon pails for the dirty oil. No more endlessly rotating the little rotary pump the Cat people fasten on the side of the engine for this purpose. No more balancing the five-gallon pails of new oil on the valve cover, trying to direct a stream of oil into a small funnel, only to have it spill all over the engine. This was heaven.

I did one of the generators first, and things went pretty well. I spilled about a cup of oil on the carpet, which made me feel bad…but hey, you carpet an engine room, what do you expect? I knew that at the end of the process I would have a pail of used filters that I could cleverly place over the stain.

I've heard that people learning to fly seldom crash; it's the people who have 250 hours and are getting a little cocky who get into difficulties. I started servicing the second generator with a certain amount of confidence.

I connected the hoses to the sump of the engine and the pneumatic pump with the "quick fits" provided. Then I connected the pneumatic pump to the dirty oil tank. Next was to flash up the compressor and open the air valve, and the amazing fluid pump would jump to life and let the transfer begin. Hell, I didn't even put on my coveralls.

The first thing I noticed was that the pump seemed to be working a little harder than usual. It was still working fine, but I had that mechanic's instinct that all was perhaps not as it should be. Also, it seemed to be transferring oil for an extraordinarily long time. I checked the valves, because I had once left one closed and the pump had seemed to labour just as it was doing now. After that, I simply stared at the whole setup for a while, and, the more time that passed, the more I became convinced there was a problem. Finally, it dawned on me that all I needed to do was pull out the dipstick and I would immediately be able to see how the oil level was dropping.

It wouldn't be easy to exaggerate the power or length of the stream of oil that blew out of the dipstick hole when I did this. Let me just say that it dented the sound-deadening material located five feet above the engine. It turns out that there is a very elementary principle that applies to all pumps: the lower hole is the intake; the upper hole is the exit. I'm glad I learned that rule and now it's yours for free.

It became immediately apparent that I had been transferring oil from the dirty oil tank into the engine. The engine, of course, was already full of dirty oil. I don't know where all of the used oil I pumped in went, and if you are kind you won't tell me.

The bilge and the carpeting were now not as clean as they'd been before I started servicing engines. I began to understand how my eight-year-old son felt when he broke the tip off my beautiful Japanese backsaw and then Scotch-taped it back on. I used several quarts of Gunk and two rolls of paper towels before I could even see the hull under the engine. All the beautiful pipes, valves and conduits that had represented the Germanic ideal of orderliness in the engine room seemed to degenerate into the Romanesque ideal of spaghetti beneath the engine room sole, and all were drenched with oil. I kept looking over my shoulder as I cleaned, even though I knew full well that the owners were happily abusing the natives in some faraway Southeast Asian sweatshop.

I did get it reasonably clean after an hour or so of wiping, but I suffered a minor setback after it was clean because I still had to undo the oil filter. Everyone knows that an oil filter should be hand-tightened, plus a quarter of a turn. This one required me to drive a three-foot-long wrecking bar through it before it would turn. "Naturally, there was some loss of oil," as Exxon is reputed to have said under similar circumstances.

Now it was time to pump in the clean oil. I checked everything I could think of. The fresh oil hose was connected to the intake of the pump. The output side of the pump was secured to the hose that led to the "add oil" receptacle on the side of the engine. I was doubly careful now, as I had learned the perils of overconfidence. I circumspectly flashed up the compressor. All seemed fine. I swung open the air valve that shifted the compressed air to the pump.

The boat builders who had put this engine room together had been very concerned with safety. Therefore, instead of having exposed belts and pulleys, everything that could possibly cause an injury was hidden behind extensive screens of expanded aluminum. Near the place where the new oil was entering the engine, there was a complicated confluence of this expanded metal protecting me from God knows what imaginary danger.

I'm having some difficulty finding a metaphor to describe adequately the action of highly pressurized oil as it was driven through several layers of this expanded aluminum (the vision of a fireboat celebrating the arrival of the Queen comes to mind). As the pressurized oil reached the end of the hose that was stuck in the engine, it simply blasted the hose backward out of its hole. In the few seconds it took me to react and shut off the pneumatic pump, untold gallons of forty-weight diesel oil were driven through the expanded metal and all over the engine room and deckhead. The deckhead was made up of several thicknesses of leaded foam for noise suppression, and that in turn was held up by aluminum sheet perforated with two or three billion tiny holes. So, while it was possible to wipe off the deckhead, the saturated lead foam would release the oil only over time, and then it would find its way through some of the billions of tiny holes, and from there continue its journey onto the engine, the engine room sole and, finally, the bilge. I'm not sure, even if I tried, that I could come up with a better way to distribute oil over time and space. And to think that all this time I could have been struggling away cranking that little rotary pump that comes with the engine.

I had three days before the owners returned…three days to Scotch-tape the tip back onto the saw.

When the owners finally did return, things were clean. The oil had been changed. The engine room log was up to date. I did a walk-through with them and I was the only one who could see the occasional drop forming overhead. One of them even said, "Things look great."

"Routine maintenance," I mumbled into my beard. "Just routine maintenance."

I worked on *Exodus* for more than a year and, by and large, it was a good job. I met many interesting people and ended up taking the boat some fairly long distances. Brad and Lisa, the owners, had planned to take the boat south to Panama and then to the Galapagos, Hawaii, then back to North America. That plan was cancelled when I pointed out to Brad that it was the same distance from

Panama to Hawaii as it is from San Francisco to Japan. This is a little-appreciated fact that I like to trot out from time to time. Panama, of course, is on the same longitude as Florida.

We did some long passages from Vancouver to the Sea of Cortez, wintered there, then headed back to southeastern Alaska and then back to Vancouver. After I left the boat, I was still included on deliveries to Costa Rica and, finally, for the new owner, from the New River in Florida to San Diego, where I quit once and for all.

....

This next story concerns our first trip. The owners lived aboard, as did I. This is not a situation I would recommend, but to be fair we did get along well until close to the end (when I had given my notice and a new skipper was being trained). On this first trip, we were still feeling each other out and, due to the fact that it involved a voyage down the west coast in the late fall, I was being quite cautious.

Now, *Exodus* was a boat that was "built to break ice," as the expression goes. We encountered all kinds of bad weather and never had any doubts about the boat during the entire time I was in charge. That didn't mean I would purposely be caught out in bad weather if I could avoid it. I'd seen 700-foot-long bulk carriers arrive in Vancouver from a trip up the west coast with their clamshell buckets ripped loose, life rails twisted, and other insufficiently secured equipment seriously damaged or missing.

On this occasion, we'd spent a month up the Columbia River in Portland, Oregon, where the owners had friends. It was a great experience for me, as I had never crossed the Columbia River bar before. Nor had I transited the river up to Portland or the locks above Portland.

We hung out in a marina in Portland while the owners carried on their always-hectic social life. Eventually, I began to feel the press of time; it was now getting into November, and we still had some of the worst areas of the trip south to cover. They finally announced that I should start watching for a weather window, as they were almost ready to depart. Sure enough, in a few days, a beautiful, large, high-pressure system began to develop to the west, and I urged them to wind things up and get going.

Alas, I was learning an important lesson about owners. We left when it suited *them*, not when it suited me. They had an important dinner the next week, and the weather would have to wait. The subsequent shit-kicking we took off Mendocino may have been an important lesson for them, but I doubt it. But that is not the story I want to tell here.

Eventually, the social conditions presented a clear horizon and we were allowed to leave Portland. We got up in the dark only to find that there was virtually zero visibility — "thick like snot," as they say. I was not terribly put off, as I was well experienced with fog and *Exodus* was a beautifully equipped vessel, with several radars, plotters, ARPA, etc. We did have a few interesting moments getting out of the marina and into the main river, but by then I was feeling good about the situation. Vessel Traffic Services was on one VHF and channel 16 on another. A large Furuno GPS-driven plotter supported the radar and could be superimposed if desired. So, although we couldn't see the bow of the boat, we were safe enough and I enjoyed the challenge of transiting the river under these conditions. Brad was also at my elbow, and had the great ability of knowing when to shut up and when to bring something to my attention. We made a good team.

The morning got light, but with no improvement at all in visibility. We hugged the north (Washington) shore, as we were required to do by the ColRegs, and had a good idea of approaching big-ship traffic because they were required to frequently report their position, speed, etc., to Vessel Traffic Services. We were not participating in the traffic system (although technically we probably should have been), but had spoken with Traffic and they knew we were there. This let us know well in advance about approaching ships even if we couldn't see them on the radar because of geography.

We passed several upbound vessels without incident. Obviously, they all had pilots on board, and we didn't hesitate to call them up on the traffic channel if we felt the need to communicate. After a while, we became aware of a large upbound ship approaching, but hidden from our radar around one of the tighter turns in the river. The ship would be altering to starboard as it made the turn and followed the course of the river. We would be hugging our starboard-hand side of the channel and altering to follow the curve of the river, for a port-to-port — or, as they say, a "red to red" — passing.

Everything seemed to be as it should be, but I called up the pilot well before either of us was close to the bend, just to establish communication and be sure he knew we were there. He responded that all was fine; he'd be watching for us and added that we should be sure to hug that starboard shore. With the plotter, we could slide exactly down the shore even though we couldn't see it, just allowing ourselves enough water to float safely and not hit any buoys.

As we approached the bend, we could finally see the ship on our radar as it swept through its turn. What I didn't understand (and I think the pilot misjudged) was that the radius of his turn was much greater than the radius of the river bend. So, as we watched on radar, this giant blob of a target swung well over onto our side of the river and kept coming.

Then on the VHF, the pilot's voice could be heard.

How to describe The Voice? I remember it best from my days at private school, when The Voice generally preceded, by seconds, a very severe thrashing. You would recognize The Voice if you've ever been arrested by a cop with a gun in his hand who isn't going to chat much longer. It's the one that doesn't want any discussion, just obedience, and it wants it *now*. It's not necessarily loud, but it brooks no disobedience or hesitation. *That* Voice.

And this voice said, "*EXODUS*, TURN NINETY DEGREES TO STARBOARD. NOW!!"

And I did. And *Exodus* slid gently into the mud of the Washington State shore. Fortunately, I had pulled back on both sticks, as the plotter indicated I would be aground, so there was virtually no impact. Reflexively, I put her in reverse. Before I could touch the throttles, I heard Brad say quietly, "Peter, look at this."

I turned around — now remember that the visibility can be measured in feet, not yards — and there was Brad staring out the back wheelhouse windows at a wall of steel sliding by our stern. We couldn't see either end, and we couldn't see the top — just an endless wall of steel seemingly inches off our stern, every weld clearly discernible. I put the clutches back in neutral and in a moment he was past us. Then I kicked her astern and we slid back into the channel and deeper water.

There was no talking on the bridge. I don't know about Brad, but for me it had happened so fast that there was no terror, only reflex. Moments later, the same voice (but turned down several notches) came on the VHF, "*Exodus*, is everything all right?"

"Everything is fine," I replied.

"Did you hit the putty?"

"We did, but no harm, no foul."

"*Exodus*, good work, That was a difficult situation. Have a good voyage. I'm out, standing by."

168

CHAPTER 24

INCOMPETENTS I HAVE KNOWN

All hat, no cattle. — Old Texan cowboy saying

Exodus had a number of owners with less of a financial interest in the boat than Brad and Lisa. One of them, Ron, had bought another smaller boat for himself and spent a summer fishing in Alaska. He normally kept the boat in San Francisco and had an American skipper to help him move it around locally. He called me up and asked me to help his regular guy bring the boat from Sitka to Seattle, and later to San Francisco.

I can't count the number of times I'd made that trip with Bluewater Adventures, as a commercial fisherman (you can see Alaska from where I fished), and with *Exodus*. I was glad to help and, without really thinking about it, asked if I was going as skipper or crew. The owner said he definitely wanted me as skipper, so that was settled.

Unfortunately, he had also told his regular guy that he was skipper. So, when we finally met on the boat in Sitka and the owner was safely in San Francisco, we had a small problem. Personally, I didn't care one way or another, but since I'd been told I was skipper, I couldn't renege on the responsibility without the agreement of the owner. The "other skipper" announced that if he wasn't the skipper, he wasn't going. At the same time, he produced an embossed business card, with colours and flags, announcing that he was a "UNITED STATES COAST GUARD CAPTAIN." I should have figured it out at that point.

There was nothing to do but phone the owner. Very pleasantly, the owner asked me if I would mind going as crew; the pay would be the same. "Of course not," I answered. All the money and none of the responsibility, I thought. Little did I know.

In the few days before we departed, I began to get a bit nervous about our leader. He had been responsible for organizing the boat, so I was really surprised that a professional skipper would store all of the bosun's supplies — pails of oil, paint, thinners, and other solvents — on top of a couple of fiddled tables that were inches above the two main engines (I know, I know…but it's a yacht). Even when I pointed out that he had effectively turned a normal fire hazard into a bomb, he didn't get it.

Privately, I sent an email to the owner saying that, if I was not the skipper, I was not the skipper, i.e., I wouldn't be held responsible for this moron's mistakes. I would do all I could to make the trip safe, but…

I'll never be able to recount all of the idiocies this fellow perpetrated, but here are a few.

....

The Inside Passage, for the most part, is pretty well sheltered. However, since we were towing the owner's $55,000 fishing skiff, we had to be careful. The first time we entered one of the long channels south, there was a fair bit of slop. I was off watch and having a nap; I awoke with the motion. Looking out over the afterdeck, I could see the skiff disappearing completely under the breaking waves. I raced to the bridge and said, "Christ, man, you'd better knock it back."

He looked at me curiously and asked, "Why?"

I pointed back at the skiff, which was porpoising enthusiastically over and under alternate waves. He shrugged, "We're towing the skiff to San Francisco, so it'll be fine in these waters."

"You may be towing it to San Francisco, but it'll be behind a car, you moron, not a boat!" Finally he relented, and we dropped back to eight knots or so.

That night we anchored in a very tight little bay. We had swinging room, but nothing more. Of course, we pulled the skiff alongside and secured it with fenders. By now, we had worked out a routine such that, when starting in the morning, I would go aft, and, as he gathered speed, I would surge the line until the painter to the skiff was fully extended. Then I would go up to the bridge.

The next morning when we got up, the fog was very thick. You couldn't see either side of the small bay in which we were anchored. He fired up the main engines and all of the electronics. I started to head aft, and then hesitated. "Let's keep the skiff alongside until we're out of the bay," I suggested. He agreed, but I wasn't actually thinking of the skiff.

On the compass shelf of this boat there were two large screens. One was a very fine 72-mile Furuno radar, and the other was an equally good plotter. All things being equal (like the range), the plotter display and the radar display will have some things in common. The shoreline, for instance, should be very similar on both machines. However, we were anchored.

I went forward, got the anchor up, and secured it. Then, as quickly as I could, I got back to the bridge so I could watch where this guy's eyes were directed. He was totally absorbed in the plotter screen. Unfortunately, if the boat is not moving, the plotter is displaying nonsense, as the indication of the aspect of your own vessel (the heading, the direction you're pointing) is dependent on motion. The GPS cannot give the vessel's heading until there is motion. I could see from the radar display that we were headed directly toward the beach, and it was already extremely close.

He reached for the sticks and — well, it's always difficult when egos are involved, and so easy when all of the crew are pulling together — it was clear this was truly amateur hour. He went ahead on both engines and I physically hauled the controls back into neutral. "Look at the radar. You're putting us right on the beach. Cross your sticks and watch the radar."

He was pissed, but on some level he understood that he would have been fucked if I'd gone aft to let go the skiff. Things were now a bit awkward on the bridge. In order to reassert his authority, he asked me to go check the fluid levels...*in the batteries*. I couldn't make this stuff up. He'd been charting the fluid levels in the batteries for as long as we'd been on the boat. Nothing else — not oil consumption, not clutch fluid, not coolant — and he had a whole notebook filled with figures. To my shame, I told him to kiss my ass.

The next morning, we were anchored in a much larger bay and I anticipated no trouble. As we prepared to get underway, I went aft and began slacking off the skiff. There was no communication between the two of us while this was happening. There was a green buoy in the middle of the bay, and, obviously, we would be leaving it to starboard as we left. However, as we surged forward (a bit heavy on the throttles, that boy), I realized he was passing on the wrong side of the buoy. Now, I didn't know what was on the wrong side of that buoy, but usually they are there for a reason. I had the skiff halfway out and it was all I could do to surge the line. I couldn't get more turns on to secure it, and I couldn't get up to the bridge to sort out the idiot.

About this time, the depth alarm started screaming, so he went hard to port to get on the correct side of the buoy. That was fine, except that the skiff was now on a slack line heading off on our former course toward the wrong side of the buoy. I was gathering in line like a motherfucker, hoping I could throw a turn on the cleat before it came tight and not have my fingers torn off, while still preventing the skiff from either smashing into the buoy or going on the wrong side. It was luck more than skill that got the job done. I wandered up to the bridge and asked if everything was fine. With a kind of sheepish laugh, he said, "Wow, I nearly went on the wrong side of that buoy." I replied, "Is that right?"

....

There's one more story I can't resist telling. We had spent a night in Nanaimo Harbour, and planned to get an early start so I could get off the boat in White Rock (just north of the border) so that he would have to single-hand for only about four hundred yards before picking up a pal in Blaine. By now, you're probably thinking I'm a total asshole for raging on about this guy's incompetence, but remember: he was the guy who wouldn't sail unless he was "The Captain." He was the guy with the embossed business card telling the world that he was a U.S. Coast Guard-certified captain. If I haven't said it before, I'll say it now: when you go to sea, you'd better be humble, for you very soon will be (I'm not sure of the origin of this sentiment, but it should be carved in granite at every maritime academy).

We got an early start, well before light. In a few moments, we eased to port around the light at the south end of Protection Island and headed for the Georgia Strait. By now, of course, I was watching this moron's every move. Sure enough, we hadn't gone half a mile past the marker, and dead ahead there was a red and green light separated by two white lights, one over the other. Dead ahead. For those not nautically inclined, this means you will be involved in a head-on collision very soon. My nautical friends know that there is only one action in this situation: you alter to starboard. There's nothing to talk about. Given the absence of other factors, you alter to starboard. We're not talking about how many angels can dance on the head of a pin; we're not talking about whether there can be two mountains without an intervening valley; you just alter to starboard. End of discussion.

At this point, I'm watching this sad sack of shit and he's doing nothing. I watch until I'm getting scared. Still he does nothing. Finally I offer, "Can you see those lights?"

He responds, "Oh yeah, that's the Tsawwassen ferry. They'll be altering to port in just a moment and going into Duke Point."

"Actually," I say, in my calmest 'we're about to die' voice, "that's the Gabriola ferry and it's going into Nanaimo Harbour directly behind us…and it might be a good idea to alter."

There was a moment of complete silence, even though we didn't have time for moments. He hesitated and then threw the wheel to port. A brief wrestling match ensued as I tried to explain Rules of the Road 101 while figuring out the best exit from the wheelhouse and which way to swim.

We made it, obviously, or you wouldn't be reading about it here, but that's how the whole trip went. I was supposed to take the boat to San Francisco, but I bailed. To his credit, he did get there.

....

I'd witnessed another example of this level of incompetence before, when I was running the Windjammer vessel (see Chapter 25). Obviously, on a ship of that size, I didn't hire the crew. When we needed an officer, the office provided one. In the instance I'm remembering, the office provided a third mate with Venezuelan papers.

We'd previously had two officers from the Venezuelan Maritime Academy, and they'd been excellent — very well-trained third mates — so we were pleased to welcome this new guy aboard.

However, I got a strange vibe from this guy. I didn't let him stand any watches by himself. He managed all right, but always worked with another officer. He was a bit of a party animal, but that's to be expected when you're young and at sea. Then someone told me that, based on his work on *Legacy*, he'd applied for a second mate's position with another gypo cruise line. I was suspicious, and thought I should bring things to a head. We were heading into Roadtown, Tortola, on a sunny day with not much traffic. A small motor launch was crossing our bow from our starboard to port on a steady bearing — a clear, simple crossing situation. Most, if not all, of the deck officers were on the bridge as we approached the town. I turned to our Venezuelan friend and said, "Who has the right of way?"

The seconds ticked past. The silence on the bridge was deafening. Everyone knew what I was doing. Finally, the third mate replied, "We do, Captain."

"Why is that?" I asked.

"Because we're bigger."

I turned to the quartermaster, a young black kid from Guyana (with a fourth-grade education, if he was lucky), and asked, "Slim, who has the right of way?"

"He do, Cap."

"Why is that?"

"He be on our starboard side, Cap."

The Venezuelan disappeared in Roadtown, never to be seen again. What I found strange is that, having bullshitted his way into a job (like I did), he wouldn't make an effort to learn the most basic shit so that he could get away with the con.

....

One last example of this kind of thing. We had been in Puerto Vallarta for a few months having some work done on *Exodus*. When it was nearly time for us to depart for northern climes, the owner asked if any of the Mexicans we had gotten to know would help us take the boat through the "Baja Bash" (it's normally tough slogging from the tip of Baja to San Diego).

I had made friends with one young guy I particularly liked, and he said he would love to make the trip. Not only that, he said he had a 100-ton licence. This was great news, so I told him we would have a crew meeting the next day and to bring his licence.

I sat everyone down and said, "I'm not trying to embarrass anyone, but I need to know each person's level of competence and I want to speak to each of you alone." Then I took them, one at a time, into a separate cabin. I had previously cut out little paper boats. I ran everyone through basic crossing situations and, naturally, my special friend knew nothing. I asked him where his licence was and, of course, it was at his mother's house.

"Look," I said, "I know you're bullshitting. You don't know the most basic rules of the road and suddenly your licence is not available. None of this matters unless I don't know that you don't know." He was too embarrassed to sail with us. The fact is, when I'm responsible for the hiring, nobody ever sails with me without first seeing my little paper boats. You'd be surprised what I am able to learn.

CHAPTER 25

....

BACK TO THE CARIBBEAN

I want to make a few notes about my time running one of the ships of the Bare-foot Adventure Windjammer fleet in the Caribbean.

The job came up after I had lost my job running a boat for Bluewater Adventures in Canada (a poorly paid but wonderful position that I fell into after ten years of commercial fishing on the west side of the Queen Charlotte Islands). When the fishing ended (collectively we killed them all, I think, although I am arguably more innocent than most, me being the worst fisherman ever born; but I tried, I tried), I cast about for work.

For background, let me explain briefly how I came to leave Bluewater.

I had more great times working for Bluewater than I could write about, but they ended up firing me. Now, I'd been fired from a variety of jobs and I never usually worried too much about it; the reality is that a lot of what happens on the water has little to do with competence and lots to do with economics and personalities. However, this one hurt.

I had been living on Cortes Island at the time, in my beautiful waterfront home with the eighty-foot dock (mentioned in Chapter 21), where I kept *Carlotta* and my fishing boat *Two Sisters*. It was truly an idyllic situation, except, of course, that commercial fishing kept me away from home every summer. Then

Bluewater came along, allowing me time off during part of every month to enjoy my home and property.

One fall, after I'd been with Bluewater for a number of years, I was required to go to Vancouver to take a course to keep my ticket current. While I was gone for the required nine days, my girlfriend of almost a decade, and the mother of my son, met and married another man. (By this time, you'll have figured out that my marriage to Dany had ended and life had moved on.)

This upset me greatly, and probably quite a bit more than it should have; I became rather depressed for a time. I won't write more about this except to say that one of life's lessons (which it took me quite some time to learn) is that we can only be responsible for our own behaviour.

At any rate, this depression of mine led to an inability to deal properly with the Bluewater passengers, and at a certain point the company was forced to let me go. At the time of this writing, many years later, we're all more or less friends again.

There I was again, in what appeared to be a recurring theme, faced with finding a way to earn a living. That's how I came to work for Windjammer.

....

This was now some time after the end of the relationship with my son's mother, and by then I was living with my wonderful friend Linda. In the course of her work as a biologist, she had met someone who'd worked for the Windjammer company in the Caribbean (Windjammer, coincidentally, was the same company that had carried the drunk who jolted me back to reality after my cosmic moment returning to Gustavia after the lightning storm) and, although I'd loathed the company when I lived in St. Barths in the '70s…well, circumstances change. So I sent them a résumé, promptly forgot about it, and started looking for work locally.

To my surprise, about six weeks later I got a phone call asking me if I could come to Miami for an interview.

Do wild bears poop in the woods? Within a day or two, I found myself on my way to Florida. I spent the night in the airport hotel, and the next day the head of personnel picked me up to take me to the company's headquarters.

Now, at no time had anyone told me what sort of job I was interviewing for. I naturally assumed it would be a mate's position, as that was all I was qualified for with my 350-ton ticket. I had borrowed a blazer from my stepfather and I thought I looked pretty respectable for a fifty-year-old hippy. The various interviews proceeded, with the only odd thing being that when the owner of the company reviewed my qualifications (the various certificates I held were contained in a Department of Transport booklet), the personnel director pointed out that I had an unlimited tonnage ticket and then quickly turned the page before the owner could examine the certificate more closely. As it happens, I do have an unlimited tonnage ticket, but it's for towing. For carrying passengers, I have a 350-ton ticket (lately bumped up to 500 tons).

I thought no more about it. The owner welcomed me "on board" and the personnel guy drove me back to the airport. Over the course of that drive, I learned that I'd just been hired to skipper the *Legacy*, the flagship of the Windjammer fleet — 300 feet long and 2,000 tons. Since the largest vessel I had ever run was a 72-foot North Sea trawler, this could be described as the maritime equivalent of someone with a private pilot's licence bullshitting himself into the cockpit of a 747 — except that I hadn't done any bullshitting.

I got back to Victoria and consulted various people whose opinions I valued. Subsequently, I sent an email back to the personnel department at Windjammer, explaining that there had been a misunderstanding: I held only a 350-ton licence and was, obviously, unqualified to run a 300-foot 2,000-ton ship. Ten minutes later I got a reply: "There has been no misunderstanding. You are the exact person we are looking for and, by the way, do not bring up this subject again."

While agonizing about whether I should push it or not about my (lack of) qualifications, one of my friends, Bill Noon (a skipper with the Canadian Coast Guard), explained to me about flags (and licences) of convenience.

Years earlier, in Panama with my pal Wolfe (the one who'd towed *Carlotta* through the canal), we had gotten it into our heads that we could go to the Panama Department of Shipping and, by giving a major backhander to someone, procure a commercial licence. When we tried this, the gentleman we were hoping to bribe was not interested, but he did inform us that if we registered a ship in Panama they would issue an appropriate Master Certificate. And this is what the Windjammer people were doing. The fact that I'd never operated a ship of this size didn't seem to interest anyone. To this day, I hold a 2,000-ton Master Certificate issued by none other than Equatorial Guinea.

Two weeks' training with a temporary skipper and I was on my own. You can imagine that I had many adventures doing this job.

Here's one.

On the second day after I had taken command, I was taking the ship from Road Town, Tortola to Gorda Sound in Virgin Gorda. This is not normally thought of as a terribly difficult place to enter (if you are in a 38-foot Moorings charter boat), but what I haven't said is that the *Legacy* was a pig to maneuver. It was a French meteorology ship that had been converted to look like a tall ship, so each of the four masts was 160 feet in height. It was twin screw, but the screws were too close together to get any joy from "crossing the sticks" (going ahead on one engine and astern on the other). They had added a much deeper keel with no fairing, with the result that she wouldn't answer her helm very well, and it was diesel electric. There were twenty-two seconds between forward and reverse — the longest twenty-two seconds of my life.

So there I was, heading toward the pass in the reef into Gorda Sound. It became clear from the GPS that a very strong current was setting us quickly to the south. I compensated and headed north of the entrance and then, at the appropriate time, put the helm down to make the entrance. Nothing happened; we continued to charge directly toward the reef. I had the sticks crossed, the helm at 30 degrees to starboard, and this stupid behemoth just plowed straight on ahead. Should I try an emergency reverse? I didn't have twenty-two seconds. You could have heard a pin drop on the bridge as the other officers prepared to watch the new guy put the ship on the reef after being in command for one bloody day. The reef got closer and closer. The water got more and more transparent. My fundament was emitting serious squeaking noises. Finally, she did pay off and we actually slid rather nicely into the anchorage. Ah, providence lending a hand again. I think I still have the pucker marks on my asshole.

I ran *Legacy* for a year. It was a big year in my life, because I had never wanted to run a ship and this felt very much like a ship to me. It's almost carved in granite that shipowners, who are invariably filthy rich, are the cheapest people on earth. The reason I was running the *Legacy*, totally unqualified to do so, was because Canadians will work for lower pay than Americans. It was an amusing coincidence that the owner of Bluewater (who fired me) and the owner of the Windjammer fleet (who also eventually fired me) were both named Burke. On *Legacy*, there was an expression among the crew that you should never, ever "get between a Burke and a buck." From my viewpoint, it fit nicely for both owners.

One of the ways in which my performance at Windjammer was evaluated was based on the amount of tips the crew received. The officers did not share the tips, but management made the assumption that, if the tips were good, the customers were happy. The tip total was always reported to management, and by the time I was skipper there was a year or two of tip history to make a baseline. The tips were collected in a large, locked box that was kept on the bar.

Almost immediately when I took over as skipper, the tip amounts started to decline. We would have a beautiful trip with great weather and great activities, and the tips would be down. Management would ream my ass because the customers were clearly not happy, and I would try valiantly to defend the crew and myself. However, the fact was that the tips — *the* measure of customer satisfaction — were down, and there was no denying it. This continued for the entire time I was with the company.

It was cold comfort to learn, a year or two later, that two or three of the junior bartenders had stolen a key to the jar and had been stealing a large percentage of the tips the entire time, robbing their shipmates and making me look like a jerk. The skipper after my tenure had to sneak the thieves off the ship in the dead of night, as they would have been murdered — *slowly* — by the crew, very poor people who were paid $500 per month on average (normally the tips would add another $500). The owners, on the other hand, had built castles in Miami with moats and live sharks to satisfy their weird egos. It's a wonderful world.

Legacy was the only ship in the Windjammer fleet that was able to enter the U.S. She was "in class" with the various maritime surveying societies, and this, of course, included the crew. The first time I took the ship into Puerto Rico, the USCG carried out a "safe manning" inspection. At this time, I had not yet received my (bullshit) 2,000-ton certificate from Equatorial Guinea, as they required physical exams and other things that took time. As a result, the Coast Guard officers inspected the certificates of all the officers and engineers, and then the Coast Guard skipper came up to the bridge to see me. He said everything was satisfactory except that he needed to see my certificate.

Well, I was totally fucked, because the fact was that I didn't have a certificate. I told him my certificate was in Miami, as Equatorial Guinea had to see it before they would issue a flag state certificate — total crap, but I was thinking on my feet. Now, I'm not a great fan of the USCG, but this officer couldn't have been more pleasant. My insubstantial 350-ton certificate was in my cabin, about ten feet from where we were speaking. The officer told me we had a serious problem, because he couldn't let us sail until he had seen my certificate and, incidentally, he had never seen a master who would let his certificate out of his possession. On the other hand, I had just loaded 125 passengers who were expecting to depart on the vacation of a lifetime, and the owner of the company was unaware that I was not qualified to run the ship. We were deadlocked.

After a while, the Coast Guard skipper said, "Look, I know the company would never hire anyone who wasn't qualified to run the ship, so contact Miami. Have them assure me that they have your certificate and I'll let you sail." Ten minutes later I was emailing the personnel guy who'd started all this, and he happily lied through his teeth to get us released.

....

I had been with the ship for five or six months when we got a pretty strange job. Normally, people booked their vacations and then showed up at the appropriate port of embarkation. This time, however, the whole ship had been chartered by one party: a sex magazine whose specialty was outsized breasts. It wasn't a magazine you could buy at a newsstand — only through subscription — and it was all about breasts. Giant breasts. Humongous breasts. And these women had not had *one* breast enhancement surgery — no, they'd had two, three or more. Whatever it took, in fact (I know this is hard to believe, but it's what they told me), to get their breasts to the requisite size. They lost me way before operation #1, though, as I have always been rather a fan of tidy, firm little breasts. Different ships, different long splices.

Anyhow, I had no idea what to expect when we got ready to load these people. It was explained to me that the way the system worked was that the passengers, i.e., the turkeys who subscribed to the magazine, were offered a chance to take a cruise with the "models" who had appeared in the magazine during the previous year. The so-called models came on the cruise for pay, and whatever arrangements they made with the passengers were their own business. My instructions were to fire any crew member who engaged in sexual congress with the models.

Well, *that* was not going to happen.

First of all, by now most of the crew were my friends. Second, my male crew members were good-looking, young, black jungle-fresh[1] studs. Who would you rather screw if you were one of the models: weird, skinny little guys with pot bellies and a breast fetish who had to take a sex tour to get their rocks off, or a young, virile member of my crew?

The whole thing got about as crazy as you can imagine. I'm sure everyone was screwing themselves blind at night, but my job was to make the ship work and keep people happy. The head model would come to me and say, "Okay, tomorrow we're doing a lesbian sex scene on the beach. We need good sand, no surf, and boats ashore at 0900." I'd sit down with my officers and we'd decide on a good beach and suitable anchorage, with not too many people.

At 0800, a couple of my crew would go ashore and stroll the beach. If they came upon Linda and Larry Lunchbucket playing on the beach with their two toddlers, they were instructed to say, "We're terribly sorry, but in an hour there will be some models and photographers coming ashore to film a truly offensive sex scene in the water just across from where you are sitting. You're welcome to watch, but if this offends you, perhaps you could move along the beach for an hour or so."

After the tour was over, I caught ten tons of shit from the head office for all the people we offended. I replied that I had consulted three other skippers in the fleet to find the most remote beaches, warned everybody on the beach that what we were doing was pretty revolting, and generally mitigated the damage in any way I could. I told them that if management chose to send me out again on such an inherently offensive job, they shouldn't be surprised if some people got offended. I never heard another word after that.

Now, "I'm liberal, but to a degree, I want everybody to be free,"[2] but I would arrive on the bridge in the morning to get the ship underway and there would be a naked, weirdly out-of-proportion female spread-eagled on the compass shelf with six men taking close-ups of her vagina with their Instamatic cameras.

There was one passenger who didn't seem to fall into the wimp category the others fit so well. He was a large, fit, black guy, good-looking and well-spoken — the kind you knew would have no trouble getting lucky on his own. After we had all been together for a week, my curiosity got the better of me and I took him aside after he'd had a few drinks. "Look," I said, "I don't mean to be rude, but it

---

[1] The Politically Correct Police have been after me for using the term "jungle fresh." Let me explain how it came about. Every week or two on *Legacy*, it was necessary to go to a small local bank on one of the islands and get $55,000 in cash. Then I had to transport the cash to the ship by taxi and put it in my office safe. I was never comfortable doing this, as it was a tremendous sum of money and would have been a big temptation for any of the local "lads." I had a young deckhand whom I liked a lot, and he happened to have the musculature of a devoted bodybuilder. I asked him if he would accompany me on these excursions, thinking his bulk might deter all but the most serious of thieves. He agreed, as it would get him away from the ship for a few hours. One day, he and his mates were chipping rust on the foredeck in the tropical summer sun, and I asked him to clean himself up and get ready to accompany me. There was a certain amount of grumbling by his mates (basically, "Why does he always get to go?"). He turned to them with his great white smile, flexed his massive biceps in a typical bodybuilder's pose, and replied, in his Trinidadian lilt, "Cause I be beautiful and jungle-fresh too."

[2] Bob Dylan, "I Shall Be Free No. 10."

seems a bit odd to me that an educated, good-looking guy like you would have to pay to get into a situation like this with a bunch of obvious losers."

He laughed and explained, "I'm an aircraft mechanic in Saudi Arabia. I get back to the States one month out of six. I make a ton of money, and I don't have the time or the inclination to sit in some bar somewhere trying to make a friend when I'll be leaving in three weeks. Here, you pays your money and you sees the show." Seemed reasonable to me. As a way to raise money for crew tips, they auctioned off the models' bras on the last night of the cruise. He paid $2,500 for a bra that would have made a medium-sized spinnaker for the boat I'm sitting on as I write this.

I really got to know — although, unfortunately, not in the biblical sense — only one of the models. I can't remember her name, but she's the one kneeling in the photo of this trip. Similarly, she was an educated, well-spoken woman who would have succeeded in any field of endeavour, so when we got to talking I had to ask her how she'd gotten herself into this line of work (I had stopped asking hookers this question by the time I was seventeen, but this was different). She explained that she was on the "A" exotic dancing circuit in Miami. After tips, she would bring home between $1,500 and $2,000 per night. Pretty good explanation. She told me that when she'd first entered the trade, her parents had stopped talking to her. In a year, after she paid cash for her first house, they started talking to her again.

She pointed to one of the other outrageously over-endowed women and explained that the woman was actually a married chartered accountant. She and her husband had gotten themselves into some financial difficulty and, like any intelligent people in such circumstances, had examined their assets. They'd found their most promising ones resting just under her chin. She wasn't screwing the riffraff, as it turned out, just getting paid for showing her tits. It takes all kinds of people to fill a freeway.

After a year with Windjammer, they let me go. They had another skipper they preferred to have running *Legacy* — a highly competent guy with whom I'd worked. Also, I had "gotten into it" on many occasions with the owner's sister, who was a shipwreck of a human being but who controlled an important aspect of the company. (If she ever reads this, I think I forgot to tell her to go fuck her hat.) They gave me a golden handshake and sent me on my way.

....

The firing itself was rather humorous. I had just taken the ship to Trinidad, where the company had a substantial (and substandard) boatyard. It was my job to get the crew out of their roles on a working cruise ship and into their roles supporting the ship in its refit. The owner of the company would be on hand. For me, it was important the crew appeared happy and ready to work, so it was not without angst that I was forced to deal with an employee issue right at that delicate time.

He was a very bright kid from Guyana — a "sea lawyer" — and I was quite fond of him. In fact, he was far too smart to be doing whatever menial job he was doing on *Legacy*, but that's the way the cards are dealt; he was happy to be eating and making enough money to send something home to his family in Guyana. In any case, he got it into his head that the crew couldn't be required to work in the shipyard because they had agreed to be seamen and not shipyard workers. Blah, blah, blah.

I took him aside once or twice and explained that he was not improving his chances of promotion or anything else with this kind of talk. He was upsetting the crew and making me look bad as a leader. Sadly, he didn't stop. Finally, on the night before we arrived in Trinidad, I called him into my office and fired him. Much to my surprise, he was very upset by this and argued strongly against the firing. I had given him ample warning, however, and I said to him, "I warned you what was going to happen and now it's happening. You're far too smart for the job you're doing and it's time for you to move along. I'm sorry."

He was pissed off, but there was nothing he could do, and by now all the crew knew that I bent over backward to help anyone who did their work and helped me.

After our arrival in Trinidad, when the ship was secure, we had a bit of a send-off party for a couple of officers who were leaving the ship. It may have gotten a bit sillier than it should have, and the next morning it was a real struggle to get my booze-ridden carcass out of the fart sack. I was not overjoyed to find the CEO of the company pacing outside my cabin waiting for me, ready to perform a big song and dance about what a good employee I had been, yada, yada. It took me a minute or two to realize that "had been" was the operative phrase. As in past tense. As in fired.

As with many companies, when you were fired by Windjammer you were history right then and there. They'd booked a suite for me at a very nice hotel, and in fifteen minutes I was walking down the gangplank with my sea bag. And guess who was walking down it with me? I looked over at the young sea lawyer I had fired the day before and said, "Hey, if you hear of any work, let me know." He grinned; he probably still thought I was a cunt, but at least he grinned.

Some years later, Windjammer went tits up. They left the ships wherever they were, along with the crew. No repatriation for the people they had been ripping off for years, just lots of umbrella drinks in Miami. I'm proud they fired me.

CHAPTER 26

....

SCARAMOUCHE

In 2006, I sold *Carlotta* to the Mohan family. Selling the boat was long overdue, as I had promised myself during her rebuild that I would never let her get into the state in which I'd found her. But I had — or at least she had run down significantly.

There are many excuses for this (divorce, poverty), but perhaps the major excuse was that I had become a commercial fisherman with another old wooden boat, and no man can serve two mistresses. The Mohans had been after me for years to sell them the boat, and eventually the realization that she was deteriorating quickly forced me to comply. Oddly, I felt very little emotion on parting with the boat that had formed such a part of — indeed, dominated — my life for thirty-five years (longer than I'd had either children or wives). And it truly had been the crucible for whatever self-confidence and self-esteem I may have developed.

I made up my mind that I would not own another boat for at least a few years. Of course, this did not preclude me from looking at boat ads.

So there I was, with a pocketful of money, when this beautiful boat came up for sale just down the road in Olympia, Washington. My girlfriend of the time was fully supportive of a fun road trip "just to have a look at it."

It turned out to be a very pretty boat and, well, what else matters? Her stern was slightly pinched, but her history (winning the TransPac) suggested that she sailed well. However, after careful consideration and given the prevailing exchange rate, I decided it wasn't realistic for me to buy her. But God, was she a nice boat: aluminum, by S&S, out of Palmer Johnson. If you know anything about sailboats, you know this is great DNA.

My girlfriend spoke up to ask if the purchase would be feasible if she took a twenty-five percent ownership share. Now, it is common knowledge that a partnership is a leaky ship, but I foolishly agreed. We pooled our money, had surveys conducted, met brokers and owners, and proceeded. Delivery was to take place on Boxing Day 2006.

(I could digress now to a short lecture on the fickleness of women, but suffice it to say that, on Christmas Eve, my friend announced that I didn't love her — actually, I would have thought I was the best judge of that — and that I was only using her. She wanted me out of her life "toot sweet.")

I was dumbfounded. I stood there with my metaphorical dick in my hand, and said, "This is crazy. Do you understand what a mess you're creating? Let me make it very clear that you own part of a boat. I don't owe you money."

It was too late to salvage the relationship, and now we were joint owners of a boat I couldn't afford to own by myself and never would have bought by myself. I thought about it for some time, and then decided the only reasonable thing to do was to buy her out, which, through some massaging of bank accounts, I managed to do. But then I had to move aboard, as now there was no way I could afford a boat and a separate place to live.

And it was good.

By this time in my life, I had spent many years sailing gaff-rigged boats and I don't think I'm being immodest when I say that I knew my way around the gaff rig reasonably well. I had sailed plenty of Bermudan rigged boats, including spending six months as skipper of *Beowulf* (Steve Dashew's 78-footer), and had done quite a few yacht deliveries and ocean crossings that involved boats with Bermudan rig. Still, I didn't feel I could sail a modern boat well, and I wanted to be able to before I died.

It took a few years to get *Scaramouche* into good condition. She needed some plating, new sails, and every piece of gear gone over from the steering to the anchor winch. The good news was that she had come with a warehouse full of equipment, and the engine had only seventy hours on it. The anchor winch was new in the box. Most important, the family from whom I'd bought the boat were "good people." I did the work and was thoroughly enjoying life aboard *Scaramouche*.

Then another major change occurred in my life: I met and began living with my girlfriend, Christy McLeod. She is everything I am not, the most noticeable of which is that she is happy and unfailingly cheerful. In all that follows, Christy is the great enabler, and her energy is in large part responsible for the successful pursuit of the various idiocies that I've pursued in my recent life.

The previous owners of *Scaramouche* had gone a long way to converting her from a fast racing boat to a comfortable cruising boat. I continued that process, even though I considered it a bit of a rape to take a fast (albeit older) racing boat and load her down with cruising gear. I struggle with the issue to this day, but when it really became evident was in 2010. That was the year in which, after about five years of ownership, I got it into my head to enter the Pacific Cup, a fully crewed race to Hawaii.

Ocean racing must be one of the most expensive sports there is, and at the time I was working for thirty bucks an hour. The first thing I thought I should do in this situation was give up any hope of winning, or even doing well. This takes off a ton of the pressure and turns what can be insanely intense into just fun. (In retrospect, I now believe this attitude is a mistake, for reasons that will become evident.)

I had wanted to enter the Vic–Maui race to Hawaii, but they didn't allow any form of self-steering. This is not a problem when competing seriously — *Scaramouche* had a crew of ten when she won her class in the TransPac in the late '70s — but now we could have only six people on board because that was the capacity of my life raft. Also, frankly, I have crossed the last ocean I ever plan to cross steering by hand. The Pacific Cup *did* permit self-steering, so I sent away for all the necessary information. Before too long, I'd signed up.

The Pacific Cup is a Class One ocean race and, over the years, a set of standards has been adopted to make the racing as safe as possible. Class One is the most stringent — with the exception of Class Zero, which applies to people who race around the world in all oceans. The Pacific Cup is from San Francisco to Oahu and, to be honest, when compared to races like the Fastnet or Sydney–Hobart, is pretty small beer. I don't mean to detract in any way from the very competitive people who drive their small boats hard and are really trying to win. However, let's face it, for a bunch like us, two days out of San Francisco you can lose your mast, your engine and all your sails, and you're still going to end up in

Hawaii; that's just the nature of the wind systems. It's not the case in other major ocean races.

However, because it was Class One, there were a thousand changes I had to make to the boat. Some made a lot of sense, while some just seemed silly to me. Jim Antrim, one of the race authorities, patiently explained to me in numerous emails why my boat must conform, and why all of the changes must be made. I was often upset at what I thought was the idiocy of some of the requirements — including the measuring system, which is simply a handicapping system so that different boats can race fairly against one another (and always defeat me, against whom the rating bodies have conspired forever). So here I was, sailing an old but fantastically strong vessel, and being forced to conform to rules designed to protect modern ultralights from sure death due largely to over-enthusiasm. But, in the end, the rules prevailed.

Since it was clear I couldn't compete seriously, due both to lack of money and lack of experience, I decided to take friends along whose company I enjoyed, regardless of their sailing experience. As it turns out, everybody loves the idea of racing across an ocean until you ask them to do it.

David Wood, an old pal of mine, helped me take the boat to San Francisco, but then had to bail out of the race due to other commitments. Cam Mitchell, who is always my first choice as a shipmate, could and would go. He brought his wife, Jen Dick, who had never sailed but was not intimidated by the thought of being the only female on a boat full of "old geezers." Charlie Cook had sailed with me a few times on *Carlotta*, and was keen enough to take a few beginner sailing lessons. During one of these lessons, he fell overboard for real, and I suppose that was a pretty good lesson for someone setting out across the ocean with no experience. Finally, to take David's place, we were introduced to Jeffrey Gould, an experienced sailor from northern California. Becoming friends with Jeff was one of the highlights of the race.

All of the above preparation took about a year and untold thousands of dollars. The Pacific Cup organization is very well thought out, and when I signed up for the race I began asking dumb questions. They put me in touch with Jim and Mary Quanci, two very successful competitive San Francisco sailors. Jim and Mary answered every silly question I had for a year (and even after the race, for reasons that will become apparent in the next chapter). *Noblesse oblige*, I suppose, although I like to think we have become friends by now.

How long did the race last? About six hours.

It's a tradition of the Pacific Cup that, upon arriving in Kaneohe Bay at the end of the race (regardless of the time of day or night), you are greeted by the Leis and Trays committee with a tray of Mai Tais. Now, given that there are radically different boats in the race — from slow and stately to eighty-footers trying to set an elapsed time record with a crew of fifteen professional sailors — and given that the race is 2,400 miles long, these poor women might have had to serve Mai Tais for weeks as the slow boats dribbled over the finish line. To avoid this very practical problem, the race committee has established a staggered start. Slow boats start first and fast boats last. Winning and losing is determined by elapsed time after the rating (handicap) is applied.

This would be wonderful if the weather was always constant, but it isn't. For instance, we sailed out of San Francisco Bay after a great start (if I do say so myself), passed under the Golden Gate Bridge, and stopped.

The next day, the class to start sailed out of the bay, carried the wind up to us, and we all got going. But now there was no hope of us ever making up the deficit of a whole day so, after all the money, all the work, and all the hassles of getting time off, the race was effectively over for us in six hours. What I didn't know at the time is that this is ocean racing. You spend tens of thousands of dollars preparing and years training, and if you do it often enough and are sufficiently prepared, once in a while the dice will roll your way. (It is a fact that the more often you can bring the aforementioned resources to bear, the more likely the dice will favour you, as "Lady Luck favours those who court her the most persistently.")

I have to say that for about four days I was horribly depressed — but then, nobody ever said learning was always a happy experience. Then, during the race, another big realization surfaced. It was this: up until this point, my whole professional life on the water had been governed by caution. I was paid to be a chickenshit. Put me in charge of your boat and I took it where it was supposed to go, safely and without damage. Unfortunately, that is not how you win ocean races. To do that, you have to let it hang out a bit. And it's knowing how much you can let it hang out that often separates the winners from the also-rans. It also separates the boats that lose their masts (and need to be rescued) from those that don't. During the race, I was ruled by caution — in hindsight, far too much caution — and it must have driven Jeffrey nuts, although he was too kind to say so. As the racers say, "In order to finish first, first you have to finish."

Of course, money also played a role. The boat that won our class had lost its mast in another race two weeks before the start (what the hell, send over another mast; it's only money). If we had lost a mast, that would have been the end of *Scaramouche* for me.

But we all had a ton of fun. I wanted to learn and I was definitely doing that. Mostly I was learning that I didn't know shit about sailing a boat fast…but that's learning too.

One of my ambitions had always been to cross an ocean by myself. I didn't tell anyone (not even Christy), but throughout the race I was constantly watching to see if I could have managed without a crew. My conclusion, when we got to Hawaii, was that the boat was not quite at the state of readiness that would be necessary for a major single-handed passage. The main issue was the Aries steering gear: although it was a back-up system, I knew in my heart that in an emergency I would never be able to coax it back to life.

After the conclusion of the race, and following a week or two of festivities in Kaneohe Bay, it was time to take the boat back to Canada. This is a trip I had made five or six times and, generally speaking, found not too challenging in the summertime. My problem was that I had no crew. Cam, who normally enjoys crossing oceans, had to get back to earning a living. On my budget, it was impossible to hire anyone, so we just hoped we could find someone who would want to do the trip, either because they needed to get to the northwest or because they wanted to experience crossing an ocean.

We did everything we could think of to attract someone, including putting our information on the various websites that advertise for crew, and posting notices at all of the yacht clubs and at the Ala Wai Small Boat Harbor in Honolulu. Nothing worked. We didn't get even a nibble.

By now, the pressure was building to leave, as the yacht club that hosts the finish of the Pac Cup wanted us gone. Still we had no hope.

Finally, a couple of people showed up. Although unlikely sailors, they were at least willing. They were dead broke and, clearly, new-age flakes, but they were enthusiastic. The man said he knew how to sail, and the woman, while not experienced, said she had never been seasick and would happily cook for the entire trip. This was something: I'm a terrible cook, and particularly hate cooking while at sea. Then I had to listen to a twenty-minute rant about how wonderful it would be to do yoga on deck with the sun rising over the sea. Oh Jesus, what was I in for? However, any storm in a port (as the saying doesn't go).

We finished up provisioning, got our ice and water, and were ready. Walking down the dock on the evening before departure, Christy, who was about to board a flight to Vancouver, asked me if I thought my crew would work out. I can clearly remember my reply: "They will be a total fucking disaster." And they were. I could rant on for pages about these two, but they're not worth the ink.

On the other hand…I can't resist describing one or two incidents just to illustrate the trip.

....

For the first day or two, things didn't go too badly. Meals appeared when they should, and the guy made some effort to help on deck and keep a good watch. It was pretty enthusiastic sailing, as it often is crossing the trade winds, but I never sail too close to the wind because it's more important to get north and pick up the westerlies than it is to force your way into the centre of the Pacific high.

Then, on day three, no meals appeared. I didn't say anything, assuming it was a case of seasickness. On day four, no meals appeared. On day five, I realized that meals were in fact appearing, for the two of them, while I was on watch — just not for me. Of course, I spoke up and the woman said she didn't feel well and couldn't cook anymore. I also soon realized that the guy was not getting up for his watches. Or, to be fair, he would get up, but as soon as I was in my bunk he would get back into his too.

Well, I had always wanted to cross an ocean single-handed and now I was, with the added problem of two loathsome slugs occupying the same space. At one point, I noticed that the woman had not been out of her bunk for three or four days. Surely she's got to get up to pee at some point, I thought; if she did, I never saw it. Her pal was now bringing her sandwiches in her bunk. We hadn't spoken in days.

Years ago, I read something about the illegality and inadvisability of single-handed sailing, and the author's conclusion was this: "If you really want to see how tough you are, sail with someone else." I was beginning to understand. Sailing across an ocean is tough enough even if everybody is trying hard and doing their share. However, the boat was now a pigsty, with two crew who would not leave their bunks (except to eat), and all of the best food and treats disappearing.

By now, I hated my crew. I woke up hating them, I spent my watch hating them, I went to sleep hating them. This was not a pleasant way to spend nineteen days on what turned out to be a rough trip.

At one point we were sitting around the saloon, busily not talking to one another. The boat was taking the seas on the beam and rolling quite enthusiastically. After a few days at sea, it is true that anyone can pick up the rhythm of the waves. You can easily anticipate a big roll even if you are inside the boat with no view outside. In this case, we all suddenly felt a much bigger wave start to heel the boat. The man and I braced ourselves against the saloon table. The woman instead grabbed the arms of her chair, which had been fastened securely to the ceiling (hull lining), but by a shipwright (me) who had never anticipated a load like this. The boat rolled and she and the chair were flung across the cabin. Her head smashed into a beautiful black walnut locker at floor level.

Naturally, I grabbed the chair (to prevent further damage to the furniture) and secured it forward. She was now wailing and moaning on the cabin sole, tears and snot covering her face. Her partner tried ineffectually to comfort her. As for me, I had seen her hit the locker. It was her mass that caused the damage and, while her mass was pretty impressive, it was just not that impressive a collision.

We finally got her up on the bunk amid cries of agony. We had a good medical kit on board and lots of appropriate drugs, and I'd had fairly good emergency first aid training (in Canada I had done Industrial First Aid and, although my ticket was way out of date, a good deal of the training remained helpful). By this time, they were both carrying on about her brain damage and how we had to call the Coast Guard and get her off the vessel.

I carried out an exam for a concussion. She hadn't vomited (a typical symptom), both pupils were the same size, and all neural systems seemed to be functioning. I concluded that there probably *was* brain damage, but that it had occurred long before her arrival on *Scaramouche*. Keep in mind that these were penniless forty-year-old adults. They didn't work, and before we'd stopped talking they had revealed their plans for travelling on the mainland by couch-surfing, indicating that they needed no money at all to do this (a method of travel commonly known as "freeloading").

With this "dreadful" head injury, they saw an opportunity to get off the boat, which they hated, and obtain a free ride to the mainland, simply by calling the Coast Guard. Further, given the possibility of a brain injury, they could get a ride the rest of the way — in their minds, via helicopter — courtesy of U.S. taxpayers (among whom they were not numbered, I assure you).

We were probably about four hundred miles from Cape Flattery at this point. They insisted I call the Coast Guard. I refused. For one thing, short of setting off the EPIRB, I didn't know how. Anyone who thinks the Coast Guard can be reached on the SSB is probably dreaming in technicolour, and the VHF was far out of range. So not only did I not want to call the Coast Guard for some imaginary injury, I couldn't.

Their puling continued until I finally looked at them and said, "For Christ's sake, you haven't looked outside for two weeks. There's a twelve-foot swell running and we're north of the Strait of Juan de Fuca. The water is freezing. You want to get into a helicopter? Here's how it happens. The helicopter lowers its basket into the sea thirty or forty feet from the boat. A rescue diver is lowered into the water. The rescue diver swims over to *Scaramouche*, puts a life jacket on you and swims you over to the basket. Now go outside for one fucking moment and decide if you want to get into that ocean for a fake fucking head injury."

This shut them up temporarily. When I came down unexpectedly from my watch outside, I found her eating a monster sandwich (a validating sign, as I suspected that a healthy appetite probably contraindicated a brain injury). Even so, as we approached Neah Bay where I was dumping them, the woman insisted that she wanted to be put ashore at the Coast Guard base to report me.

"Sorry," I said, "this is post 9/11. I wouldn't approach a Coast Guard base without prior communication, as they would probably blow us out of the water. But I will let you off just next to the base and you can report me all you want."

It was like something out of a cartoon as we approached the dock in Neah Bay. They stood on the deck with all their luggage lined up against the lifeline. I pulled alongside and they jumped for it and ran. You think I'm exaggerating, but they *ran* (or in the case of the woman, waddled) up the dock. The boat wasn't even tied up.

I tidied things up and basked in my solitude. I had a shower — the first one in nineteen days. I had a drink — the first one in nineteen days. I went up on deck to put my feet up in the cockpit. There, beside the boat, were two young Coasties. I completely lost it, "Did that fat fucking cunt call you?!" I shouted at them with my eyes bulging and spittle flying.

They leapt back from the maniac, holding up their hands in supplication, "No, no, we're just here to do a safety inspection."

I calmed down and welcomed them aboard.

One thing about being a Class One ocean racer is that you are way overqualified to have any worries about failing a Coast Guard inspection. Not only do you have flares, you have SOLAS flares; not only do you have an in-date life raft, you have a SOLAS life raft; you have more fire extinguishers than required, and in date; and so on. I explained why I was upset. They were perfectly decent young kids, and were impressed by the state of the safety equipment on board.

After the Coasties saw that the safety equipment was more than adequate, they said, "All right, we just need to look at your head valve and you're free to get on with your day."

One thing about our American brothers is they have a strange fascination with a boat's head. The Coast Guard never wants to find the valve in the "overboard" position. I have tried endlessly to point out that, before contact — that is, before the arrival of the white man — there were about 50,000 natives living on the coast of BC, Washington and Alaska who all used the intertidal zone as a toilet. Since we've killed most of the natives and there are not anywhere near 50,000 boaters travelling the coast, we are, in fact, running a large poop deficit. They should be applauding our use of the head. Ah, well, "you can lead a whore to culture, but you can't make her think."

I knew my valve was in the wrong position, as we had just arrived from deep sea. With no better idea popping into my head (no pun intended), I said that the head had been broken for weeks and we had been using a bucket.

"Oh well, I suppose there's nothing to inspect then. Enjoy your stay in Neah Bay."

CHAPTER 27

TYMAC

At just about the same time that I bought *Scaramouche*, I was once again look-ing for a job to support my boat habit. Up until then, I had pretty much gone wherever I needed to earn a living, but this time it was a little different. My mother and stepfather (her husband after Bob's death) were getting pretty old. They managed on their own, but only with the support and attention of my brother and me to take care of shopping, trips to the doctor, and all the usual things the elderly need help with.

My search for work was thus naturally restricted to the Vancouver area where they lived, and that presented a big problem. I had never had much trouble get-ting work as long as I was willing to travel, but everybody with qualifications like mine wants to work in Vancouver. All of the big tug companies, such as Seaspan and Rivtow, were cutting back. I really had no choice, so I started calling some of the smaller companies. In fact, the first call I made resulted in an invitation to interview, and by the next day I was employed by Tymac Launch Services.

In my previous careers, I had run both sailboats and motor yachts ranging from eighty to one hundred feet in size and worth millions of dollars, and the Windjammer ship I skippered was three hundred feet in length with a crew of forty-five. So, do you think it was a comedown to find myself running badly maintained, bashed-up water taxis?

I know my friends seemed a little shocked, but it turned out to be a pretty good job. Living in town, I could have a social life and a car, as well as take care of my parents. I also really enjoyed many of the guys with whom I worked. The hours were long: eighty-four hours per week once I'd worked my way up to a permanent position (although then I got the following week off). It turned out to be the longest permanent job I ever held.

I've always worried that my attitude toward safety on the vessels I've run professionally has perhaps been a little too casual. In those days, however, Tymac made me look like a safety inspector. Never have I seen a company that cared less for the well-being of its employees. I will give a few examples, and let you judge whether my various responses were reasonable.

....

One of the regular jobs was to take personnel out to the ships in the harbour. Often the company required that the boat stand by until whatever work they were doing on board was finished. This could be for one hour or it could be for ten hours; it could be at ten in the morning or two in the morning — any time at all. The boat operators, unsure of the length of their stay out in the harbour, would bring food, drink, books, etc. The caveat was that we couldn't tie up and we had to remain awake.

A thinking person might wonder how we went to the toilet. Easy: we hung our butts off the swim grids. This could be rather embarrassing on a Sunday afternoon surrounded by weekend sailors, but think about 0300 on a black February morning, with horizontal rain and a four-foot swell running. You'd often be working alone, so a slip would very likely be fatal.

My first assault on the Tymac Health and Safety Committee raised the dangers posed by working alone at night. Management responded that since we were always working alongside ships, the ships could be relied upon to rescue us in the event of a problem. This was total nonsense, and so derisive an answer that I was rendered temporarily speechless. Every employee had experienced blowing the boat's whistle for hours or pounding with hammers on the hull — anything to get somebody to lower the gangway. At night, the ships' crews were (big surprise) inside, where it was warm and dry.

As mandated by law (as opposed to by management), the Health and Safety Committee met monthly. Labour was represented on the committee, but they were all "company men" who looked forward to an hour or so away from their regular duties. Accidents happened often, but they were always viewed as discrete events and not part of a pattern. One employee, for example, drove a forklift off a barge into sixty-five feet of water. Technically, he was required by the safety committee to wear a seatbelt, but if he'd complied the company would have been short one employee. Rescued by the crew of the cruise ship he was alongside, he left in an ambulance. Another employee was swept off the top of a giant garbage bin by a colleague using a forklift; major surgery and metal pins put his knee back together. A report that one of the tug's exhaust systems was shedding asbestos dust into the engine room was conveniently lost by management.

Tymac was a small, privately owned company, and the owner was a massive man who physically intimidated everyone. Whenever he lost his temper, which was regularly, he practically foamed at the mouth. However, we were also a union company, and this provided some protection from arbitrary firing. Also, some years ago I had come up with a personal financial plan that, while not unique (I'm sure many others do the same), gave me some measure of security. It was this: I figured out what it cost to live for six months, and I kept that amount liquid and in my current account. Not so easy for wage-earners with kids and mortgages, but easy enough for me at this stage of my life. I called it my "fuck-you money," and it gave me the freedom to bear down on the Health and Safety Committee, an Orwellian group if ever there was one.

There was a Health and Safety suggestion box in the crew lunchroom. Presumably, this was so that people could make suggestions or complaints while remaining anonymous — a noble idea of which I took full advantage. It took me only a few months to realize that nobody ever emptied the box. I had dated my first list of suggestions, and it sat in the box for two years, only being recovered by management when I initiated The Great Memo Scam.

Work was going on normally, and I was acquiring some good boat-handling skills. One of our jobs was to back barges down a narrow alleyway of water to the ramp, where they were loaded and unloaded. Yes, you read that correctly: you are attached to the barge with a towline, and it's necessary to shorten up the line and back up the barge. The tugs were crap, and the barges were often barely afloat, but I never tired of watching some of the twenty-year employees carry out this job. I found that as I got older, new skills were difficult to master, so, although I could execute this manoeuvre successfully, I always had to pay close attention and it never came naturally. Likewise, putting people on board ships was something we did many times each day. It was a piece of cake to come alongside a gangway on a calm, sunny day, but in thirty knots of wind and a contrary tide with a five-foot swell running, it took a lot of skill and some calm nerves.

One particular job I really came to enjoy was putting the pilots on board ships underway at night. During my first years at Tymac, we used regular launches, and for reasons that might lose some of the non-mariner readers, we had to load them onto the pilot ladders from the aft deck of the launch. Anyone with boat-handling experience may doubt that this is possible, because the water is moving toward you at six to ten knots and trying to push the bow away from the ship. Once this separation occurs, you're gone from the side and, in the best of circumstances, the pilot can't board; in the worst of circumstances, he's swimming. However, with just the right application of throttle and helm, the stern can be held indefinitely against the ladder.

In keeping with the Tymac tradition of ignoring all safety considerations, nobody was actually trained in this skill. I caught on because I carefully studied how the old-time operators did it. Probably because I'm a fairly experienced mariner, I picked up on the tricks quickly. This was fortunate because, at Tymac, one day you were a deckhand and — perhaps the next night — somebody didn't report for work, it would be blowing thirty knots, and now you're the skipper loading a pilot onto an eighteen-inch-wide rope ladder in a six-foot swell at eight knots alongside an eight-hundred-foot steel ship.

My obsession with the Health and Safety Committee persisted. I think my first complete victory was around the question of toilets. I wrote them a letter pointing out that the year was 2006 and people couldn't be expected to shit off the swim grid and that, in the vast majority of drownings involving men, the victim was found with his zipper down. (I always joke that the hypothesis accepted by most people is that the dead guy was taking a leak; another might be that he fell into the water and got bored waiting to drown.)

Much to my surprise, management responded immediately by buying plastic buckets with toilet-seat lids so that people could actually use the toilet without risking their lives. Victory number one. I should probably point out that in the interim the company had changed hands and the new owner, besides not being physically aggressive and intimidating, was much more open to safety concerns. However, it would still take time to bring Tymac screaming into the eighteenth century.

At the time I'm writing about, I had probably written ten different letters to the Health and Safety Committee. What had I gotten in return? Toilet seats. But it was a start. The problem was that we still had the same management culture.

Every week when the new shift started, there would be some idiotic memo about safety. There were no ladders on the boats to reboard in the event of falling overboard; instead of responding to this, they insisted we all needed to wear shoes with safety toes. All of my suggestions for safety improvements were ignored, yet they would send people home for not wearing fluorescent vests. The memos were endless, and no doubt it appeared to the new (but absent) owner that the company was concerned about safety. However, it was always trivial stuff and involved little or no company money.

Finally, I had my break-through moment. I copied the company memo format on my laptop and started issuing my own idiotic memos. I would pin them up where the safety memos were normally posted. I would do this right at shift change, so that when they realized someone had issued a bogus memo, they wouldn't be able to tell which shift he was on.

TO: ALL EMPLOYEES
FROM: ████████████████
DATE: OCT. 26, 2010
RE: SAFETY REPORTING

Some employees are still having difficulty distinguishing between safety and maintenance issues. Maintenance issues are a result of company neglect, safety issues are a result of employee error. For example, some of the tugs are kept afloat by their bilge pumps. This is a maintenance issue. If a tug sinks while you are operating it because a bilge pump fails, this is a safety issue (and a report will be entered into your permanent employee record).

Maybe another example will help. As you know, we are rebuilding the #11 [boat]. We are using gas engines and legs, so we can look forward to another ten years of maintenance issues. If an engine should fail while you are offloading cargo near the stern of a ship, this is a maintenance issue. But if the wheelhouse should then strike the counter of the ship and be damaged, this is a safety issue (and a report will be entered into your permanent employee record).

If you have either a maintenance or a safety issue, write it up completely. Then you can either put it in the safety committee box in the crew room (where it will be safe for years) or bring it to my office and put it in the wastepaper basket under my desk (I've read these things for years and my lips get very tired).

TO: ALL EMPLOYEES
FROM: ██████████████
DATE :   OCT. 31, 2010
RE: NEW LAUNCH DESIGNS

As you know, we are about to order the new launches. Some of you have been scribbling suggestions about their design on the crew notice board. Please understand that we have to communicate our needs to both naval architects and the builders themselves, so if you have suggestions for the new boats, please type them. This will help you to think clearly about what you want to say, and of course makes it easier for us to understand.

We DO need your input. Many of you have worked for us for decades and all that experience is very valuable to us. So please, TYPE up your design suggestions and, if you are at home, print them, and then you can simply slip them into a convenient wastebasket at home, or bring them into work and put them in the wastebasket in the crew room. My email at work is tymac@notugstoomanylaunches.com. If you are at work using the computer in the crew room, please use my email address and then use the Adobe Acrobat pdf format. After you have written up your suggestions, simply click DELETE.

It is NOT necessary to sign your name, as we treat all suggestions from employees equally regardless of your time with the company.

This might be a "you had to be there" moment, but you have to imagine the committee pontificating about safety and then doing everything possible to prevent a single dime from being spent on it. I don't know if I succeeded, but I was trying to just skirt the edge of idiocy, so probably more than half the employees seriously believed these memos were issued by management; even the president of the company is reputed to have said, "What is that idiot [the manager] saying now?" Still, I'm pretty certain humour is a better response than self-righteousness; in fact, whenever I start feeling self-righteous, I know it's probably because I'm doing something wrong.

I want to make it clear that the Tymac of today is a far different company than it was when I started working there. The new owners spend money like drunken sailors, both on new equipment and on safety. They listen to the workforce and respond. It still takes time, of course, but it's a big turnaround from the previous mess.

Once, before the company acquired new equipment, a deckhand and I were towing a barge with a lube oil truck on board. Many of the ships in Vancouver load grain, and petroleum-laden trucks are not allowed on the wharfs where this is taking place (I was never sure why they weren't allowed, except that grain dust is very explosive). This gave Tymac quite a bit of business towing the trucks on our small barges to the side of the ship away from the dock.

Once the barge was secured alongside, we would secure the tug to the side of the barge. Then our job was finished until the truck driver had pumped his lube oil onboard. Usually this took a few hours, during which we could sleep or read or stare into space.

When one particular truck arrived earlier than scheduled at Tymac, the tug was having an electrical problem that was being worked on by the maintenance crew. We needed the tug right away and, naturally, asked if it could be used in its present state. It could be, we were told, but the panel with all the switches, gauges, etc., would be hanging down, and not fastened properly under the compass shelf.

Everything went well with the tow. The barge was secured alongside the ship and the tug alongside the barge. My deckhand got his head down on the only available bunk, and I put my feet up on the compass shelf and dozed in the skipper's chair. I didn't sleep for long, though, awakening with my feet on fire. Smoke and flames were pouring into the wheelhouse from the hanging instrument panel, and my feet were on top of it.

Leaping up, I grabbed the fire extinguisher and, aiming it at the area that appeared to be the source of the fire, I squeezed the handle. The handle fell off in my hand. It was company policy that the tugs remain idling while alongside ships (this was possibly because we were never sure if they would start again once shut off). My deckhand rushed outside and threw open the engine room access hatch to turn off the engine, but acrid, poisonous fumes spewed out, driving him back. Meanwhile, I got the truck driver to stop pumping and give me one of his extinguishers. We blew it off, but the fire slowed only momentarily. In a moment of asinine bravery, my deckhand managed to get far enough into the engine room to activate the fuel shutoff, and slowly things got under control. We were fortunate, because this was a tug that had been built in the 1920s: the wood was saturated with fuel oil and the fire could easily have gotten out of control.

Later, another tug towed us back to Tymac and nothing more was ever said except a lame attempt by management to suggest that my sleeping foot had somehow activated the starter motor of the (already-running) tug. Ever since I had begun at Tymac, I had made it a policy to report honestly if I damaged a piece of equipment, so they knew this wouldn't fly. Remembering the memos, they probably hesitated to poke the sleeping bear. I suspect they learned that sending crew out in a tug halfway through a repair job was not the smartest idea they'd ever had.

Not long after this, I went to the head of the Health and Safety Committee with a letter that stated that, "in his professional and personal opinion," the tugs at Tymac were safe to operate. I asked him to sign the letter. He refused, and I never towed another barge for the company.

....

There were a ton of funny moments at Tymac, as some of the crew were very bright and enjoyed bizarre humour. One of the most memorable for me, however, didn't involve the other crew at all.

Have you ever wondered what happens to the 10,000 empty pop bottles generated on a cruise ship every week? Or what happens to the tons of paper produced daily, or the tons of food waste? Well, I will tell you. Tymac happens to it. Tymac does virtually all of the light towing in Vancouver Harbour. It does all of the pilot boat activity, as well as having a lock on most personnel movements between ship and shore. But where Tymac really makes its money is in removing garbage and recyclables from cruise ships.

This was not very enjoyable work, and in the end I managed to get out of towing the garbage barges by refusing to get the port security clearance that was required after 9/11. Still, for a few years prior to that, I did my share of running them, just like everyone else. It was dirty, hot work in the summer, and we usually wore coveralls that looked as if we had bathed in the garbage by the end of our twelve-hour shifts.

During my year running *Legacy* for Windjammer Barefoot Cruises, when I was completely "at sea" with a crew of forty-five and more than a hundred guests, I was able to succeed in part because I had a particularly wonderful Chief Mate, Jonathan Burrage. He did his job beautifully and supported me to the fullest. I don't know if he was aware of how totally out of my depth I was then, but if he did it didn't seem to matter to him. We remain friends to this day.

Jonathan wanted to pursue a career at sea. When I eventually parted ways with the Windjammer organization, I went on to run various yachts and tugs, while Jonathan continued in the cruise ship industry.

Inevitably, during my time at Tymac, the day came when I realized that the ship from which I was removing garbage had Jonathan on board as an officer. I asked the environmental officer who supervised the garbage transfer from the ship to call the bridge and tell Jonathan I was working his ship.

Here was a moment rivalling the meeting of Stanley and Livingstone. Jonathan appeared at the refuse port in the ship's side, in the crisp, white, spotless uniform of a cruise ship's first officer, to be greeted by his former boss and captain wearing a hard hat, greasy boots and gloves, and filthy coveralls, from a barge overflowing with garbage.

A good, ironic laugh was had by all. But what the hell — friends are friends. And we do what we have to do to eat.

CHAPTER 28

....

THE SINGLEHANDED TRANSPAC

"A bug light for weirdos."

I mentioned earlier that I had always wanted to do a single-handed ocean crossing, and the time to do it was fast approaching, if only because I was now sixty-four years old and the sailboat seemed to get about two feet longer every year. It is a well-established fact that a single person can sail almost any size of vessel if enough effort is put into the design of the systems — think of some of the early OSTAR races in which the largest vessel was 236 feet long (*Club Mediterranee*). However, that costs a pile of money, and I was still earning thirty bucks an hour. Still, when I first read the quote above, I knew that the Singlehanded TransPac was for me.

The race was from San Francisco to Kauai, a distance of about 2,300 miles. An argument could be made that San Francisco to Kauai is not trans-Pacific, as a truly trans-Pacific voyage would be San Francisco to Japan. However, there is the race from Long Beach to Oahu that has been run for many years, and it is universally known as "the Transpac." Thus, the Singlehanded Sailing Society is justified in calling their race the Singlehanded TransPac, as a mistake everybody makes is not a mistake.

I managed the preparations as I always did, by doing all the work (except the welding) myself, and by scouring the used marine stores and classified ads when I needed gear. I also entered a couple of local single-handed races to get a feel for things, only to discover that, despite the occasional good result, I could not sail the boat at anywhere near its potential. This has been my whole history with *Scaramouche*: rare flashes of good speed interspersed with a lot of humiliation. (As an example, only a few weeks before writing this, I entered a couple of local races in which the race committee had picked up the marks and gone home before we finished the race.)

Anyone who is still reading and knows anything about sailing will see that there is a bit of a conflict in *Scaramouche*'s development. Ironically, I had just spent six years turning an old race boat into a cruising boat — only to take her racing. This is why the people in the Pac Cup were laughing up their sleeves at us. I joked that we were the only entrant that had a drill press on board — except that it wasn't a joke: we *did* have a drill press on board. I couldn't get out of the cruising mentality, where every eventuality is planned for and reflected by the gear on board. Interestingly, one of the people who laughed the loudest and most publicly at our efforts in the Pac Cup turned back after two days because of an electronic equipment failure. Cold comfort.

After our return from the Pac Cup, I spent the next two years preparing for the single-handed race to Hawaii. Of course, during that time we did a lot of local cruising and, in order to do the TransPac, it was necessary to do a qualifying sail. The summer before the race, Christy and I took the boat up the coast in leisurely fashion so I could make one great leap by myself outside Vancouver Island. The rules required that I be one hundred miles offshore and the trip no fewer than four hundred miles long.

I live on one of the most beautiful, convoluted, biologically diverse coastlines in the world, so it's a bit strange to me that many people have spent their whole lives in the major cities nearby and seen nothing of its rugged beauty. Christy is one of those people, and I'm glad to say that she fell in love with the coast just as I had done many years before. We took a couple of weeks to wend our way north to Shearwater, where we left the boat and returned to work for a week. Then I flew north to make my first single-handed voyage of any distance.

The organization that puts on the SHTP supplies a logbook (or form), and the thinking is that if you fill it out regularly on your qualifier, it would be hard to fake. I filled it out religiously, for I dreaded going to all of this trouble and expense and then not being allowed to race.

The qualifier was interesting, but nothing more than that. I departed St. John Harbour on the central coast with a settled forecast for a couple of days and then the possibility of gales developing. Due to personality issues (I suppose), I have spent lots of time sailing alone, so I was not particularly nervous. The gales never did develop, and I thoroughly enjoyed my three-day solo sail. Since I'd spent so much time on the coast, I knew more or less where the dragger fleet would be working and I could plan my sleep so that I was rested for the area off Bamfield (where the concentration of large fishboats was the greatest). I sailed over 12 Mile Bank — the same place I had made landfall upon arriving in *Carlotta* many years before (when a kind fisherman had given us our position and a lovely big salmon). Not a troller was in sight.

I had read on the Internet that participants in European single-handed qualifiers take pictures of themselves with the plotter next to their heads so that the boat's position and their face are in the same frame — a kind of geographic selfie that would be very hard to fake. I did that when I was a hundred miles off Cape Cook to prove that I did get a hundred miles offshore as the rules required, as well as a couple of other times just to be thorough.

Arriving back in Vancouver, I assembled the necessary documentation and, with my logbook, sent it all off to the SHTP official in California. I heard nothing back. I emailed and got no response. I phoned: nothing. Finally, I tracked down another member of the SHTP race committee and told him that I had submitted everything required (including the only copy of the log proving I had made the voyage), gave him the name of the person I had sent it to, and explained that I wasn't getting a response. He replied that the person in question had moved to the east coast and had nothing to do with the organization anymore.

So...I had just spent a good part of my summer, along with inestimable amounts of money and effort, with nothing to show for it. The person in California was very sympathetic, but the rules were the rules. The previous cretin was unresponsive to personal emails, so I was in a bit of a quandary. Then I remembered the pictures.

I dragged out my digital camera and there, in colour, was a series of photos showing my progress down the coast, including the boat a hundred miles off Cape Cook. The race committee also requested my résumé, and that clinched things (most of the first-time participants did not have a ton of offshore experience nor any professional qualifications).

We were set to go for the following spring. I spent the winter improving the boat as much as I could (or could afford). I never doubted the boat, as it is fantastically strong. I, on the other hand, am not a particularly strong specimen, so my worries were more about my own ability to handle difficult situations than about anything dreadful failing on the boat. I had the sails examined by professionals, which was expensive. However, my sailmaker understood what I was trying to do, so the sails were way over strength and this was something I never regretted (you will see why later).

I built a small platform so that I could sleep in the cockpit either fore and aft or athwartship; that effort turned out to be a waste of time. I also had a large struggle getting my electronics into the state I wanted. The new AIS system kept reporting me thirty miles inland, named something different, and showed me going at forty-two knots. Bit by bit, though, everything came together.

In May 2012, we had a going-away party in False Creek, then the usual suspects and I headed down the coast toward San Francisco. My plan, as is my habit for these coastal passages, was to wait in Neah Bay (located at the extreme northwest corner of the lower forty) until a good westerly developed, and then head out. The First Nations band that runs Neah Bay has an excellent community centre, so every morning I would row ashore, check the weather on their free computers, and, if it didn't suit, go for a walk. In this instance, we were only there for a couple of days when a nice high-pressure system developed far enough north. We were off like a dirty shirt.

I've done the trip so many times that the various voyages run together in my mind, but one thing they almost all have in common is that it blows like hell off Cape Mendocino. This trip was no exception. I don't have any instrumentation to indicate wind strength (except possibly my asshole slamming shut), but I would guess we probably had about thirty knots of wind as we approached the gybing point off San Francisco. Now, one thing that I absolutely didn't cheap out on was my autopilot system. It is a WH Autopilot that I had learned about when I was skipper of *Beowulf*. I don't agree with everything Steve Dashew says, but he does buy the absolute best for his boats. That's what I wanted for crossing the Pacific by myself.

We gybed off San Francisco on a filthy, dark night and now, with the wind on our beam and three reefs in, we stormed toward Drakes Bay and shelter. It was just then that the autopilot failed. Let me clarify. The WH Autopilot is a wonderful tool, but that doesn't guarantee the workmanship of the moron (that would be me, in this case) who installs it. The three-quarter-inch stainless steel bolt that secured the autopilot hydraulic ram to the quadrant broke, and we were forced to hand-steer for the next few hours until we slipped into Drakes Bay to get some much-needed sleep .

This was the best thing that could have happened. To have it break when I had two strong, knowledgeable pals on board was preferable, by far, to it breaking in the middle of the Pacific with only me on board. I took some pictures of the installation and fired them off to WH.

Will (the W of WH, and the owner) has a unique management philosophy. If you phone between eight in the morning and midnight, he guarantees that he will personally answer the phone. This could have its drawbacks, as I was to learn, but for troubleshooting it's hard to beat.

When Will got the pictures of my installation, he fired an email back in large red type: "Whoever made this installation is a total idiot who does not understand hydraulics and certainly doesn't understand lever arms. Do not under any circumstances proceed to sea with the setup as it is!!!!"

Mea culpa.

He then proceeded to make a series of suggestions about how the situation could be improved. In my own defence, I had already put about 10,000 miles on the installation with no trouble. However, in the early spring I'd had Bob Perry design an enlarged rudder blade for the boat. The boat, being an early IOR design, doesn't track very well downwind, so this makes the autopilot work a lot harder and use a lot more electricity. I enlarged the blade by more than thirty percent and that helped, but there is no free lunch, and now the steering loads were heavier (although applied less often). This doubtless caused the bolt to fail given the enthusiastic breeze in which we found ourselves.

There could be no fooling around. I took Will's point and went to KKMI, the most expensive yard I've ever dealt with. In a few hours they had built an aluminum support system for the bolt (which I'd had remade larger and out of shaft stainless), complete with flying buttresses and all manner of wonderful engineering to strengthen the system. The welding was artwork. And I was glad — poor, but glad.

The day of departure grew closer. We had a ton of small jobs to do, but essentially the boat was ready and I was anxious to get going. The race committee sponsored a few events to encourage camaraderie between the skippers; this was fine, but basically I had been preparing for a year and it was time to sail. At one of these events, I ran into a sailor I had met in Canada who was also entering the race. Our initial meeting had not been a happy one, but when I saw that he was participating I swallowed whatever rancor I was harbouring and tried to be friendly.

The great day finally arrived. We had shifted from the Richmond Yacht Club to the Corinthian Yacht Club in Tiburon. Thus, with the start line directly in front of the club, it was only a matter of motoring away from the dock. It was lucky for me that there had been a rule change in the race. In prior years, they would wire your prop closed so that there was no chance to cheat by using power at any point. Let me rephrase that: you could use power, but anyone inspecting your prop would immediately see that the wire had been severed. I would have had trouble getting out of the dock area into which I was tucked without power, so it was a big help that the committee had decided it was a Corinthian sport and people simply wouldn't cheat. I'm sure they were correct.

A kiss for Christy, a few handshakes, and I was away at last. Main up, engine off, and I cruised the start line waiting for my starting signal. We had been warned that there was also a major San Francisco schooner race going on and that the courses had a certain amount of overlap. One result of the two races taking place on the same day was that every photo boat in the Bay Area was out shooting pictures of the knuckleheads sailing to Hawaii by themselves, along with the beautiful schooners bashing along in the twenty-knot breeze.

I have always been terribly critical of people who go sailing and leave their fenders dragging in the water; it seems so slovenly and unseamanlike. Therefore, I was grateful, after sailing around for an hour having many pictures taken of my lovely boat, and thoroughly enjoying all of the attention, when a woman on one of the photo boats leaned over and, in what was meant to be a stage whisper, said, "*Scaramouche*…pick up your fenders."

When you go to sea, you'd better be humble, for you very soon will be.

At long last, the gun for my class fired and we were off. I had no real strategy for exiting San Francisco Bay. As usual, there was a strong westerly pouring through the Golden Gate, and we had a strong ebb tide. I expected a big lump because of the wind-over-tide situation, but it never materialized. Tack after tack, I made my way toward the bridge. Christy had put three bottles of Gatorade in the cockpit, and they were gone in about the first fifteen minutes. I don't think I've ever cranked on winches so hard in my life.

This was when all of the information I'd received from my friend Jim Quanci and his wife Mary, who had patiently answered my plethora of silly questions during the Pacific Cup race, came to my aid. Jim, who is a wonderful sailor (and eventual winner of my class, and overall winner, too), had told me to stay basically in the middle once past the bridge, and definitely not to get close to either shore given that the winds would be light there. I wish I had asked him that before the Pacific Cup, and things might have turned out differently.

It was a classic departure from San Francisco: far too much wind (for me, at least), fog as thick as snot, and lots of deep-sea traffic. Surprisingly, it all went pretty well. I passed some of the smaller boats in a class that started before me. Just west of the bridge I was tacking over toward Mile Rock. I was getting closer to the shore than I wanted to be, and was terrified of losing my wind. I glanced over my shoulder as I prepared to tack, and there, close on my starboard quarter, was another competitor.

It was the "General," a Singlehanded TransPac legend: at the time, eighty-two years old and undertaking his twelfth single-handed race to Hawaii. We were both on starboard, but if I tacked he would have the right of way. Stupidly, I tacked, hoping I could either pass ahead of him or duck under his stern. In fact, as I completed my tack, I realized I could do neither. Fortunately, I always keep an air horn in the cockpit — well, "always" except for those times when I desperately need it, such as right then. I hollered and screamed, trying to get his attention, as I was now right in front of him and couldn't clear him by my actions alone. He finally looked up, threw in a quick tack, and we were safe. He gave me a friendly wave, but I felt like a complete incompetent: two hours into the race, I had port-tacked a guy whom everyone loved and who could, if he chose, have me disqualified from the race. I was absolutely embarrassed to have made such an amateurish mistake.

(After our arrival in Hawaii, in fact, the first chance I had to get him alone I apologized as profusely and humbly as I knew how. He looked at me as if I was from outer space. "You were on starboard. It was my fault," he said. "No," I said, "You were on starboard. I was on port and it was me who tacked just in front of you." He thought for a minute, and said, "I guess you're right; 'nother beer?" I had been agonizing about this for the whole voyage, and he couldn't give a rat's ass.)

Anyway, just after that incident the wind began dropping off and the fog thinned. I was happy with both developments. I was completely exhausted, and it was good to be able to see oncoming traffic. At the same time, I felt the boat was doing quite well. The last competitor to start was in an Open 40. He was not really competing with us, as his rating (handicap) made it impossible for him to win, but he was hoping to set a course record (which he did). He passed me in the early evening and I remember thinking, well, he's passing me, but I don't think he's passing me as fast as he should be.

For the first three days of the race, I was doing extremely well. I was even in front of Jim Quanci, and that's probably the only time in this life *that* will happen. The wind built somewhat, but it was a lovely beam reach and *Scaramouche* was flying. The Moore 24s and the Olsens would blow me out of the water as soon as the wind was strong enough for them to plane, but as long it was a matter of waterline length I could do very well.

The route to Hawaii is raced so often and the weather systems are so constant that good sailors have written articles about the best route. Regrettably, it is all nonsense now that climate change has reared its ugly head.

Typically, after the second or third day, the wind should have built in what is called the "fast reach" part of the course. It didn't. In fact, it went fairly light, but that didn't prevent a big swell from dominating the sailing. My sails are eleven-ounce Dacron and they began to slat. The wind came around behind, and I set the spinnaker pole to square off the genoa. As the boat rolled to port, both sails would collapse; then, as the boat rolled to starboard, both sails would fill with a report like a shotgun blast. I'd never heard anything like it in all my years of sailing. I flattened the sails as much as possible, then rigged vangs and preventers to hold the boom steady, but nothing I could do seemed to help. It drove me mad. There was no escaping these explosions as both sails slammed full. This went on for a week, and I honestly thought the boat would be torn apart. This is where I need to thank my sailmaker, as the strong sails really paid for themselves; lesser sails would certainly have been shredded to bits.

The competitors all spoke to each other every evening and reported our positions. This was a condition of competing. I couldn't believe after three days that I (ignoring the Open 40) was leading the fleet. I had no trouble believing that I was losing position after position from the third day on. But I couldn't give a shit. I just wanted that slamming to stop.

I knew it would stop when we reached the trades, but the trades had moved way south and I didn't get into what I would call real trade-wind sailing until a couple of days out of Kauai. By then, I never wanted to see this fucking ocean or the fucking Singlehanded TransPac ever again.

What I should have done was reach off to the south and put the spinnaker up. It's an asymmetrical in a sock, and pretty easy to handle even single-handed. This would have quieted the sails, increased speed (and distance). Had I done this, with any luck the VMG would have remained the same or improved, and I would have reached the stronger trades sooner — and the slatting would have stopped. I didn't do it, however, because I'm afraid of the spinnaker. Jim Quanci had his spinnaker up and was going like billy-be-damned, but Jim Quanci is a very experienced ocean racer. His boat is ten feet shorter and he is ten years younger and, well, I say all this only as a way of explaining my lack of nerve. I was disappointed in myself.

By the tenth day, I started to pick up the trades and then really began to make some ground, but by that time any hope of doing well had long ago expired. Before the race, I had made a big deal out of not being competitive. I insisted I would be happy just to complete the course with no injury or major damage. I had also set two other goals: I wanted to do the race without burning any fossil fuels, and I wanted to have one day over two hundred miles.

I accomplished none of this. Early on in the race, I had my autopilot incorrectly adjusted and it was drawing far too much power. It took a couple of days for me to figure out what was wrong, and by then I'd had to run the engine a few times in order to charge the batteries. The wind was so light that I never got anywhere near two hundred miles in a day (perhaps in the one-eighties, but not much more).

I *did* succeed in not sustaining any serious injuries myself, or damage to the boat. The only incident of interest occurred early one morning about two-thirds through the race. I woke up with the dawn (I was sleeping inside) and stuck my head out to see that all was well. By looking at the motion of the wheel, it is easy to see how well balanced the boat is, or, put another way, how hard the autopilot is working. I was pleased to see that the wheel was barely turning.

Wait a minute.

The wheel wasn't turning at all. How could that be? We were on course. I could see from our wake that the rudder was working. But the wheel remained absolutely stationary.

As I climbed back to the cockpit, the penny dropped. This had happened before. The wheel is on an axle with a key in a keyway that ensures that, when the wheel turns, the axle turns, and that turns a sprocket over which runs a chain that…you get the idea. There is a small bolt that secures the wheel on the key, and if that comes loose the wheel can slip past the keyway. The autopilot will continue to steer the boat, but the wheel just rotates uselessly on the axle.

Without thinking (I had just woken up, after all), I gave the wheel a tug. It came off in my hands and there was a small metallic clunk indicating that the axle and attendant gear had just fallen down inside the binnacle. Oh fuck.

Now here I was in the middle of the Pacific Ocean with no manual steering. The question was how to recover the whole top end of the steering gear that had fallen down inside the binnacle. First, I had to disassemble all the nav gear that was mounted above the compass, then remove the compass from its home at the top of the binnacle. Then I had to loop some light lines around the gear that had fallen down and raise the gear high enough that I could slip the wheel back on the axle. Finally, I needed to secure the small bolt to prevent this from happening again.

All of that took a couple of hours, and for once I was glad the boat was down by the head[1] from all my various tools and toolboxes. I might not win any races, but there wasn't much I couldn't fix.

The funny conclusion to this story is, after securing the small retaining bolt, I forgot all about the problem; after all, I had fixed it. Long after arriving in Kauai, Christy and I sailed the boat to Honolulu. We had a terrible trip across the in-famous channel that separates the islands, and it was two in the morning when we pulled into the Ala Wai Small Boat Harbor. I was fairly tired after a tough, thirty-hour sail, and Christy was definitely not feeling her best. The halfwit in the office had been unable to describe where our slip was, and there was a stiff breeze blowing across the entrance to the slips. Finally, I said, "The hell with it, we'll go in any empty slip." I chose one, started my final turn, and the wheel came off in my hand. I had secured the bolt in the incorrect hole, so after all my repairs it was just as bad when I finished as when I started. Who's the halfwit?

One other interesting event happened during the race. Earlier I mentioned the other Canadian with whom I'd had a disagreement back in Canada. We'd kissed and made up in Tiburon before the start of the race, and of course his was

---

[1] Editor's note: "Down by the head" is a nautical term used by commercial mariners to mean overloaded.

one of the boats whose position I kept note of as the race progressed. Before the race, though, some of our discussions did make me wonder about his experience level; however, if the race committee was happy, I was happy.

On about the fifth day into the race, I noted that he wasn't reporting in on our daily radio schedule. There could be a thousand reasons for this, and it would only become worrying if his tracking device stopped transmitting. By the seventh day, the race committee reported to us that he was okay but had been taken off his vessel by a container ship, and was headed back to San Francisco for medical treatment. We didn't get the full story until we'd all arrived in Kauai.

It went like this. He had developed a bad infection in his butt or leg. It got worse and worse until he had trouble breathing. In a conversation with me later, he said he'd visualized the white blood cells attacking the infection (but I guess that didn't work out too well). He tried calling the USCG on his SSB, with no luck, and finally set off his EPIRB. The Coast Guard directed a ship to take him off, and this was done beautifully by one of the Matson container ships that ply between the islands and the mainland. As he mounted the accommodation ladder on the ship's side, he gave his boat a push away, with one sail up and the self-steering gear still pointed toward Hawaii.

Once on the ship, the skipper got in touch with the high seas medical aid organization that keeps a doctor on call at all hours. The doctor quickly diagnosed a staph infection and, over the sat phone, gave the master instructions in administering antibiotics by injection. In just a few hours, the patient started to feel better. After that, it wasn't too many hours before he started worrying about his boat.

The tracker on board his boat was still working, so we could see it heading perfectly for Maui (I pointed out that he had picked up a couple of places in the race since getting off his boat, but no one was amused). He could now email us from the ship, and tried to solicit someone to rescue his boat. The race committee had the ability to make his tracker signals private, i.e., available only to the committee, so there was no chance of anybody "salvaging" the vessel.

In Kauai during the race, it was a tradition that we all meet under a palm tree every day at five to drink beer and greet those who'd just arrived. The talk, of course, was often about the sick Canadian — how he was doing and how amazing it was that his boat just kept coming exactly on course for the north shore of Maui. At this point, we had a communication from the USCG. If the vessel entered the twelve-mile zone and was still "Not Under Command," the

Coast Guard was going to blow it out of the water — something like our Alaskan brothers, whose state motto is "If it moves, shoot it. If it doesn't, cut it down." The Coast Guard's idiotic (over)reaction was probably due to pollution concerns, but this was a thirty-five-foot sailboat with probably ten gallons of diesel fuel on board that would evaporate in minutes in the Hawaiian sun. Not exactly the *Exxon Valdez*.

By luck, one of the racers had connections with the Coast Guard and pointed out that if they wanted to alienate every recreational boater in the world, they were going about it the right way. The message was received, and the Coast Guard did a 180-degree attitude adjustment. From then on, they were all sweetness and light.

This evolving drama unfolded at a fairly modest rate of knots, and each day under the tree we would hear the most recent communication from the sick Canadian — that is, the latest of his messages beseeching us to save his boat and, of course, relaying its last reported position. Finally, one of the racers, who perhaps had more resources than some of us, said, "We've got to save this guy's boat." He had to fly back to work, but he agreed to finance the rescue. A couple of the younger studs volunteered to do the actual job.

They flew to Maui and chartered a sport fishing boat. About twelve miles off the north coast of the island, they found the sailboat. They boarded it with a few groceries, sailed it to Honolulu, tied it up at the Waikiki Yacht Club docks, then went about their lives. Meanwhile, the Canadian had made a full recovery in hospital in San Francisco. He flew to Honolulu, and there was his boat all tied up safe and sound. He bought some fuel and food, and a few days later continued his trip to the South Pacific — crisis averted through the good works of fellow sailors.

As you have probably gathered, I did not do well in the race. That didn't bother me much, but what did bother me was that I had made such a poor effort.

At the awards dinner, each competitor had to stand up and give a small speech. I was caught completely off guard, having not been told this was required. Fortunately, I had gotten seriously into the before-dinner drinks, so the silver-tongued devil had his way. I announced to the assembled: "I have always fancied myself something of a writer, and so I've been trying to think of a metaphor for the race. All I can think of is that it is like teenage sex. You're proud you did it, but a little embarrassed by your performance. And when I was a young man and indulging in teenage sex, I often sought solace afterward in alcohol and drugs. I don't see any reason that should change now. Thank you."

....

As I'm writing this in the winter of 2013, I think I may try just once more to rescue my self-esteem by entering the Singlehanded TransPac for a second time. Again, I'm not that interested in beating anyone to Hawaii, but I'm very interested in feeling that I shot my best shot.

Let me amend that: I'm not interested in beating anyone…with the possible exception of my friend Steve on *Frolic*, who was just a little too happy about beating me last time.

....

AUTHOR'S NOTE

I did end up racing again in the 2014 Singlehanded TransPac. The story of that summer could be a book in itself, but just to conclude this one, I will mention that Steve, my pal on *Frolic*, once more soundly humiliated me on the race course. He sailed a beautiful, smart race. In my personal opinion, there should be a heavy handicap applied to those who practise beforehand and then try really, really hard…but no one listens to me. At one point he said that his primary motivation was the line in the book (above): "I'm not interested in beating anyone…with the possible exception of my friend Steve on *Frolic*…."

However, even a blind pig finds an acorn occasionally, and indeed I found an acorn in the race: being first to finish and being awarded the Jack London Trophy. I'm sure this is the only time in this lifetime that my name will appear on the same trophy as Steve Fosset's. *Sic transit gloria mundi.*

Above: *Big O* (now *Ocean Light 2*) moored in Cabo San Lucas, circa 1997.

Below: *Exodus* at La Pas, Baja, Mexico, date unknown.

Carlotta at anchor, Cortes Island, BC, 1998.

Carlotta on her grid in Gorge Harbour, Cortes Island, BC, 1998.

Peace in Gorge Harbour following the Great Chainsaw Massacre, 1998.

Captain of *Legacy*, Road Town, Tortola, 1999. *Photographer unknown*

Legacy in Aruba, 2002. *Photo by Jurek Zarzycki*

Left: Aboard Windjammer's *Legacy* cruise ship in Jost Van Dyke, British Virgin Islands. Below: Excuse me…I'm just trying to use the radio. Both circa 1999. *Photographer unknown*

Scaramouche at the start of the 2012 Singlehanded TransPac. *Photo by LaDonna Bubak, Latitude 38 magazine*

The author rowing back to
Scaramouche in Maui, 2013.
Photo by Christy McLeod

Christy on *Scaramouche* in
Kauai after the finish of the
2012 Singlehanded TransPac.

AFTERWORD

Returning the Favour

Since I was ten years old I've been enjoying stories about the sea. Appendix 2 will give you some idea of the authors I've loved, and it's my hope that a few people will enjoy these little stories I have now taken the time to tell.

Sitting here typing this at sixty-six years of age, I can hear the clock ticking. *Scaramouche* will be for sale soon, and every year it's harder and harder to resist the pull of the rocking chair. I think again of all of my sailing heroes, and many of them kept kicking the can well into their seventies and "I think I can, I think I can"…but who knows.

Tight bowlines,
Peter

ACKNOWLEDGMENTS

Good times, and riches, and son-of-a-bitches
I've seen more than I can recall.
— Jimmy Buffet, "Changes in Latitudes, Changes in Attitudes"

It is a wonderful custom after writing a book to take the opportunity to thank those who helped make the book possible. It would be even more fun to name all of the bastards who made your life miserable, but that's not the custom.

If you've made it this far through the book, you'll know that in my life I've done a certain amount of tilting at windmills. Every so often, and much to my surprise, some of those windmills have tilted back. I've been fortunate to have a small group of friends who, over a number of years, have opened their door to find a small, puling bucket of puke cowering on their doorstep. That would be me, back from some idiotic adventure that had gone wrong. So, for Jim and Judy, Anne, and Denetiah, a big thank you for a thousand meals, a thousand offers of shelter and succor, and very occasionally, a much-needed kick in the ass. John Stocker has been more than a good friend; guru might be a better term. Peter Divers lent me his skill and friendship. Cam Mitchell was, and is, the best shipmate I could ever hope for, and Jen Dick is the best shipmate enabler (if there is such a thing). David Wood has always made his skills and knowledge available, and kept his criticisms to himself. Mad Man Murphy and Sandra kept me fed and showered during my time in St. Barths, and remain great friends to this day (although we are now orbiting around different stars). MMM was especially supportive of this book.

I'm very fortunate to be able to count among my friends Ed Lien. Ed spent much of his professional life as master of a Canadian Coast Guard buoy tender. He is now with the Pacific Pilotage Authority. While writing the book, I often turned to Ed when I was unsure of a technical issue, and invariably I had an answer by return email. If you still run across any technical errors, we'll find someone to blame (just not Ed or me).

Through the wonders of Facebook, I met my editor and book designer Jane Keyes. Jane immediately got right behind the project and, although we did not meet face-to-face until the book was published, she not only edited and designed the entire book but also gave me much-needed emotional support when it occasionally seemed the project would never end. Thank you, Jane.

APPENDIX 1 • HISTORY OF *CARLOTTA*

The following short history of *Carlotta* is reprinted verbatim with the gracious permission of the Mohan family, who owned *Carlotta* after me and did an absolutely wonderful job, not only of restoring her to her original beauty, but also of compiling an accurate history of her that was, on occasion, in conflict with previously published information. Photos have not been included, but visit **http://www.pilotcutter.ca/history.html** to view the full website. It's well worth the time for those interested in pilot cutters.

....

1899 *The Solway*

An agreement was signed June 23, 1899 between the boat builder William H. Halford of Gloucester England and the Cumberland Sea Fishery Committee to build a 'Police Boat' or 'Protection Cutter' for the use of Officers to patrol the fisheries in the Cumberland area.

Halford's yard had previously built at least three Bristol Channel pilot cutters, including the St. Bee's and the Britannia. Unlike many other pilot boats that sported an offset bowsprit, some of Halford's pilot boats were unique in featuring a bowsprit that housed directly over a raked stem. The new boat was to be built to the same scantlings, materials, design and layout as the Halford pilot boats.

As work progressed there was some difficulty in getting Lloyd's to perform a scheduled survey of the boat going together. The Cumberland Sea Fishery wanted someone to report frequently on the progress of the yard, and the task was given to a Mr. Brinkworth — a retired Pilot who worked as the Dockmaster in

Gloucester. On November 15, 1899 the boat was launched and christened *The Solway*. It measured 50' long on deck, with 13' beam, 8' draft and 28 tons.

Following the launch the boat was found to be under ballasted by about four tons. Halford argued that he had fully completed his end of the contract and after much dispute the Fisheries Committee added the remaining ballast themselves, having to contract another boat builder in Whitehaven to raise the cabin sole to make room for additional lead weight.

Although the boat had been assembled and rigged in the manner of a pilot boat, the Officers delivering the boat from Gloucester to Whitehaven found the rigging, interior, and some of the gear on board to be inadequate. They had the boat surveyed, and were quick to point a finger at Brinkworth for not supervising Halford more closely. Brinkworth responded (noting his 25 years experience in the Pilot service with all manner of craft) that the recommendations of the recent survey were *"no more a neccessity to the boat than a side pocket to a shark."*

1900

By July 13, 1900 the Sea Fisheries had tendered out the repairs for *The Solway* and in the end were satisfied with the work done. She was worked in the River Solway and off the coast of Cumberland by a crew of four to seven men and a Master. The Whitehaven Shipping Registry lists the vessel's employment as 'Police duty' under license number '2' and she was painted black with a vermillion cove stripe.

1907 *Carlotta*

June 20, 1907 — *The Solway* was transferred to ship chandler John Thomas Kee of the Isle of Man. The Certificate of Registry with Whitehaven Port was cancelled July 3, 1907 as the Sea Fisheries Committee believed the policing duties would be better served by a steam-powered vessel.

It is believed a 'Lady Vivian' found the boat at Whitehaven, converted her to a yacht and registered her anew under the name *Carlotta* at Ramsey, Isle of Man due to alterations. Sometime after this Vivian shot and killed an intruder in her home and as a consequence to this trouble sold the yacht.

1907 records

David A. Croall of The Sports Club, St James' Square, London as owner and the vessel registered in Ramsey.

1908

During this time *Carlotta* was associated with several prominent people, including the notorious financier Clarence Hatry. One of the key events leading up to the 1929 Stock Market Crash was the collapse of Clarence Hatry's empire in Britain. In 1930 he was sentenced to 14 years penal servitude for forging municipal bonds and obtaining money by fraud.

1913

Carlotta won the 1913 Royal Cornwall Yacht Club Regatta under the ownership of A.R. Hoette. The Mercantile Navy List and Maritime Directory of 1913 gives the owner as William H. Rogers of Bickford Grange, Penkridge, Staffs.

The 1914 and 1915 Lloyd's Register of Yachts shows the owner of *Carlotta* as W.G. Luke of The Anchorage, Hamble, Southampton. In 1919 Beken of Cowes photographed *Carlotta* under full sail in company with the 'Banba' — a yacht built in Southampton in 1897. To date it is the earliest photo record of *Carlotta*.

1920

Carlotta is reported being owned by a property developer named John Rene Payne of 17 Regent's Park Terrace, London. He was known as 'Fiddler Payne' as he used to play his violin (one of three Stradivari that carry the Payne family name) in the still of the early morning and evenings aboard *Carlotta*. He sailed *Carlotta* out of the Royal Burnham and Royal Corinthian Yacht Clubs with a full compliment of paid hands. *Carlotta* was beautifully kept and took part in all the cruiser races. She underwent a complete re-rig which included having her bulwarks cut down — as a low flat sheer was fashionable at that period. She was also fitted with what was known at the time as a 'Marconi topmast' — a hollow spar fitted into a metal cup on the top of the mast. In 1922 Carlotta won the 'Round-the-Island' race with a £120 Silver Plate. During this time *Carlotta* was racing against International Twelve-metres on the Essex Coast. Eventually Payne sold the yacht and went on to own a succession of William Fife Twelve-metres — the yachts *Vanity I through Vanity V. Carlotta* appears on the Royal Yacht Squadron list from 1923 to 1928.

1925

John Standish Surtees Prendergast Vereker, the 6th Viscount Gort — more commonly known as Lord Gort — is reported to have loved the yacht and preferred to live aboard rather than ashore in the family's East Cowes Norris Castle. Lord

Gort was a British soldier who served in both World War I and II, rising to the rank of Field Marshal and receiving the Victoria Cross. In 1940 he led the British Expeditionary Force to France and subsequently the retreat from Dunkirk. It was aboard *Carlotta* that he wrote *The British Army Training Manual*. He lavished care and money on *Carlotta* and fitted her with every comfort and convenience.

1929

Shows the retired Lieutenant Colonel, the Honourable Christian Henry Charles Guest of London as the registered owner.

1933

George Henry Jordan of Southlands, Monmouth is shown as owner on the sixth of December 1933 but only for a very short term as Sir Thomas Hewitt Skinner of London is shown as owner December 22 of the same year. At this point *Carlotta* was given a magnificent swept teak deck.

1935

Beken of Cowes once again took several photographs of the yacht.

1937

Bessie and Aleck Bourne of London bought *Carlotta* to replace their aging *Idris* — another smaller ex-pilot boat. In 1938 Aleck Bourne (a noted gynecologist) performed the operation of abortion without fee on a young girl not quite 15 years of age who was raped by a group of British soldiers. Bourne was charged with unlawfully procuring abortion but later acquitted of all charges.

The Bournes would spend the summers sailing around the coasts of Northern Europe in the North Sea, the Channel, the Baltic and the coast of Brittany. One summer was spent sailing right around England. A silent home movie documents these travels.

During a stay in Brest in 1939 the radio receiver on board broke down. Without much concern the Bournes took a leisurely course southwards down the Britany coast. At Concarneau, a large port where they finally met civilization again, they received a telegram from London:

RETURN HOME IMMEDIATELY. WAR IMMINENT.

They promptly sailed North and left the boat in the care of friends at St. Peter Port on the island of Guernsey thinking that *Carlotta* would be safer here than on the mainland.

1940

The ownership was transferred to three gentlemen in Guernsey: Commander Lewis Tobias Peyton-Jones, Mr. Harry Lyster Cooper, and Timothy Patrick Moriarty O'Callaghan. Far from being a safe haven, the Channel Islands were the only British territories to be occupied by the Germans. On a Sunday in June 1940 the Germans landed at the airport.

1942

The yacht was found laid up in a canal basin dock near Fleetwood in 1942 by Richard Twist. Twist paid 1000 guineas and became the next registered owner. Twist sailed her out of Strangford Lough, Northern Ireland for about four years with his friend Harry Pitt — a master helmsman who scorned the use of the engine. During these years they sailed mostly among the Hebridean Islands, Scotland, and Ireland. Twist claimed that a porpoise once swam across her deck in a Scottish squall!

He later chartered *Carlotta* out of St. Mawes, Cornwall with his wife Nellie (who incidentally could set all sail and singlehand the boat) with frequent voyages to France. *Carlotta* was laid up at St. Mawes beside the Laurent Giles designed cutter Dyarchy every year when out of season. The following season the Twists would always leave on May the first "whatever the weather" as Richard used to say.

Sometimes they used the laborious process of a block and tackle to raise the anchor. Mrs. Twist would take the business end over her shoulder and walk the length of the deck until the anchor was aweigh, at which point Mr. Twist would shout "Avast there!" She seemed to like it. Apparently one season Twist could not afford anti-fouling so he used sheep dip instead that year.

Some fast times Twist made with her were from Wicklow Head in a N and NE wind to Longships in twenty-four hours. Another time she was off the Manacles on the South Cornish coast at 7:15 am and was abeam the Abervrach lighthouse at 6:00 pm. This was under trysail in a strong NW wind. In September 1950 in the North Channel a hurricane force wind over an ebb tide made the sea white all over and the *Carlotta* was laid down until the masthead truck was almost hitting the waves. Another time in the Sound of Bute a williwaw put her over until the water came up to the deck skylights.

She was also sailed out of some tight corners, notably inside of Caladh Island in the Kyles of Bute, as well as going South to North through the rocks inside the

Raz de Sein — a terror of sailors from the very earliest of times. In the Middle Ages, when a ship had safely passed through, one of the sailors would blacken his face pretending to be Father Neptune collecting tolls. This bit of tomfoolery was later extended to crossing the equator.

Twist was a regular contributor to *Yachting Monthly* and wrote several articles of his adventures in Carlotta during the 1950's and 60's. He taught Adlard Coles (who in 1947 founded his own nautical book publishing firm and wrote many pilots, narratives and the classic world-famous *Heavy Weather Sailing*) and Sir Max Aitken (son of Lord Beaverbrook — proprietor and founder of the *Daily Express newspaper*) all they knew about North Biscay and its ports. Twist would often consult for French Naval officials and correct the inaccuracies of their charts!

1969

The Twists kept *Carlotta* for twenty-seven years. They lived aboard for seventeen years and spent the off-seasons living at Elwynick, St. Anthony. Richard Marsden Twist died at St. Anthony in Roseland, Cornwall October 28, 2003 aged 94.

1970

Twist sold *Carlotta* to two young men from Golant, Cornwall. The two men ignored a warning from Twist "not to leave the boat up on legs" and she fell over and came into a deplorable state of decay with many frames smashed.

1973

Canadian Peter Heiberg found *Carlotta* in the Fowey estuary. Heiberg had been searching for this type of vessel for some time having sailed aboard the Bristol Channel pilot cutter *Marguerite T* with his friend — owner Les Windley. Heiberg bought *Carlotta* and spent the next four years replacing frames and restoring her at Thomas' Ponsharden Yard at Falmouth. He removed the dark, compartmented, falling-apart, Japanese Oak interior and gutted the boat for the most part. He replaced twenty-eight futtock ends, seventeen planks, sixteen deck beam ends, refastened the hull throughout, refastened the deck, fitted new bilge stringers, re-caulked where necessary and fitted a small transom where the end of the counter had gone rotten.

The restoration was a full time job for Heiberg. At one point he felt close to giving up and traveled all day by train to the other end of England to visit his friend Les Windley for words of encouragement. As he made his way down to the harbor he spied the *Marguerite T* from afar and was so overcome by her beauty that he turned around and went straight back to Falmouth full of inspiration — without even visiting his friend!

1977

In the summer of 1977 Heiberg set out to Vancouver, British Columbia but was thwarted by a severe storm in the Bay of Biscay. The following summer he set out again but was forced back to Falmouth. On a third attempt he reached Vigo, Spain and sailed on to the Caribbean island of St. Barts where he proceeded to win every category in the Old Gaffer's races for the next two years.

After two years Heiberg pointed west again through the Panama Canal to Hawaii. Eventually he reached Vancouver after a quick passage averaging 180 miles a day — without an auxiliary. He then tried to make the boat earn her keep by chartering and offering sail-training to distressed juveniles — possibly becoming the only vessel to be towed by rowboat completely around Texada Island since Captain Vancouver's voyage! *Carlotta* was a regular winner in the Old Gaffer's races in English Bay, Vancouver, B.C.

Peter Heiberg's relationship with *Carlotta* lasted for over 30 years — the entire time without an engine or any other modern conveniences installed. He has proven that an old gaff rigged boat need not be thought of as a slow, clunky, old tub — as he raced *Carlotta* competitively and made many long passages aboard her

2004

Heiberg sold *Carlotta* to Barbra, Jasper and Stephen Mohan. Long time admirers of *Carlotta* and pilot cutters, the Mohan's jumped at the chance to be *Carlotta*'s next custodians. After one year of sailing and living aboard on the Sunshine Coast of British Columbia attention was turned to necessary long term repairs. The Mohan's began the process of restoring *Carlotta* with an eye towards the original workboat she was in 1899.

2009

August — The hull and decks are completed and the mast had been stepped. A small party was held at the Hotel dock in Lund with a traditional Celtic band, Champagne smashed on the bow, a few sea shanties belted out by the Lund Shanteymen, and cake for everyone!

2009

October — *Carlotta* sails again! There are still many jobs to do — including rigging of the topmast, building a windlass and constructing the interior. On board for the first sail is Richard Campbell from England — wearing the same red sailing smock that his father wore when sailing on *Carlotta* back in Cornwall in the 1950's with the Twist's.

2011

October — The interior is completed and the Mohan's move back aboard *Carlotta*!

Carlotta's story with thanks to: Joan Ostry, Robert Simper, Charlie Ford, Peter Maxwell, Tim Pratt, Richard Campbell, Hugh Conway-Jones, Dick and Juliette Rymer Cooper, Peter Heiberg and many others.

APPENDIX 2 • READING LIST

Ad hoc, ad loc and quid pro quo. So little time — so much to know!
— Spoken by Jeremy in Beatles movie *Yellow Submarine*

Below are listed all the books that are currently on my shelves. Lots of them have travelled many miles with me and are mildewed and ugly and musty-smelling — and I love them all the more for that. I haven't typed complete information about each book because, with Google and the various wonderful used book sources now online, anyone can find and obtain any book at very little expense or effort. I have included a brief description where warranted. The vast majority of the books listed here are worth a read, although some are dated and will interest some people more than others.

....

Technical books on the gaff rig

The Lonsdale Library of Sports, Games and Pastimes, Volume 15 — Cruising and Ocean Racing, E.G. Martin & John Irving
A much-neglected source that is full of information on boats and sailing from an earlier time. Recommended to me by Commander Tom Blackwell.

Hand Reef and Steer, Traditional Sailing Skills for Classic Boats, Tom Cunliffe

Classic Boat Seamanship, Martin Tregoning

Elements of Yacht Sailing and Cruising, Alec Glanville

Gaff Sail, Robert Simper

Gaff Rig, John Leather
This was the bible when I was re-rigging *Carlotta*. My copy is destroyed from sitting on deck in the rain tying Matthew Walker knots and cow hitches in the dead-eye lanyards.

Gaff Rig Handbook, John Leather

Books of historical interest but not necessarily historical books (often but not always involving the gaff rig)

Messing About in Boats, John R. Muir
The first person to describe in detail the correct method to use the Appledore Roller Reefing Gear (God bless him). A great read.

Sail, The Surviving Tradition, Robert Simper

Yachting and Cruising for Amateurs, Frank Cowper

Inshore Craft of Britain, Vol. 1&2, Edgar J. March

Yachtsman's Omnibus, Calahan

Yachting, Bullen and Prout

When a Loose Cannon Flogs a Dead Horse There's the Devil to Pay, Olivia Isil

The Fore and Aft Rig, Morris

Spritsail Barges of the Thames and Medway, March

The Origins of Sea Terms, Rogers

The Great Coal Schooners of New England 1870–1909, Parker

A History of Seamanship, Phillips-Birt

Sixteen Times Round Cape Horn, Hibberd

American Sailing Coasters of the North Atlantic, Morris

Vintage Boats, Lewis

Technical books on boats, sailing, racing and seamanship

Best of Uffa, Guy Cole, ed.

Sailing Boats, Uffa Fox

Sailing Theory and Practice, C.A. Marchaj
Marchaj writes the definitive books on the physics of sailing. If you're like me and can't understand the "proofs," just go with the flow, his books are still great reads and very helpful for understanding our sport.

Aero-Hydrodynamics of Sail, Marchaj

Elements of Yacht Design, Skene
Because of my interest in boats old and new (and books old and new), I have a first edition, a fourth edition and an eighth edition. Very different; all great. The later additions are called Skene's *Elements of Yacht Design* by Francis S. Kinney. Many relevant tables and packed with useful information.

Practical Coastal Navigation, Comte De Miremont
Of historical interest only.

His Book, Rod Stevens
This book was published posthumously by Rod's family. Rod played a major role at Sparkman and Stevens, and this is an incredibly informative book, although he is obviously old at the time of writing and rambles a bit toward the end. Available free online.

The Best of Sail Trim, Sail Magazine (anthology)

Sailboat Racing Rules, McDermott

When the Crew Matter Most, Erroll Bruce

Racing With Cornelius Shields, Cornelius Shields

Practical Yacht Handling, Tabarly

Seamanship, Norris D. Hoyt

How to Sail, Carl D. Lane

The Boatswain's Manual, William McLeod

Further Offshore, John Illingworth

Storm Sailing, Jobson

Offshore Cruising Encyclopedia, Steve and Linda Dashew
Steve brings a critical mind to bear on almost all sailing issues, and is not afraid to trample icons. Although I don't always agree with him (anchoring), he is always thought provoking and insightful. I was lucky enough to skipper the 78-foot *Beowulf* for six months, and I really came to appreciate exactly how innovative Steve and Linda are.

The Circumnavigators Handbook, Dashew & Dashew

Mariner's Weather Handbook, Dashew & Dashew

Bluewater Handbook, Dashew & Dashew

Singlehanded Sailing: The Experiences and Techniques of the Lone Voyagers, Henderson

Ocean Cruising Survey, Cornell

Simonsen's Navigation, Simonsen

Sea Sense, Henderson

World Cruising Routes, Cornell

The Sea Around Us, Rachel Carson
Nothing to do with sailing except…well, everything.

Oceanography, Grant Gross
See comment above.

The Living Sea, Jacques Cousteau
See comment above.

The Ship Captain's Medical Guide, Department of Trade
There are much more relevant and timely books available now, but this one sailed
thousands of miles with me.

Nicholl's Seamanship and Nautical Knowledge, Cockcroft.
Not very relevant unless you are interested in deep-sea ships.

The Offshore Game: Today's Ocean Racing, Edward F. Cotter

Race Your Boat Right, Knapp

Elementary Seamanship, D. Wilson Barker

Tait's New Seamanship, U.K. Board of Trade

Ships and Boats, The Nature of Their Design, Douglas Phillips-Birt

Boats, Oars, and Rowing, R.D. Culler

Introduction to Sailing, Mitchell Jr.

Basic Sailing Skills, Giffin

Survival At Sea, Wright

Safety and Survival at Sea, Lee and Lee

Heavy Weather Sailing, Coles
This is a must-read, although I believe the newer editions are better given that more
knowledge is gained yearly. Later editions are by Bruce.

Sails, Howard-Williams

Sailing in Windy Weather, Henderson

Manual of Seamanship 1937, Lords Commissioners of the Admiralty

One-Design Class Handbook, Scharff (1961)

Naval Architecture, Lovett (1905)

The Symmetry of Sailing, Garrett

Dinghy Racing, Fitzpatrick

Boat Data Book, Ian Nicolson

Cruising Under Sail, Hiscock
This book and the following volume were our bibles when preparing our boats for
ocean voyaging in the '70s. I noted that there was some resentment from earlier pio-
neers, I'm thinking of Frank Casper on *Elsie,* as well as Tom Blackwell. I don't want to
speculate on the why of this, as everyone was only too happy to share their knowledge
with us (including Eric Hiscock and Susan, whom I met while rebuilding *Carlotta* in
Falmouth in '78).

Voyaging Under Sail, Hiscock
See comment above.

Ships, Bowen

Manual of Sailboat Racing, McDermott

Desirable and Undesirable Characteristics of Offshore Yachts, Rousmaniere

Sailing to Win, Bavier, Jr.

The Racing Edge, Turner and Jobson

Ocean Racing Around the World, Hammond

Boat-Mans Handbook, Bottomly

How to Be a First Rate First Mate, Sloane and Coe

The Sailing Yacht, Baader

The Ocean Sailing Yacht, Street

The Complete Canvas Workers Guide, Grant

The Efficient Deckhand, Wright

Safety at Sea, Day

Suggestions to Captains, Mitcalfe (1901)

Blue Water Yacht Navigation, Coutts

The Way of a Yacht, Hollingsworth

Weather for the Mariner, Kotsch

Understanding the Yacht Racing Rules, Perry

The Offshore Racer, Jones

Sail Power, The Complete Guide to Sails and Sail Handling

Self Sufficient Sailor, Lin and Larry Pardey

Thoughts on Small Boat Racing, Ogilvy

Little Blue Book of Sailing Secrets, Isler

Blue Water, Griffith & Griffith

The Splicing Handbook, Merry

Weather for the Mariner (3rd ed.), Kotsch

The Sailor's Weather Guide, Markell

Instant Wind Forecasting, Watts

Passagemaking Handbook, Rains and Miller

Designed to Win, Marshall

Celestial Navigation for Yachtsmen, Blewitt

Basic Astro Navigation, Dixon

Cruising Rigs and Rigging, Norgrove

The Rigger's Locker, Toss

The Rigger's Apprentice, Toss

Chapman's Nautical Guide "Knots," Toss

Singlehanded Sailing, Evans
Great book that can be downloaded for free.

Sail and Rig Tuning, Dedekam
I can't recommend this small book enough.

Modern Marlinspike Seamanship, MacLean

The Ashley Book of Knots, Ashley
An encyclopedic work, but I find the drawings sometimes hard to follow; nonetheless, it should be in everybody's library.

Simple Sun Shooting, Bateman

Books on pilot cutters

The Sailing Pilots of the Bristol Channel, Peter J. Stuckey

Triumph and Tribulation, H.W. Tilman
Bill Tilman visited *Carlotta* during the rebuild; unfortunately, I chose that day to be off buying supplies, and missed meeting a great man and one of the true believers.

Adventures Under Sail, H.W. Tilman

Ice With Everything, H.W. Tilman

Topsail & Battleaxe, Tom Cunliffe

Cruising books from back in the day

Yacht Cruising, Claud Worth
This book is truly one of the classic cruising books, and sits on my bookshelf next to R.T. McMullen's *Down Channel*. Loaded with technical information, but also cruising stories.

Down Channel, R.T. McMullen
If you're a cruising sailor and want to see whose shoulders you're standing on, start here.

Ocean Passages
I have a first edition from 1896, and a current edition. Personally, if planning a long voyage now (and who isn't), I would rely on the various Pilot Charts. I just like old books.

Amaryllis, G.H.P. Muhlhauser

The West in My Eyes, Annie Van de Wiele

The Bombard Story, Dr. Alain Bombard

The Fight of the Firecrest, Alain Gerbault

In Quest of the Sun, Alain Gerbault

Sailing Alone Around the World, Joshua Slocum
A charming Yankee bullshitter who definitely "draws too much water" — but what the hell, a must-read classic.

The Cruise of the Teddy, Erling Tambs

Wind Aloft, Marin Marie

The Venturesome Voyages of Captain Voss, Voss

A Voyage of the Sunbeam, Lady Brassy

Boat building and repair books

The Repair of Wooden Boats, John Lewis

Simplified Boat Building, Harry V. Sucher

The Finely Fitted Yacht, Mate

Marine Diesel Engines, Calder

The First Ferro Boat Book, Pete Greenfield
I only include this book because I suddenly realized, while I was reading it, that I'd helped to plaster the boat in the book. I'd forgotten all about it.

Fitting Out, Percy Woodcock

Wooden Boats Restoration and Maintenance Manual, Scarlett

Clinker Boatbuilding, John Leather

Modern Shipfitter's Handbook, Swanson
Anything but modern.

Simple Boat Building, Prout

Ship Wiring, Scull
I cannot conceive of any reason to get this book or the next.

The Practical Principles of Naval Architecture, Rabl

NLGA Standard Grading Rules for Canadian Lumber, National Lumber Grades Authority

Make Your Own Sails, Bowker and Budd

Boatbuilding, Howard Chapelle

Rules and Regulations for the Construction and Classification of Wood and Composite Yachts, Lloyd's Register of Shipping, London

The Care and Repair of Hulls, Verney

Glossary of Shipbuilding and Outfitting Terms, Eddington

The Ship's Husband, Calahan

Tools of the Maritime Trades, Horsley

The Big Book of Boat Canvas, Lipe

The Stripper's Guide to Canoe-Building, Hazen

Marinize Your Boat, Nicolson

The Big Book of Marine Electronics, Graves

Modern Wooden Yacht Construction, Guzzwell

Handbook of Rigging, Rossnagel

Good Boatkeeping, Aiken

The 12-Volt Bible for Boats, Brotherton

Good yarns, both fiction and non (you be the judge)

They Sailed Alone, Macdonald Harris

Sopranino, Ellam & Mudie
Recommended; great story if you like small-boat voyaging.

The Salt-Water Men, Schull

Schooner Master, Carnahan

Godforsaken Sea, Lundy
Fantastic story of the Vendée Globe.

Shackleton's Stowaway, McKernan

The Perfect Storm, Junger

The Pacific, Ambrose

Oyster River, Millar

The Water in Between, Patterson

Sea Change, Nichols

Defining the Wind, Huler

The Impossible Voyage, Chay Blyth

Voyage, Sterling Hayden
I love these books.

Wanderer, Sterling Hayden

The War With Cape Horn, Alan Villiers

Moderm Mariners, A.J. Villiers

The Set of the Sails, Alan Villiers

Alone Across the Atlantic, Francis Chichester

Along the Clipper Way, Francis Chichester

The Romantic Challenge, Francis Chichester

Gypsy Moth Circles the World, Francis Chichester

The Lonely Sea and the Sky, Francis Chichester

Atlantic Adventure, Chichester

Voyage of the Century, Simpson and Angeloglou
About Chichester.

In Gramma's Wake, Girl Stella's Voyage to Cuba, Frank Mulville
Great story of a Looe Lugger by a thoughtful man.

Captains Courageous, Rudyard Kipling

Polar Passage, MacInnis and Rowland

Against the Sea: Great Adventure Stories
From the pages of *Motorboating & Sailing.*

Adrift, Steven Callahan

Great Stories of the Sea and Ships, N.C. Wyeth (ed.)

The Brassbounder, Bone

Tom Chatto, Second Mate, Philip McCutchan

The Sea Chest, Critchell Rimington

Song of the Whale, Rex Weyler
I've known Rex for many years and still enjoy his great books.

To Save a Whale, Robert Hunter and Rex Weyler
Bob Hunter was a good friend. Because of his encouragement and editing skills, I sold my very first magazine article. He was also a minister of The Whole Earth Church and, as such, officiated at my wedding. The marriage didn't last so long, but people are still talking about the reception.

Warriors of the Rainbow, A Chronicle of the Greenpeace Movement, Robert Hunter

At One with the Sea, Naomi James

Survive the Savage Sea, Dougal Robertson

Very Willing Griffin, David Blagden

A Treasury of Sea Stories, Gordon C. Aymar (illustrations by Rockwell Kent)

N by E, Rockwell Kent

Sheila in the Wind, A Story of a Lone Voyage, Hayter

The Brendan Voyage, Tim Severin

Redburn, Herman Melville

White Jacket, Heman Melville

Billy Budd, Sailor, Herman Melville

Typee, Herman Melville

The Young Mariner Melville, Gould

Hornblower and the Atropos, C.S. Forester

The Cruise of the Cachalot, Frank T. Bullen

Makora, H.E. Goodwin

Longitude, Sobel

Ship of Force, Evans

Desperate Voyagers, Tokayer and Swartz

Post Reader of Sea Stories, Day Edgar (ed.)

Yankee's Wander-World, Irving and Electa Johnson

The Creation of Cloah Sark, Johnny Clougher

John Paul Jones, Samuel Eliot Morison

A World of My Own, Robin Knox-Johnston

Arctic Dreams, Lopez

Home Port Victoria, Jupp

The Secret Voyages of Sir Francis Drake, Bawlf

Great Voyages in Small Boats, Solo Transatlantic, Ann Davison, David Lewis & Hannes Lindemann
I'm not sure if I have a copy, but the other books by Ann Davison and David Lewis are not to be missed.

The Curve of Time, M. Wylie Blanchet
A classic true tale from my neck of the woods, loved by all who read it and especially by women.

Because the Horn is There, Miles Smeeton
Of course, all of Smeeton's books are required reading. I fell in love with the family's adventures when Miles gave a talk and showed a film at my boarding school in 1958.

The Misty Islands, Miles Smeeton

The Sea Was Our Village, Smeeton

Trekka Round the World, Guzzwell

Adventures, Blizzards, and Coastal Calamities, Snow

Schoonerman, Capt. Richard England

Sou'West & by West of Cape Cod: The Classic Evocation of New England Shore, Sea, and Islands — From Point Judith to the Head of Buzzards Bay, Llewellyn Howland

Red Dog & Great White, Inside the America's Cup, Clark

Death Sails the Bay, Feegel

Come Wind or Weather, Clare Francis

The Whale People, R. Haig-Brown

Moby Dick, Herman Melville

Best South Sea Stories, Day and Stroven (eds.)

Hakluyt's Voyages, Hakluyt

The Happy Return, Forester

The Penguin Book of Sea Stories, Richards (ed.)

Victory, Conrad

The Princess Story, Hacking and Lamb

The Rover, Joseph Conrad

Across Three Oceans, Conor O'Brien

The Boat, Walter Gibson

The Eternal Voyagers, Robert Mirvish

To the Great Southern Sea, W.A. Robinson

Whistle Up the Inlet, Rushton

Storm Passage, Webb Chiles

A Steady Trade, Tristan Jones
We all know what a terrible liar Tristan was, but what great stories.

Adrift, Tristan Jones

Saga of a Wayward Sailor, Tristan Jones

A Star to Steer Her By, Tristan Jones

Outrage, The Ordeal of Greenpeace III, David McTaggart
I knew David when he first got involved with GreenPeace. David visited *Carlotta* in Mashfords Boatyard during the rebuilding.

The Walkabouts, Mike Saunders

Drum, Simon Le Bon & Neil Cheston

The Rage to Survive, Jacques Vignes

Luxton's Pacific Crossing, Luxton

The Bedford Incident, Mark Rascovich

Cape Horn, The Logical Route, Bernard Moitessier

The Long Way, Moitessier

The Twelve Meter Challenges for the America's Cup, Norris D. Hoyt

Princess, Joe Richards

The Eternal Darkness, Robert D. Ballard.

The Tugman's Passage, Edward Hoagland

South With Scott, Capt Edward Evans

BC Commercial Fishing History, Forester
If you've read this book, you'll know why there are a few books on fishing included.

Striper, Cole

Fishing With John, Iglauer
An extremely accurate description of the troll fishery described in this book, as well as a good read.

Harvest of Salmon, Landale

Working on the Edge, Walker

Practical Shipbuilding, Holms
Probably of little interest to the current reader.

Treasure Island, Robert Louis Stevenson

The Eye of the Wind, Peter Scott

Fidelio, My Voyage to a Distant Shore, Rodger Birdwell

The Water in Between, Kevin Patterson

The Boat Who Wouldn't Float, Farley Mowat

West Viking, Farley Mowat

The Black Joke, Farley Mowat

The Riddle of the Sands, Erskine Childers
A thriller that still reads beautifully.

The Golden Keel, Bagley

Ramage's Mutiny, Pope

The Ship that Died of Shame, Monsarrat

My Old Man and the Sea, Hays and Hays

A Web of Salvage, Brian Callison

Great Adventures in Small Boats, Klein and King

South by Java Head, Alistair MacLean

Sailing to Freedom, Veedam and Wall
This book is *not* about middle class cruisers escaping the mortgage.

Best of South Sea Stories, Day and Stroven (eds.)

The Sea Wolf, Jack London
Don't miss this one if you like London.

Where the High Winds Blow, Walker
Not a sailing book.

The Other Titanic, Simon Martin

The Great Iron Ship, Dugan
Isambard Kingdom Brunel remains a great hero of mine. The railway bridge over the Tay in Cornwall, the speed of the trains in Cornwall — for better or worse, we owe it all to this genius. "Not only was he a great engineer but he was pretty handy with an 18" bastard file."

Darken Ship, Monsarrat

The Speedwell Voyage, Poolman

Just Cruising, Liza Copeland

Keepers of the Light, Graham

Endurance, Lansing

Island Race, McCarthy and Toksvig

Paddle to the Artic, Starkell

On the Wind's Way, Snaith

The Story of the Sea, a Man, and a Ship, Nicolson

One-Off, A Story of Yacht Racing, Midlands

Moods of the Sea, Solley and Steinbaugh (eds.)
Poetry.

Sailing to the Edge of Fear, Dye

The Hungry Ocean, Greenlaw

You Are First, Kinney
The S&S story.

By Way of the Wind, Moore

Scaramouche, Sabatini
This has nothing to do with sailing, but my present boat and many others are named after the book. Could it be because the opening sentence is "He was born with the gift of laughter and a sense that the world was mad"?

The Mauritius Command, Patrick O'Brian

Master and Commander, Patrick O'Brian

Mainsail to the Wind, Galvani

The Arctic Voyages of Martin Frobisher, McGhee

High Seas, High Risk: The Story of the Sudburys, Norris

Mutiny, A Brief History, Woodman

Rounding the Horn, Murphy (ed.)

The Log of Bob Bartlett, Bartlett
Must-read for Canadian mariners.

Unsolved Mysteries of the Arctic, Vilhjalmur Stefansson

Sailing, Edward Heath
Writer, conductor, incredibly successful sailor — and, oh, I nearly forgot — Prime Minister, Heath is a true renaissance man. I would never vote for him (Tory), but truly admire the man.

Two Against Cape Horn, Hal Roth

Two On a Big Ocean, Roth

The Man Who Loved Schooners, Boudreau

Memories From the Sea, friends of Paul Erling Johnson
Paul was a good friend in my St. Barth's days, and was very knowledgeable about the gaff rig and wooden boats in general. He was always ready with advice. He designed the Venus line of gaff-rigged cruising boats.

Coffee table books of beautiful boats

Yachts Under Sail, Alfred F. Loomis

The Racing Schooner Westward, Hamilton-Adams

A Panorama of Gaff Rig, Leather and Smith

The Big Class Racing Yachts, John Leather

Bluenose, Backman

Great Yachts, Lord Feversham

The America's Cup 1987, Fisher and Ross

The Macmillan Book of Boating, Wallace

Wind and Water, Onne van der Wal

The America's Cup 1851 to the Present, Beken of Cowes

William Fife, Pace

Splendour Under Sail, Holland

10216701R00140

Printed in Great Britain
by Amazon